John Hughes and Eighties Cinema

John Hughes and Eighties Cinema

Teenage Hopes and American Dreams

Thomas A. Christie

Crescent Moon

Third edition 2012.
© Thomas A. Christie 2009, 2011, 2012.

Printed and bound in the U.S.A.
Set in Book Antiqua 10 on 14pt and Gill Sans.
Designed by Radiance Graphics.

British Library Cataloguing in Publication data available for this title.

Christie, Thomas A.
John Hughes and Eighties Cinema
I. Title
791.4'33

ISBN-13 9781861713896

Crescent Moon Publishing
P.O. Box 1312
Maidstone, Kent
ME14 5XU, Great Britain
www.crmoon.com

Contents

Acknowledgements

Having grown up through eighties and having great nostalgic affection for the age, working on this project has been something of a labour of love for me, and to revisit the many varied works of John Hughes is also to revisit the styles, the music and the whole ambience of life in an eventful and tumultuous decade that still casts a long shadow on world history even today. So it gives me great pleasure to thank the following people for all of their help, support and advice during the writing of this book:

Thanks first and foremost to my sister Julie and my aunt Mary, both of whom were there for me in the eighties and – I'm very thankful to say – are still here for me now. I would also like to give a special word of thanks to my late mother Sandra. She offered such heartfelt encouragement when I was writing the first edition of this book, I know without question that she would have been so pleased that it was to be released in a new and expanded version years after she had passed away.

To Alex and Kelley Tucker, two of the best friends you could ever hope to be in contact with, and my finest (and definitely wittiest) source of popular cultural news and views on the other side of the Atlantic. They are two extraordinarily talented people, and equally good pals.

To Ivy Lannon, who didn't *quite* know me in the eighties (close though), but who has kept in touch with me ever since. We're still regularly exchanging views after all these years, a fact for which I am eternally grateful.

To Alistair and Linda Dalrymple, two good pals of mine from the beautiful county of Northumberland, and whose friendship I will always value greatly.

To Denham and Stella Hardwick, two dear friends who I will always enjoy catching up with. Whether it's Rotary Clubs or performance theatre, Denham and Stella hold a wealth of information between the two of them, as well as great camaraderie, and are a pair of very special people.

To Douglas Allen, my friend and fellow film enthusiast. Douglas is the wisest and most knowledgeable mentor any film student could hope to work with – and as coincidence would have it, we first met while I was writing a Masters dissertation about geopolitical themes in James Bond films which had been directed during (when else?) the eighties!

To Eddy and Dorothy Bryan, two great friends with an incredible joy for life. You can always learn something new from just five minutes talking to Eddy and Dorothy, and I'd like to thank them for all of their interest in this project as it took form.

To Dr Elspeth King, Margaret Job, Michael McGinnes and all of my friends on the staff of the Stirling Smith Art Gallery and Museum. As well as boasting a vast array of objects of historical and cultural interest, the Smith is also an institution which has great respect for the eighties, given that it lived through not just the 1980s, but the 1880s as well. I for one have little doubt that it'll be around for at least the 2080s too – and with any luck, for many decades beyond that.

To my transatlantic friend Rachael McClure, not only because I promised her that she'd get a mention this time, but also due to the fact that as a big John Hughes fan, she's more than earned an appearance here. (After all, she's seen *Ferris Bueller's Day Off* more than five times now... and still laughs.)

To Barrie and Sandra Sturmey, two terrific pals of mine from Northumberland who, quite frankly, deserve a warm mention in everybody's book – but as luck would have it, they'll have to settle for a mention in mine!

To Professor Rory Watson and Dr Scott Hames of the University of Stirling, for their fellowship and advice – and also their patience at the time I've spent writing this book simultaneously with my PhD thesis. (And when you consider that my thesis is about the study of popular genres of contemporary

Scottish novels, you realise just what a stretch that actually is!)

And last but certainly by no means least, to the director of Crescent Moon Publishing, Jeremy Mark Robinson, for his unstinting support and kind agreement to me working on and completing this project in all three of its editions.

Once again, a sincere thank you to one and all!

This book is dedicated to my beautiful, long-suffering and mercifully very patient sister
Julie Christie
(no, not that one)

"Youth would be an ideal state
if it came a little later in life."

Herbert Asquith (1852-1928)

"Nostalgia is a thing of the past."

Anonymous Graffito

Photo of John Hughes by Paul Natkin (1990).

THE BREAKFAST CLUB

WEIRD SCIENCE

Sixteen Candles

Uncle Buck

pretty in pink

PLANES, TRAINS AND AUTOMOBILES

MR. MOM

VACATION

MATTHEW BRODERICK

FERRIS BUELLER'S DAY OFF

BUELLER... BUELLER... ED

THE GREAT OUTDOORS

SOME KIND OF WONDERFUL

YULE CRACK UP!

CHRISTMAS VACATION

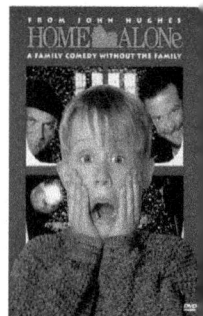

HOME ALONE
A FAMILY COMEDY WITHOUT THE FAMILY

Chicago, the setting for many of John Hughes' movies
(above and overleaf)

FOREWORD

John Hughes annoyed the crap out of me when I was a teenager.

Strange admission considering this is an overview of the man's oeuvre. Bear with me.

When Tom originally asked me to do this foreword, I was honored beyond belief. He wanted an American perspective – someone who was once a teen living through the go-go, me-first, greed-is-good 80s. I was only too happy to comply.

(Mind you, I should have written the above paragraph over a month ago. I now find myself haphazardly typing words, hoping they form something resembling coherency. Deadlines and blind panic do not a happy partnership make, but they are effective motivators.)

Hughes' CV still runs the full gauntlet of the 80s teen experience. His stories were often told from the misfit's point of view, which was pretty much everyone I ran with. Every indignity a teen could suffer was included: Flying spitballs, somnambulist-inducing teachers, sadistic siblings and even more sadistic bullies. Vindictive principals. Obtuse parents. Rich kids, poor kids, smart kids, not-so-smart kids. Nothing was left out of the mix.

I rented *Ferris Bueller's Day Off*, one of my personal favorites. Even before putting it in the DVD player, I thumbed through my memory rolodex to a Saturday afternoon in 1986, when I first saw it at the now-extinct Northgate Six Cineplex. There in the dark I learned three valuable life lessons:

1.   Licking one's palm is, in fact, an effective method of faking an illness.

2.   The 1961 Ferrari 250GT California is choice. If you have the means, I highly recommend picking one up.

3.   If you happen to be watching a parade in Chicago, feel free to climb aboard a float and start singing 'Twist and Shout'. No one will stop you as they'll all be too busy dancing on Michigan Avenue.

I was enjoying the film until I came to the scene where Cameron accidentally kicked the Ferrari off its jacks, promptly causing it to careen backwards into automobile oblivion. While I still enjoy his St Crispin's Day speech ('I am not going to sit on my ass as the events that affect me unfold to determine the course of my life'), I can't help but think Cam never got a chance to make his stand. In my imagination, his rotten dad simply chucked him out that giant broken window and told the police he was suicidal.

Overreaction, you say? Sure, but what of it? I related to Cameron. I *was* Cameron. Having his storyline unresolved caused me to lose at least three hours of sleep every night for the next six years afterward. What happened to Cam? It wasn't enough for me to assume he'd be okay. I had to *know*.

Inspired, I started writing down a litany of Hughes complaints I'd developed through the years. A sampling: Andie had no business choosing Blane over Duckie. Bender and Andy would have killed the other Breakfast Club members and fought each other for supremacy, a la *Lord of the Flies*. And although it was an incredibly romantic gesture, buying Watts a pair of earrings with his college money was the stupidest thing Keith could have ever done.

Suspension of disbelief goes only so far. I must have fried twenty Barbie dolls with battery cables before I came to the sad conclusion that I was never going to build my own magical supermodel.

Fast forward to a middle-aged man who has long since given up skinny ties and skinnier jeans. Time clarifies things. As a teenager, I didn't fully realize Hughes was telling an entire generation of late Boomers and early Xers that life was a very messy affair, filled with defeats as well as victories. His lessons are still there for the taking: *Love often hurts, but fight for it anyway. Don't miss your opportunities for happiness. Stand up to your fears, even when they knock you down.*

Tom Christie knows this. What you hold in your hand is not some dry work typed by a stenographer, but a labor of love from an imaginative scholar. Tom writes honestly and with authority because he genuinely understands and appreciates his subjects. You can tell with every syllable.

At long last, I can stop worrying about Cameron. In Tom's world, he made out fine. How could he not? Maybe Cam even owns and loves his own Ferrari – but loves his son even more.

No doubt he keeps that car under armed guard, of course.

Alex Tucker
Chattanooga, Tennessee, USA
22 October 2008

P.S. Blane? *Seriously??*

Alex Tucker is a graphic artist and animator. You can see his work at www.alextucker.com.

INTRODUCTION

Think of the American cinema of the 1980s, and your mind is instantly bombarded by dozens and dozens of vibrant, flamboyant moving images from this most distinctive of cinematic decades. You might be thinking of films which became blockbuster classics such as *The Empire Strikes Back* (Irvin Kershner, 1980), *Raiders of the Lost Ark* (Steven Spielberg, 1981), *Back to the Future* (Robert Zemeckis, 1985), or possibly even *Batman* (Tim Burton, 1989). It was a decade that gave birth to some inimitable film franchises – one need only call to mind John Rambo's explosive first appearance in *First Blood* (Ted Kotcheff, 1982), the harrowing exploits of Officer Murphy in *Robocop* (Paul Verhoeven, 1987), or even the improbably long-running knockabout antics of Cadet Mahoney and his fellow recruits which began with the raucous *Police Academy* (Hugh Wilson, 1984). Looking back, the list seems almost inexhaustible. From *Dirty Dancing* (Emile Ardolino, 1987) to *Gremlins* (Joe Dante, 1984), and from *A Nightmare on Elm Street* (Wes Craven, 1984) to *Fame* (Alan Parker, 1980), there's little doubt that if you love the world of cinema, there was at least one title released during the course of the eighties which captured your imagination.

It was against this creatively abundant background of the eighties film world that audiences were first introduced to the work of influential director and screenwriter John Hughes (1950-2009). Today he remains just as well known for the scripts he created for hugely popular family films throughout the 1990s, including *Home Alone* (Chris Columbus, 1990), *Beethoven* (Brian Levant, 1992) and *Dennis the Menace* (Nick Castle, 1993), sometimes written under his pen-name of Edmond Dantès. But whether active as a producer, screenwriter or director, even these highly successful commercial accomplishments couldn't hope to compare with the artistic diversity and cultural significance of his output throughout the eighties.

Although it is easy to remember Hughes for his meteorically successful teen movies right the way through the decade, including *The Breakfast Club* (1985) and *Ferris Bueller's Day Off* (1986), he was every bit as adroit in his handling of madcap suburban satires such as *Mr Mom* (1983) and *Uncle Buck* (1989), his wry observations of the great American holiday in *National Lampoon's Vacation* (1983) and *The Great Outdoors* (1988), the trials of an exasperated everyman commuter in *Planes, Trains and Automobiles* (1987), and the expectation of anxious new parents in *She's Having a Baby* (1988). Throughout the course of Hughes's career, there has rarely been a lack of variety in his choice of subject matter, and even years after his death his films have retained their cultural significance when so many other movies and franchises from the eighties have long since passed into obscurity.

Hughes's teen dramas are remembered today with particular fondness, not least by members of Generation X who grew up through the eighties and many of whom now look back on era-defining films written by Hughes – such as *Pretty in Pink* (Howard Deutch, 1986) and *Some Kind of Wonderful* (Howard Deutch, 1987) – with considerable nostalgic affection. But Hughes's social commentary didn't stop with his insightful filmic exploration of American youth at the time; looking back at his cinematic output over the course of the decade, he seems just as concerned with piecing together a mosaic of different aspects of the American character, employing comedy both ribald and sophisticated – along with an affectionate interpretation of his country's idealism and eccentricities – to create a compelling series of optimistic snapshots of life in the United States throughout the eighties. It is a social and cultural patchwork which has proven to be as inventive as it is enduringly memorable.

This text takes a look at all of John Hughes's films throughout the 1980s; not only the features that he directed, but also those for which he provided the screenplay. It does not discuss his occasional prose work, nor does it examine any of his early television writing for episodic series such as ABC situation comedies *Delta House* (1979) and *At Ease* (1983). Although Hughes has become especially well recognised for his directorial output throughout the eighties, the ample evidence of his outstanding writing skills extended from the early years of the decade all the way through to the time of his death in 2009, and as this book will argue, the contribution which Hughes's critically-acclaimed screenwriting brought to modern American cinema arguably exceeds his commercial successes (extensive though they were) as a producer and director.

Although this book's primary focus is upon the first decade of Hughes's engagement with the world of cinema, it is important to note that he did of course remain active in the film industry well into the nineties and beyond. It has long been observed, however, that a pronounced tonal shift occurred in his career between the late eighties and early nineties, where a conscious move was made from the keenly-drawn social and cultural observations of his earlier work (most especially his teen films from 1984-87) towards the comparatively light family comedies which he was to write and produce throughout the 1990s. Although the following chapters examine his eighties output exclusively, this is in no way intended to diminish the cultural value of his later work. Although it is true that the bulk of his screenwriting and production efforts during the nineties were markedly different from that which had come before, the majority of those films met with huge commercial success at the box-office (some monumentally so, such as *Home Alone* and its sequel), and proved that although the composition of his intended audience may have changed, Hughes himself remained determined to deliver high-quality motion pictures and was never inclined to underestimate the critical discernment of viewers.

Common to all of Hughes's films was an obvious and infectious enthusiasm for his country. A discernible pride in the United States always seemed apparent from his palpable affection for American cultural customs and traditional values, and even when his social satire was at its most serrated – as in the *National Lampoon's Vacation* films – audiences were never left with much doubt that his mockery concealed a deep and abiding admiration for what made America great in Hughes's eyes. The nation's cultural riches (as seen throughout the Chicago of *Ferris Bueller's Day Off*), the beauty of its natural landscapes (as glimpsed during *Planes, Trains and Automobiles*) and of course the wide-eyed but always sincere patriotic fervour of characters like Clark Griswold all combined to emphasise and celebrate the uniqueness of the United States during the era of the Ronald Reagan White House, the home electronics boom and the heyday of high capitalism.

By analysing these motion pictures and discussing their social and cultural significance in the wider context of the decade, Hughes's importance as a film-maker will be considered, and his prominent and lasting contribution to American cinema assessed. The book concludes with a detailed analysis of *Ferris Bueller's Day Off*, a film which is considered to be among Hughes's most critically successful works and also one of his most structurally refined. As mentioned earlier, the 1980s were a remarkable time in American film-making; a fascinating artistic period which, deeply influenced by the socio-economic environment of the world around it, can never come again. John Hughes's work is one of the reasons why the American cinema of the eighties became so distinctive, and – both popular with critics and financially successful at the box office – it is difficult to overstate his significance in commercial film-making during this exciting period in the industry's history.

1

NATIONAL LAMPOON'S CLASS REUNION (1982)

American Broadcasting Company

Director: Michael Miller
Producer: Matty Simmons
Screenwriter: John Hughes

MAIN CAST

Gerrit Graham	-	Bob Spinnaker
Michael Lerner	-	Dr Robert Young
Misty Rowe	-	Cindy Shears
Blackie Dammett	-	Walter Baylor
Fred McCarren	-	Gary Nash
Miriam Flynn	-	Bunny Packard
Stephen Furst	-	Hubert Downs
Mews Small	-	Iris Augen

John Hughes was born on Saturday 18 February 1950 in Lansing, Michigan. After graduating from Glenbrook North High School in Northbrook, Illinois, he attended the University of Arizona, but left higher education to begin a successful career in comedy writing and, later, advertising.[1] It was in the late seventies that he was invited to join the writing staff of the satirical *National Lampoon* magazine, one of the great American popular cultural icons of that decade, and still a highly recognisable trademark today. A bitingly satirical take on American politics, society and culture, at its height *National Lampoon* was regularly selling issues in the hundreds of thousands on a monthly basis, and throughout the seventies the magazine became a marketing phenomenon, spawning a number of commercially successful spin-offs including a radio show (*The National Lampoon Radio Hour*, 1973-74), off-Broadway theatrical production (*National Lampoon's Lemmings*, 1973), numerous tie-in books, and several vinyl record albums.[2]

With the *National Lampoon* brand name becoming ever more profitable as the seventies progressed, it seemed almost inevitable that a breakthrough into commercial film-making would be made, and in 1978 two features were released under the *National Lampoon* banner. The first was a TV movie entitled *Disco Beaver from Outer Space*, while the other, far more prominent production was John Landis's raucous campus comedy *National Lampoon's Animal House*, which received a cinematic release. Starring John Belushi, Tim Matheson, Tom Hulce and Peter Riegert, the film was an incredible commercial success and would eventually prove to be one of the most profitable films of the decade.

Given the instant cult success of *Animal House*, further releases were planned which would bear the *National Lampoon* brand name, and some years later *National Lampoon's Class Reunion* went into production. However, whereas the screenplay of *Animal House* had been the collaborative product of three *National Lampoon* writers – Douglas Kenney, Christopher Miller and Harold Ramis (who would go on to script many commercial hits throughout the eighties and nineties) – the next film from the

National Lampoon stable was to have only one screenwriter: John Hughes, penning his debut motion picture film script.

The film's action takes place in the dilapidated gymnasium of Lizzie Borden High School (presumably named after the ultimately-acquitted key figure in the infamous Fall River axe murders of Massachusetts in 1892 – the school's motto is 'A Cut Above the Rest'). Although the school has long been closed down and is now in a derelict condition, special dispensation has been granted to Bob Spinnaker (Gerrit Graham) to host a class reunion there for his graduating class of '72. The purpose of this reunion, we soon discover, is to enable Spinnaker – an arrogant, over-achieving windbag – to regale his erstwhile classmates of his success as a yacht salesman since leaving school a decade earlier.

Spinnaker's highly unconventional peers all dutifully emerge in response to their invitations, and every outrageous stereotype imaginable proves to be present and correct. There's Hubert Downs (Stephen Furst), a jovial but lecherous slob who's always on the lookout for his next (or indeed, any convenient) conquest. Then there's Bunny Packard (Miriam Flynn), a snootily aloof cheap-point-scoring harridan who turns the simple act of handing out name-badges into a creative launchpad for some inspired bitchery. Meredith Modess (Shelley Smith) is the pretty but bland class beauty who now advertises hosiery, while Gary Nash (Fred McCarren) is the affably good-natured but stultifying insipid class geek who no-one else can even vaguely remember. Strangely enough, the above are among the most normal of the class; some of the more outrageous remainder of their peer group include Iris Augen (Marya Small), an unlikely temptress who is visually impaired, partially deaf and mildly nymphomaniac, and Delores Salk (Zane Buzby), who once had trouble with her physical mobility but now enjoys considerably improved health after discovering the surprising benefits of demonic possession.

The evening gets off to a rather bland start, due to stilted conversations between people who barely recognise each other after ten years, some authentic 'celebratory' school meals, and an achingly self-congratulatory slideshow presented by Spinnaker, the self-appointed master of ceremonies. Not even a surprise performance by the legendary Chuck Berry (appearing as himself) is able to ignite the party. However, the lethargy soon dissipates with the unexpected arrival of Dr Robert Young (Michael Lerner), a specialist from a local infirmary for the criminally insane. Young comes bearing disturbing news: it transpires that Walter Baylor (Blackie Dammett), a former class nerd who had been subjected to a staggeringly cruel prank on his last night of school in 1972 – a prank which was so traumatic that it was subsequently to turn him insane – has escaped from medical supervision. Young fears that Baylor has infiltrated the school reunion with homicidal intentions, determined to exact belated revenge on his old classmates.

Young's fears soon become manifest when one of the group, new-age religious devotee Milt Friedman (Steve Tracy), is found murdered. Panic then sets in when the rest of the classmates, desperate to escape being the next in line for Baylor's retribution, discover that all of the exterior doors in the school have been securely locked. The mismatched band quickly try (and largely fail) to organise an escape attempt, but as time ticks away and more of their number are picked off, will any of the group manage to survive their ill-advised reunion?

Hughes's script for *National Lampoon's Class Reunion* is an interesting one to observe, particularly in comparison to his later work; although the film's budgetary limitations are sometimes quite clearly on display (as an early attack by Baylor, brandishing an obviously-tinfoil knife, clearly demonstrates) and the action suffers in comparison to the gleeful Bacchanalian frenzy of its celebrated predecessor *Animal House*, there is still some entertainment to be had here. The structure of the film is markedly more simplistic than those of Hughes's later screen-plays, and is impaired at times by a sense of choppiness due to the fact that no one character is ever given ample time to develop satisfactorily. However, there are some early flickers of the sophisticated dialogic interplay which was to characterise Hughes's later features, such as stoner classmate Chip Hendrix's (Barry Diamond) dazed discourse on Jungian psychology, and some acidic put-downs traded between the waspish Bunny and the increasingly arcane, borderline psychotic Delores. Special mention too must go to Hughes's inspired demolition of Spinnaker's character over the course of the film; the always-watchable Gerrit Graham does a commendable job of articulating the arrogance and pomposity of the overbearingly self-righteous would-be socialite, milking his delusions of grandeur for all they are worth. Spinnaker, who is reluctant to put himself in the slightest risk of danger at any stage but who will take the credit for anyone else's accomplishments without hesitation, is one of the film's most memorable characters; his ersatz upper class accent, always-impeccable appearance and constant, laboured name-dropping make him an amusing figure of fun, and an effectively larger-than-life counterpoint to the well-intentioned but chronically dull Nash (a nicely judged tongue-in-cheek performance by Fred McCarren), who overcomes his lack of personality in order to become the unexpected hero of the hour.

One of the most noteworthy aspects of *National Lampoon's Class Reunion* is the fact that the film proves so difficult to place into any one particular genre. The humour is usually bawdy, but at times almost knowingly subtle. At other times, it borders on the surreal. Certainly the film's parodic horror element is difficult to square with other frantic gross-out comedies which would come to populate the genre in the early eighties, such as *Screwballs* (Rafal Zielinski, 1983) and *Bachelor Party* (Neal Israel, 1984). Yet the exaggerated absurdity of the situations that are presented (Baylor's lair in the school basement, for example, is decorated with all the trimmings of traditional horror film conventions including a full set of medieval armour) erode any attempt at a growing sense of peril that might otherwise be expected from typical low-budget horror fare. The irony of this is certainly not lost on Hughes – at one point the trapped classmates, growing tired of incessant panicking at their inability to escape Baylor's clutches, eventually end up playing a game of bingo. Yet for all its occasional inventiveness, the film is permeated with an inescapable undercurrent of simply going through the motions; in particular, the plot twist near the climax is signposted quite significantly in advance, and is almost rather postmodern in its blatant implausibility (even for a pastiche).

Michael Miller's direction is always competent, at times lively, and by and large the production is efficient enough to overcome the budgetary limitations which occasionally creep into view. A theatrical director prior to entering the film business, Miller was at the time perhaps best known for features which included *Street Girls* (1975) and *Silent Rage* (1982). Likewise, the cast – although largely bereft of well-known performers – are clearly performing to the best of their ability, and do seem in many cases to be enjoying the larger-than-life farcicality of the film's perplexingly odd situations. Talented character actor Gerrit Graham had been active in TV and film since the sixties; also a screenwriter, he had appeared in films as diverse as *Demon Seed* (Donald Cammell, 1977) and *Cannonball!* (Paul Bartel, 1976), and in later years would feature in an even wider variety of features including comedy *Big Man on Campus* (Jeremy Kagan, 1989) and science fiction thriller *The Philadelphia Experiment II* (Stephen Cornwell, 1993). He has also made a great many appearances in television programming across several genres. Michael Lerner had also made many appearances on TV and film before appearing in *National Lampoon's Class Reunion*, among them being satire *Alex in Wonderland* (Paul Mazursky, 1970) and thriller *Borderline* (Jerrold Freedman, 1980). Stephen Furst has been active not only as an actor, but also as a producer, writer and director. Although he has made appearances in many films, his best-known role amongst many viewers has been his regular part as Centauri ambassadorial assistant Vir Cotto in J. Michael Straczynski's influential, ground-breaking science fiction television series *Babylon 5* (1993-98). Additionally, Furst had also appeared in

National Lampoon's Animal House, though the trials of the hapless lothario Hubert are a marked contrast from the ill-fated wimp that he had played in the previous film, freshman Kent Dorfman.

National Lampoon's Class Reunion did not fare well with critics at the time, facing a reception which varied from the indifferent to the hostile,[3] and indeed more recent appraisals by film commentators have been equally unsympathetic following the film's release on DVD.[4] Although *Class Reunion* was never to develop the same loyal cult following that *Animal House* retains even today, it is nonetheless an interesting evolutionary link in the *National Lampoon* filmic chain, which would eventually lead to a whole franchise of cinematic offshoots throughout the eighties. For Hughes, the film marked a competent if understated beginning to a screenwriting career that would shortly see him catapulted into the commercial big time. The next time that he would return to script a *National Lampoon* feature, his efforts would meet with infinitely greater success in the eyes of critics and the public alike.

Historical Context

National Lampoon's Class Reunion was released in the United States on 29 October 1982. Perhaps the most prominent concurrent film release that day was Malcolm Leo and Andrew Solt's satire *It Came from Hollywood*, starring Dan Aykroyd and John Candy. Due to the proximity of the Halloween season, two horror films were also making their first appearance in cinemas on that date. They were Larry Cohen's horror film *Q*, starring Michael Moriarty and Candy Clark, and Gary Graver's *Trick or Treats*, featuring Jackie Giroux and David Carradine. Topping the American Billboard Charts at the time of release was John Cougar with 'Jack and Diane'. In the news that week, the People's Republic of China announced that its population had exceeded one billion individuals, sixteen-colour EGA graphics cards became available for IBM-compatible PCs, and Portugal's government agreed upon revisions to its national constitution.

'The screenplay, by John Hughes, is a lot more vulgar and dopey than it is genuinely comic, and most of it is too flat to sustain such a busy lineup of characters. Still, it's reasonably cheerful.'

Janet Maslin, *The New York Times*, 30 October 1982.

'All involved with Class Reunion are to be whipped in the public square until they make a newer, better movie. Oh wait, some of them already have. John Hughes is off the hook.'

Norman Short, *DVD Review*, 28 March 2000.

'Class Reunion may have been a box-office bomb, but writer John Hughes later redeemed himself.'

Leah Collins and Miranda Furtado, *The Montreal Gazette*, 7 April 2012.

2

MR MOM (1983)

Sherwood Productions

Director: Stan Dragoti
Producers: Lynn Loring and Lauren Shuler
Screenwriter: John Hughes

MAIN CAST

Michael Keaton	-	Jack Butler
Teri Garr	-	Caroline Butler
Frederick Koehler	-	Alex Butler
Taliesin Jaffe	-	Kenny Butler
Courtney and Brittany White	-	Megan Butler
Martin Mull	-	Ron Richardson
Ann Jillian	-	Joan
Jeffrey Tambor	-	Jinx

Mr Mom was to mark a change of pace in Hughes's early career. Although a comedy, as *National Lampoon's Class Reunion* had been, this feature was to enjoy a greater budget, a selection of well-known actors – including its talented up-and-coming star – and would come to enjoy greater critical interest. Directed by Stan Dragoti, best known in the early eighties for his successful horror pastiche *Love at First Bite* (1979), *Mr Mom* would demonstrate that Hughes's screenwriting talents had developed beyond the frantic comical mayhem that had been depicted in his debut feature.

Life is sweet for Jack Butler (Michael Keaton) and his wife Caroline (Teri Garr). Jack is employed as a successful engineer at a Michigan car manufacturing plant, while Caroline – a marketing graduate – is a homemaker looking after their three young children. However, their comfortable suburban existence is shaken when the company that employs Jack, hit by an economic recession, unexpectedly lays him off. His shifty manager Jinx (Jeffrey Tambor) insists that due to market pressures there is no practical alternative other than dismissal, but Jack is unconvinced.

Jack finds it next to impossible to find alternative employment in town, due to other companies in the manufacturing industry being affected by the same detrimental economic situation. However, an unforeseen answer to their financial woes soon materialises when Caroline, having dusted off her marketing credentials in order to share the hunt for employment, is offered a job at a prestigious advertising agency. Although Jack is justifiably proud of his wife's achievement, and glad that his family unit has renewed financial support, he feels unprepared for the new domestic role that lies ahead of him as he gets ready to swap places with Caroline and become a stay-at-home father.

At first, Jack throws everything into his responsibilities, taking charge of the school run, grocery shopping, housework and baby care – amongst many other tasks – with varying degrees of ineptitude. However, he soon begins to wonder how Caroline was ever able to balance all of the household duties that he finds himself faced with, especially when he encounters a number of minor domestic disasters including his infant daughter gorged on chilli, the quite possibly possessed vacuum cleaner, and a washing machine malfunction that soon leads to a rapidly flooding basement.

Meanwhile, Caroline finds herself under pressure from her new employers, awkwardly sandwiched between sleazy director Ron Richardson (Martin Mull) and his glacial PA Eve (Carolyn Seymour). The advertising agency she works at is full of disillusioned, cynical hacks, worn out by the rapidly changing consumer market, and the optimistic Caroline – freshly back to the sector – quickly meets with sneering derision from her new colleagues. However, she perseveres, and her innovative take on the advertising process – informed by years as an end-user of the kind of grocery produce that the agency is trying to sell – soon wins the respect of her peers, as well as the unwanted romantic attentions of Ron.

Back home, Jack finds himself slipping into a quagmire of daytime TV soap operas and domestic monotony, where the highlight of his week is a communal card game with a collection of Caroline's friends. The house, along with his appearance, soon becomes dishevelled as Jack begins to coast through life on autopilot. But Caroline – though exhausted from her own heavy workload – eventually pulls Jack back from the brink of ennui, forcing him to reconsider his priorities and take a greater sense of worth in his outlook.

Just as he has returned to a state of workable self-respect, however, things become even more complicated. Traces of foul play begin to emerge at the car manufacturers when Jinx's management comes under harsh scrutiny; Jinx hopes to rely on Jack to cover for his dishonesty, but what exactly will Jack be willing to risk for a chance to return to employment? Meanwhile, Caroline hits the big time when she manages to sell a pioneering advertising package to a tuna manufacturer, forcing her to spend ever longer periods away from home. But as the shady Ron begins to make his move on her, will Caroline risk her family in order to safeguard her prosperous new career?

Mr Mom is a solid high-concept feature, which benefits greatly from strong performances by its two likeable leads. Although Michael Keaton already had an established TV acting career at the time, encompassing many shows including *The Mary Tyler Moore Hour* (1979), *Working Stiffs* (1979), and *Report to Murphy* (1982), his film career was still in its formative stages when *Mr Mom* was released. He had earlier appeared to some acclaim in macabre comedy *Night Shift* (Ron Howard, 1982), alongside Henry Winkler, and of course would later achieve worldwide success with his performances in films such as *Beetlejuice* (Tim Burton, 1988), *The Dream Team* (Howard Zieff, 1989), *Pacific Heights* (John Schlesinger, 1990), and – most notably – the monumentally profitable blockbusters *Batman* (1989) and *Batman Returns* (1992), both directed by Tim Burton. His high-energy performance and obvious enthusiasm for the part enhance his screen presence considerably, and help to elevate the film beyond its initial premise, lending it additional substance. His accomplishment is matched by Teri Garr, who likewise provides an appealing and at times touching performance. Garr had been nominated for the Best Actress in a Supporting Role Academy Award for her performance in *Tootsie* (Sydney Pollack, 1982), and had given many television performances by the time of *Mr Mom* as well as appearing in a wide variety of films over the years. Her recognised comedic talents meant that she was particularly well known at the time for humorous roles in films such as *Young Frankenstein* (Mel Brooks, 1974) and *Oh, God!* (Carl Reiner, 1977), to name but two. However, she was perhaps most recognisable to audiences for her prominent appearance as Ronnie Neary in *Close Encounters of the Third Kind* (Steven Spielberg, 1977).

The film's supporting performances are also strong, particularly in the case of Martin Mull who turns in an admirably seedy performance as smarmy yuppie Ron Richardson. An extremely prolific actor on American television throughout the seventies and eighties, Mull was also known to audiences for his appearance as one of the disc-jockeys in the radio industry-themed *FM* (John A. Alonzo, 1978). Ron's understated rivalry with Jack in particular is handled with relish by both Mull and Keaton, with both actors clearly enjoying the testosterone-fuelled one-upmanship which brews between the two men throughout the course of the film. Smaller roles are every bit as well presented, especially from Carolyn Seymour's nicely observed turn as the icily condescending Eve, Christopher Lloyd's eccentric turn as Jack's fellow engineer Larry, and Jeffrey Tambor as the twitchily mendacious Jinx. Special mention however must go to the talented child cast, Frederick Koehler, Taliesin Jaffe and twins Courtney and Brittany White, who provide totally sound support throughout the film and often steal the show (not least in the movingly humorous scene where Jack has to engage all of his fast-talking skills of persuasion to coax Kenny into parting with his beloved security blanket).

Hughes's script for *Mr Mom* displays substantial advancement in comparison to his debut screenplay, both in terms of style and content. The snappy dialogue evident in *National Lampoon's Class Reunion* became wittier and more sophisticated for his second feature, and Hughes's natural eye for effective characterisation is readily apparent in his skilful contrast between Caroline's developing professional success and Jack's entertainingly-depicted descent into domestic mundanity (and his eventual self-reinvention as he strives to make the most of his new household-based existence). From Jack's growing addiction to cheesy daytime soap operas to his attachment to his trademark housework shirt – which almost becomes a kind of supporting player in its own right – Hughes's attempts to portray the film's characters as quirky, three dimensional beings are vitally important in counterbalancing the restrained sentimentalism which creeps in throughout the course of the third act. Likewise, Caroline's efforts to fight off Ron's unwelcome affections are mirrored amusingly with Jack's desperate attempts to repel Joan (Ann Jillian), an amorous divorcee, which reinforces the couple's dedication to each other even in spite of the new stress which has unexpectedly been placed on their marriage.

There is also a fair amount of subtle social commentary in evidence throughout *Mr Mom*. Having himself been a native of Michigan, Hughes knew only too well the vital importance of heavy industry in the state, to say nothing of the effect of economic turbulence on the manufacturing sector, and thus the consequences of the layoffs at the car factory where Jack is employed are handled with thoughtfulness and more sensitivity than might be expected from a comedy feature. It is interesting, for instance, to note how much more sympathetically the factory's assembly line workers are treated in comparison to the agitated duplicity of Jinx and his superiors, to say nothing of Jack's encounters with other similarly redundant engineers who have found themselves – with their social baseline thoroughly disrupted – every bit as lost as he has become.

Mr Mom met with mixed reviews on its release. Whereas some critics praised Keaton's performance talents (with the caveat that the film's episodic nature rarely gives him the opportunity to engage them quite as fully as might be considered possible)[1], others found the central concept to be rather laboured in its execution and generally over-reliant on incident at the expense of comic realism.[2] That said, critical reception of *Mr Mom* has thawed considerably in recent years, with some modern reviewers noting the film's nostalgic charm and ability to encapsulate Midwestern domestic attitudes of the time.[3] The film also won the Best Family Motion Picture Award for a Comedy or Musical Presentation at the Young Artist Awards in 1984, along with a nomination for Best Young Motion Picture Actor in a Feature Film at the same awards ceremony for Frederick Koehler in his role as Alex Butler.

Mr Mom can be seen to mark a significant gear-shift in Hughes's early career. With its dryly observant depiction of unexpectedly disrupted middle-class domestic lives and a timely if subtle commentary on the economic instabilities affecting America in the early eighties, the film provided many opportunities for him to demonstrate his perceptive command of characterisation and acute awareness of social mores. These aptitudes would be further engaged in his script for another, much more prominent feature which was to be released that summer of 1983: *National Lampoon's Vacation.*

Mr Mom made its first appearance in American cinemas on 22 July 1983, alongside Joe Alves's action sequel *Jaws 3-D*, which starred Dennis Quaid, Louis Gossett Jr and Lea Thompson. Headlining the Billboard Charts that week was The Police with 'Every Breath You Take'. In current affairs at the time, France performed a controlled atomic test explosion at Muruora Island, a violent storm curtailed a concert by Diana Ross in New York City's Central Park, the first solo helicopter circumnavigation of the globe was made by Dick Smith, and Prime Minister Wojciech Jaruzelski announced the end of nineteen months of martial law in Poland.

Representative Critical Opinion

'If they'd taken these characters and their situation and followed through on the implications, on a believable level, they might have come up with a true human comedy. Instead, everything is pushed too far, [and] situations are overwritten and over-directed.'

Roger Ebert, *The Chicago Sun-Times*, 22 August 1983.

'John Hughes, who wrote the much funnier screenplay for *National Lampoon's Vacation*, comes up with only a few novel touches.'

Janet Maslin, *The New York Times*, 26 August 1983.

'Even with Erma Bombeck-style domestic humor like *Mr Mom*'s got in spades, Keaton consistently rises above the mawkish material (as written by a pre-Shermer John Hughes) and turns a turkey into a treat.'

Scott Weinberg, *DVD Talk*, 24 April 2006.

3

NATIONAL LAMPOON'S VACATION (1983)

Warner Brothers

Director: Harold Ramis
Producer: Matty Simmons
Screenwriter: John Hughes, based on his short story 'Vacation '58'

MAIN CAST

Chevy Chase	–	Clark W. Griswold
Beverly D'Angelo	–	Ellen Griswold
Anthony Michael Hall	–	Russell 'Rusty' Griswold
Dana Barron	–	Audrey Griswold
Imogene Coca	–	Aunt Edna
Randy Quaid	–	Cousin Eddie
Miriam Flynn	–	Cousin Catherine
Eddie Bracken	–	Roy Walley

National Lampoon's Vacation was to mark a major progression for both the *National Lampoon* film franchise and for John Hughes's early screenwriting career. Based on Hughes's earlier short story 'Vacation '58', which had appeared in *National Lampoon* magazine back in 1975, the film was to present a much more focused and controlled comedic experience than the unremitting anarchic chaos of *National Lampoon's Animal House* or Hughes's own script for *National Lampoon's Class Vacation,* and was to benefit enormously from a number of excellent performances (including most especially that of its outstanding lead actor).

The film was directed by Harold Ramis, an experienced and successful writer for *National Lampoon* magazine who had also been responsible for co-writing the screenplay for *National Lampoon's Animal House.* Also a producer, Ramis would go on to write and direct a number of successful features throughout the eighties and nineties, perhaps the most prominent of which was *Groundhog Day* (1993), starring Bill Murray, which met with major critical acclaim on its release. Ramis was additionally active as an actor during the same period, and was particularly well-known to audiences in the eighties for his distinctive performance as the eccentric parapsychologist Dr Egon Spengler in Ivan Reitman's massively popular fantasy comedies *Ghostbusters* (1984) and *Ghostbusters II* (1989).

National Lampoon's Vacation centres on the well-intentioned but ill-fated Clark W. Griswold (Chevy Chase), who has arranged a two week break from working in the food additive industry to take his family on a dream holiday to the famous Walley World theme park in California. Clark is heedless of his wife Ellen's (Beverly D'Angelo) warnings that it would be easier to fly there, given that their Illinois home is a dauntingly long drive of almost two and a half thousand miles from their intended destination. But Clark is unperturbed by the prospect of the journey, determined at all costs to spend some dedicated family time on the road with his two young teenaged children (who, it is readily apparent, would much rather be vacationing in Hawaii instead).

Even a mix-up with the purchase of a new car for the long expedition, which lands the family with a hideous pea-green station wagon instead of their intended long-haul vehicle, does nothing to dampen Clark's eagerness for the mammoth road trip ahead.

Sadly for Clark and family, however, his meticulous planning of every detail of the trip is unable to deflect an inordinate amount of bad fortune from heading their way. Although he has devised a jam-packed schedule that draws in visits to any number of well-trodden national tourist attractions, none of which go even remotely to plan, it is the unexpected assortment of detours that cause the greatest amount of pandemonium. From unforeseen excursions into areas ranging from violent inner-city neighbourhoods to the arid deserts of Arizona, Clark will allow no disaster – no matter how severe – to derail his rigidly-planned agenda. As their erratic vacation progresses, Clark and his family encounter long-lost relatives (who, they soon realise, probably should have remained lost), are confronted by issues of life and death – rather more directly than any of them would have anticipated – and attempt to relax in some of the most uncomfortable accommodation ever to be found in North America. Clark even finds time, improbably enough, to be bewitched by a beautiful woman in a red Ferrari (Christie Brinkley). Yet when the Griswolds, against all odds, finally find themselves in California – scarred, bruised, jaded but still largely unbroken – they soon discover that the Walley World experience isn't quite what any of them were expecting...

If there's one thing that can't be disputed about *National Lampoon's Vacation*, it is that the film belongs entirely to Chevy Chase. As the well-meaning but hopelessly beleaguered Clark Griswold, he delivers a terrifically observed performance which never flags. Chase throws everything but the kitchen sink into his portrayal of the sincere, steadfastly family-oriented father, and his comic timing is absolutely impeccable. (Witness, for instance, the slow-motion disintegration of Clark's glasses as he engages in a hopelessly awkward 'meaningful' father-and-son discussion with teenager Rusty (Anthony Michael Hall) following a car crash in the wilderness of Arizona's Monument Valley.) Clark's occasional bouts of hysterical profanity, his obsessive fixation on reaching California at quite literally any cost, and even his apparent dalliance with the notion of adultery are all executed so ham-fistedly by the character – and played so sublimely by Chase – that it is difficult to judge this oddball protagonist's increasingly erratic actions too unsympathetically. Indeed, Clark's inspired descent into semi-deranged mania as he edges ever closer to his intended destination – which plays like Joseph Conrad's *Heart of Darkness* as performed by the Marx Brothers – is an unforgettable experience to behold.

The film's reception with the public was also considerably enhanced by Chase's significant profile as a performer; he had enjoyed enormous popularity as one of the original cast members of NBC's *Saturday Night Live*, and his writing for the show had earned him a number of Emmy Awards throughout the seventies. In the world of cinema, he had met with critical acclaim for his appearances in films such as *Seems Like Old Times* (Jay Sandrich, 1980), written by Neil Simon, and *Under the Rainbow* (Steve Rash, 1981). In 1979, he had been nominated for the Best Motion Picture Acting Debut (Male) Award at the Golden Globes for his perform-ance in the comedic thriller *Foul Play* (Colin Higgins, 1978), and had also worked with *Vacation* director Harold Ramis a few years beforehand, in the celebrated golf club comedy *Caddyshack* (1980).

National Lampoon's Vacation also benefits greatly from a top-notch supporting cast. Beverly D'Angelo puts in an excellent performance as Clark's put-upon wife Ellen, whose fusion of practicality and seemingly endless reserves of patience creates the perfect foil for Clark's hare-brained idealism. D'Angelo had enjoyed a successful film career, having appeared in films as diverse as *Annie Hall* (Woody Allen, 1977) and *Hair* (Milos Forman, 1979), and like Chase was a recognised face to audiences of the time. Anthony Michael Hall and Dana Barron also deliver remarkable performances as the Griswolds' endlessly stressed children, Rusty and Audrey. Hall's laconic delivery and eye-rolling despair at his father's fruitless efforts to keep his vacation schedule on track are brilliantly realised, and Hall would of course go on to collaborate with Hughes on a number of other occasions throughout the eighties. Barron too makes the most of Audrey's line in sarcastic wisecracks and her sibling rivalry with Rusty; although she has marginally less screen time than Hall, Barron nevertheless delivers a rock-solid supporting performance.

The film also features a wildly entertaining patchwork of exceptional cameos from a number of character actors. Foremost among them is Randy Quaid, who comes very close to stealing the show as the unforgettable Cousin Eddie. Succeeding in the intricate task of creating a character that is both repellent and oddly endearing at the same time, Quaid makes the sequences at Eddie's run-down home in Kansas one of the highlights of the film. With his unreservedly cack-handed cadging and unsanitary line in barbequing, Eddie is a character who stays in the memory long after the film has concluded, and it is easy to see why the character was revived for subsequent entries in the *Vacation* series. Other high-profile appearances included Brian Doyle-Murray, a veteran of *Saturday Night Live*, as the manager of Kamp Komfort (a distinctly 'un-komfortable' holiday camp in Colorado), and Eugene Levy – appearing as a car dealership rep – who would later go on to appear in *Splash* (Ron Howard, 1984) as well as *American Pie* (Paul Weitz, 1999) and its numerous sequels. Veteran stage, TV and film performer Imogene Coca creates an impressive performance as the faintly monstrous Aunt Edna, who hitches a ride with Clark and family only to get rather more than she bargained for on the journey. The film also provided a very early role for Jane Krakowski as Eddie's daughter Vicki; Krakowski would later appear in *Fatal Attraction* (Adrian Lyne, 1987) as well as – most notably – a cast regular on David E. Kelley's legal comedy-drama series *Ally McBeal* (1997-2002). And John Candy, who had appeared to great acclaim on *Second City TV* (1976-81) and who would later go on to achieve success in films such as *1941* (Steven Spielberg, 1979) and *Stripes* (Ivan Reitman, 1981), appears in a notable extended cameo as Lasky, the queasy Walley World security guard who finds himself on the receiving end of Clark's hyperactive wrath. Like Anthony Michael Hall, Candy would work with Hughes again on a number of features over the years to come.

Aside from the many skilled performances on display, the film has numerous other praiseworthy qualities, including Ramis's excellent location work which juxtaposes America's stunning natural scenery and famous landmarks with the deeply unconventional venues of the Griswolds' less than successful side-trips across the country. Hughes's script manages, without ever overstating the point, to emphasise the huge gulf that exists between Clark's expectations of the perfect holiday experience (which, one is left in no doubt, the character views as a kind of Holy Grail of ideal commodities) and the grim realities that he is actually faced with. Not even the most peculiar concatenation of ill fortune and bad coincidences can dent Clark's infectious enthusiasm, and Ramis judges the comic timing of each scene perfectly, fully utilising the maximum potential for amusement. His keen eye for satire is also very much in evidence throughout; take, for instance, the avuncular appearance of Roy Walley (Eddie Bracken) at the film's conclusion, whose distinctive moustache and affably wholesome countenance might be considered strangely reminiscent of a certain other world-famous American theme park creator. Ralph Burns's original score is also a lively accompaniment to the film's madcap action, as is the catchy theme song, 'Holiday Road' by Lindsay Buckingham, which features throughout the course of *National Lampoon's Vacation*.

Although humour is one of the most subjective concepts in all of criticism, *National Lampoon's Vacation* was greeted favourably by most reviewers, many of whom were to praise the film's sharp observational comedy – a skilful mix of all-out absurdity and pseudo-realistic situations which would be faintly recognisable to anyone who had ever suffered a holiday disaster.[1] Commentators also focused particular praise on Chase's superlative command of comic intensity.[2] Perhaps because of the film's distinctively eighties sensibilities and fashions,[3] modern reviewers have retained this generally positive appraisal of *National Lampoon's Vacation*,[4] with relatively few dissenting voices.[5]

In economic terms the film has performed well with audiences, both at the time of its cinematic debut and following subsequent releases on DVD, and Ramis and Hughes's ingenious method of subverting familiar elements from family films into a darker, edgier comedy experience made *National Lampoon's Vacation* a firm favourite among many cineastes. Just as the film became one of the best-known features to carry the *National Lampoon* brand name, so too was it to mark a high point in Hughes's early career. Along with the success of *Mr Mom*, it marked him out as a writer of both great comic skill and observant character interpretation, and denoted the beginning of his rise to mainstream success in the American film industry.

National Lampoon's Vacation was released in the USA on 29 July 1983. Also making their first appearance in cinemas were Eric Rohmer's drama *Pauline à la Plage* (*Pauline on the Beach*), featuring Amanda Langlet; Peter Yates's fantasy adventure *Krull*, with Lysette Anthony and Francesca Annis, and Noel Black's comedy *Private School*, which starred Phoebe Cates, Betsy Russell and Matthew Modine. 'Every Breath You Take' by The Police was still at the top of the Billboard Charts, where it would remain until 2 September 1983. Appearing in the news at that time, Laurent Fignon won the Tour de France, flashes of light were observed occurring in the atmosphere of Jupiter's moon Io, the USSR performed a nuclear test at Semipalitinsk, and NASA launched the Telstar-3A satellite.

Representative Critical Opinion

'Most of the gags are more subdued, the sorts of cartoonish witticisms that might turn up in a magazine parody. The screenplay, by John Hughes, keeps these witty but simple.'
Janet Maslin, *The New York Times*, 29 July 1983.

'The film can be awfully dumb at times, yet it's oddly appealing in one of those guilty-pleasure sort of ways as well, thanks largely to a screenwriter and a director who allow their star, Chase, to deliver his uniquely laid-back style of comedy.'
John J. Puccio, *DVD Town*, 17 August 2003.

'It's no masterpiece, but compared to the toothless comedies of its era, its attack on American mythology seems almost worthy of Preston Sturges.'
Dave Kehr, *The Chicago Reader Film Search*, 18 May 2010.

4

NATE AND HAYES (1983)

Paramount Pictures

Director: Ferdinand Fairfax
Producers: Lloyd Phillips and Rob Whitehouse
Screenwriters: John Hughes and David Odell; screen story by David Odell, based on a story by Lloyd Phillips

MAIN CAST

Tommy Lee Jones	-	Captain 'Bully' Hayes
Michael O'Keefe	-	Nathaniel 'Nate' Williamson
Max Phipps	-	Captain Ben Pease
Jenny Seagrove	-	Sophie
Grant Tilly	-	Count Von Rittenberg
Peter Rowley	-	Louis Beck
Bill Johnson	-	Reverend Williamson
Kate Harcourt	-	Mrs Williamson

Nate and Hayes heralded a rather unconventional side-step in Hughes's career; after the considerable success of his past two features, both of which had focused on different aspects of domestic life to generate comedic entertainment, here he was to leave the United States far behind and make an unexpected switch to the less familiar territory of the swashbuckling adventure film instead. The result would prove to be a feature unlike any other that Hughes would be involved in throughout the course of his prolific filmography.

Temporarily moving beyond the familiar territory of contemporary American social mores and his trademark sophisticated comic observation, *Nate and Hayes* would see Hughes engaging with the kind of fast-paced historical action adventure that had become increasingly popular in the early 1980s following the monumental success of *Raiders of the Lost Ark* (Steven Spielberg, 1981). Although Ferdinand Fairfax's film could not hope to match the sheer energy and structural refinement of Spielberg's masterpiece, the film would nonetheless feature many spirited action set-pieces, strikingly beautiful location work, and some engaging turns from its central cast – not least a lively, full-blooded performance from Tommy Lee Jones in the role of protagonist Captain 'Bully' Hayes.

Nate and Hayes (also released under the title of *Savage Islands* in some international markets, including the United Kingdom) additionally marked a rare instance where Hughes was to collaborate with another writer on a feature film. This co-writer was David Odell, who had been one of the writers on TV's hugely popular *The Muppet Show* (1976-81) and who had also penned the script for much-loved family feature *The Dark Crystal* (Jim Henson and Frank Oz, 1982). Odell would later go on to write the screenplays for two other high-profile eighties films, *Supergirl* (Jeannot Szwarc, 1984) and a big-screen adaptation of children's animation *He-Man*, entitled *Masters of the Universe* (Gary Goddard, 1987). Together, Hughes and Odell would create a fictionalised and gleefully embellished account of the adventures of real-life American-born pirate Captain William 'Bully' Hayes (c.1829-c.1877), including an explanation of how he came to take command of his famous vessel, the *Leonora*.

The lion's share of the film's narrative takes place in flashback, as Hayes – captured by Spanish colonial authorities after a botched rifle-smuggling operation for a rebelling tribe of natives leaves his crew dead or missing – relates his story to a spellbound constabulary clerk. Hayes (Tommy Lee Jones) explains that the chain of events that led to his incarceration began when he accepted a contract to ferry a young clergyman, Nathaniel Williamson (Michael O'Keefe), and his beautiful fiancée Sophie (Jenny Seagrove), to a Christian mission deep in the South Pacific. The affable Sophie quickly strikes up a rapport with the charming rogue Hayes, whereas the prim Nathaniel is much more reserved.

Hayes delivers the two young lovers to the remote mission run by Nathaniel's uncle and aunt (Bill Johnson and Kate Harcourt) before weighing anchor. Tragically, however, Nathaniel and Sophie's wedding is barely in progress when the settlement is attacked by the brutal Ben Pease (Max Phipps) and his cutthroat band of pirates. Seeking to incarcerate the native villagers and sell them into slavery, Pease's men murder the Reverend Williamson and his wife and mistakenly leave Nathaniel for dead. However, upon discovering that Sophie has survived the slaughter, Pease decides to kidnap her for his own undisclosed ends.

Nathaniel regains consciousness and, discovering that sites across the settlement have been emblazoned with a blackbird emblem, erroneously concludes that Hayes is responsible for the murder of his family. Taking to sea in a makeshift raft, he is quickly shipwrecked and only narrowly manages to survive when Hayes's ship – more by good fortune than design – happens to cross his path. Once aboard, Nathaniel angrily confronts Hayes, only for the captain to explain the true nature of the situation. Hayes and Pease had once been business associates, but a violent disagreement led Hayes to accidentally (and rather intimately) maim Pease. Pease consequently never forgave Hayes for his actions, and resolved from then on to implicate Hayes in every criminal action that he was to participate in.

Hayes tails Pease's ship, the *Leonora*, into a rough and ready free port. Once docked, Hayes seeks out Pease in order to confront him, while Nathaniel steals aboard the *Leonora* in search of his missing bride. It quickly transpires that Pease has already smuggled Sophie off the ship. However, Nathaniel discovers a hidden note from her which details Pease's intended destination: Ponape. Unknown to Nathaniel, Pease has struck a deal with Count Von Rittenberg (Grant Tilly), who seeks to expand Prussian colonial influence in the area by establishing a base in Ponape, a territory occupied by fearsome cannibalistic tribespeople. Pease has had prior dealings with the King of Ponape (Prince Tui Teka), and offers to act as intermediary for the Prussians in exchange for a sky-high fee. Reluctantly, the Count agrees to his demands in the hope that a treaty can be brokered.

Hayes eventually manages to track down the elusive Pease, and his crew quickly make short work of the outlaw pirate gang. However, they are unable to prevent Pease's escape with Sophie on a steam-powered Prussian gunboat. Hayes's ship, the *Rona*, is no match for the speed of the ironclad vessel, and as such he commandeers the *Leonora* in order to keep pace with his adversary. At Ponape, Pease's best attempts at diplomacy are unable to convince the cannibal king to allow a Prussian settlement. Offers of shrunken heads and other arcane gifts are unable to satiate his greed. Pease and the Count only succeed in convincing the king to co-operate in their plan when they offer him Sophie as a human sacrifice. He readily agrees to this, and Sophie is bound to an esoteric pulley-driven device which will plunge her into a fire-pit in praise of the cannibal gods. Fortunately, Hayes and Nathaniel arrive with their crew and overpower the natives, freeing Sophie only moments from her death.

Pease and the Count once again manage to escape Hayes's

grasp and make it back to the Prussian gunboat. Nathaniel fears that the *Leonora*, a wooden sailing ship, will be no match for the powerful steam-powered vessel, particularly as it is armed with a substantial rocket turret. A tense game of cat and mouse then ensues as the Count and the gunboat's captain (Peter Vere-Jones) pursue the hastily escaping *Leonora*. It is only by taxing Hayes's ingenuity to the very limit that he and his crew are able to overpower the Count's forces and finally win the day.

Back in his prison cell, Hayes concludes his story by explaining that he was ultimately to return Nathaniel and Sophie to civilisation before adapting his business practices to encompass more benevolent activities. The latter, it seems, has come about through a combination of the influence of Nathaniel and Sophie's virtues and the result of his hard-fought victory over the venal Pease. Hayes's account is then brought to an abrupt end with the arrival of prison guards, much to the clerk's dismay. Yet even as he is led out to face his execution at the gallows, it seems that fate has one final surprise in store for Bully Hayes.

In the grand tradition of the action adventure genre, the plausibility and rigidity of *Nate and Hayes*'s plotline are often readily subordinated to eye-catching set-pieces and frantic, entertaining incident. It is therefore to the film's benefit that Hughes and Odell's script maintains a genial, appealing approach to characterisation which lends the action a pleasantly tongue-in-cheek knowingness. The frantic escapades in *Nate and Hayes* are greatly enhanced by the presence of a skilled central cast of performers, foremost among them Tommy Lee Jones as the sardonic, wayward but ultimately honourable Hayes. Jones had been a veteran of film and television from the mid-1960s, but had achieved greater prominence in the eyes of the film-going public by the early eighties thanks to critically acclaimed performances in films such as *The Eyes of Laura Mars* (Irvin Kerschner, 1978) and *The Rainmaker* (John Frankenheimer, 1982), an adaptation of the N. Richard Nash play of the same name. In recent years, Jones has gone on to achieve enormous success in the film industry due to high profile appearances in films as diverse as *Heaven and Earth* (Oliver Stone, 1993), *Batman and Robin* (Joel Schumacher, 1995), *Men in Black* (Barry Sonnenfeld, 1997) and more recently in *No Country for Old Men* (Joel and Ethan Coen, 2007). He was awarded an Academy Award for Best Actor in a Supporting Role for his barnstorming performance as Marshal Sam Gerard in *The Fugitive* (Andrew Davis, 1993), and has additionally received Oscar nominations for Best Supporting Actor in *JFK* (Oliver Stone, 1991) and Best Actor for *In The Valley of Elah* (Paul Haggis, 2007). Jones's rendering of Hayes, with his pronounced southern drawl and idiosyncratically laid-back attitude to the piratical havoc which regularly surrounds him, makes for a distinctive and likeable protagonist. Much is made of Hayes's personal code of ethics, and the fact that he considers himself a businessman first and foremost, with piracy merely an occasional and incidental means to an end. Jones is especially adroit in his handling of the on-deck banter with Hayes's rag-tag crew, and performs even better when sparring (both verbally and literally) with Hayes's old adversary Ben Pease, who proves to be a worthy and entertaining opponent; Max Phipps's depiction of the sinister, dishevelled rival captain is memorably droll and creepy in equal measure. The devious Pease also functions effectively as a counterpoint to the pompously buffoonish Count Von Rittenberg. Grant Tilly delivers a calculatedly amusing performance as the militaristic aristocrat with imperialistic designs on the South Pacific, and the slow-motion puncturing of the Count's self-important grandiosity is one of the film's main sources of comic relief.

There is also an effective contrast between the eccentrically unorthodox Hayes and the strait-laced earnestness of Michael O'Keefe's Nathaniel 'Nate' Williamson. O'Keefe was well known to audiences for his prominent appearance in the popular *Caddyshack* (Harold Ramis, 1980) and his Academy Award-nominated supporting performance against Robert Duvall in *The Great Santini* (Lewis John Carlino, 1979), and his rendering of Nathaniel provides a suitably spirited foil to Jones's protagonist, with the snootily pious Harvard-educated clergyman becoming progressively less stuffy and more adventurous as the film's plot advances. Also satisfying is O'Keefe and Jones's characters' on-screen chemistry with Jenny Seagrove's glacially calm Sophie. Seagrove appears to take much playful pleasure in her character's seemingly unbreakable composition in the face of ever-increasing adversity (even when mere seconds away from a fiery death), and she underplays Sophie's natural sense of irony with great panache. The nicely understated love triangle which she unwittingly creates with Nathaniel and Hayes is also entertainingly handled by all three actors, particularly by Jones.

Yet for all of the screenplay's dry wit and pleasing performances from the cast, it cannot be denied that viewing *Nate and Hayes* sometimes feels like an oddly unbalanced experience. Lacking the finesse of Hughes's later work, the film's pace is occasionally uneven, with sporadically awkward transitions between frenetic drama and chatty exposition, and a few of the action sequences appear leaden and overtly signposted. Yet the film never seems to have much pretension beyond presenting an efficient slice of escapist entertainment, and in this it almost always succeeds. Director Ferdinand Fairfax makes the most of some phenomenal location work, not least in a scene where a stranded Nathaniel stands isolated on a rocky outcropping deep in the empty ocean, and the shipboard scenes are all treated with noteworthy accuracy of period detail. The beautiful scenery which forms the backdrop to much of the film's action is easily the equal of other maritime adventure films of the same period, including features such as acclaimed naval drama *The Bounty* (Roger Donaldson, 1984), and the set design is highly competent throughout. Trevor Jones's stirring soundtrack is also worthy of mention, providing a suitably bombastic accompaniment to the action, no matter how intense or chaotic it may be.

Even with its larger-than-life heroes and villains and an imaginative willingness never to let history get in the way of a good story (Jones's performance lays emphasis upon rather more honourable characteristics than the history books tend to recognise in the real Hayes), *Nate and Hayes* ultimately did not perform well at the box-office, falling immeasurably short of blockbusters such as *Indiana Jones and the Temple of Doom* (Steven Spielberg, 1984) which would dominate cinemas the following year. However, the film did share many formal qualities with other action films of the period,[1] most especially *King Solomon's Mines* (J. Lee-Thompson, 1985), which starred Richard Chamberlain and featured a number of common factors, not least a charmingly unconventional fortune hunter as the central character and an eclectic range of imperialistic Prussians in antagonistic roles.

Nate and Hayes met with a lukewarm reception by commentators at the time of its release, with reviews ranging from the pedestrian[2] to the unabashedly hostile.[3] However, in spite of its lack of commercial success, the film did eventually establish something of a cult fan-base which has rehabilitated its critical reputation to a degree in recent years.[4] This has been further enhanced by an international DVD release in 2006, which was to introduce the film to an entirely new audience[5] following other, higher-profile pirate-themed features such as *Cutthroat Island* (Renny Harlin, 1995) and most especially *Pirates of the Caribbean: The Curse of the Black Pearl* (Gore Verbinski, 2003) and its sequels.

As mentioned earlier, *Nate and Hayes* formed an interesting departure for Hughes, as it presented a genre and style that he was never to engage with before or since. Although his characteristic flair for sharp, intelligent dialogue was to shine through at various points in the film, *Nate and Hayes* is about as far from a traditional John Hughes film as it is possible to imagine, and indeed today it remains one of the most obscure features in his oeuvre. However, one other probable reason for its lesser-known status may be the fact that it was to find itself sandwiched between the huge success of *National Lampoon's Vacation* and *Sixteen Candles*, his next film which was to prove – even today – to be one of his most immediately recognisable.

Nate and Hayes was first released to American audiences on 18 November 1983, a date which was to provide cinemagoers with no shortage of choice. Released on that day were horror films including Richard Fleischer's *Amityville 3-D*, Jackie Kong's *The Being*, Robert Hiltzik's *Sleepaway Camp*, and Umberto Lenzi's *Incubo sulla Città Contaminata* (*City of the Walking Dead*). Additionally, there was family entertainment in the form of Bob Clark's *A Christmas Story*, Paul Lynch's suspenseful *Cross Country*, and also drama with John G. Avildsen's *A Night in Heaven* and Gleb Panfilov's *Vassa*, an adaptation of the Maksim Gorky play. Perhaps most prominently, Barbra Streisand's *Yentl* was to make its cinematic debut on this day; it would later go on to win an Academy Award. Meanwhile, Lionel Richie was headlining the Billboard Charts with 'All Night Long (All Night)'. In that week's current affairs, the first cruise missile was sited in England's Greenham Common, the Turkish Republic of Northern Cyprus was proclaimed, and Harm Wiersma retained his reigning title at the Checkers World Championship.

'You know you're in trouble when people are carrying swords and talking like TV game-show contestants. The movie uneasily occupies a niche between swashbuckling pirate movies and *Raiders of the Lost Ark*.'
Roger Ebert, *The Chicago Sun-Times*, 22 November 1983.

'[*Nate and Hayes*] tries unsuccessfully to be that buoyant, rollicking pirate movie we all remember having seen in our youth and which they don't make anymore.'
Vincent Canby, *The New York Times*, 18 November 1983.

'Aside from a humorously uncomfortable performance by Tommy Lee Jones (and a hilariously unconvincing one by O'Keefe), there's very little in *Nate and Hayes* that isn't cheesy, silly, or downright obnoxious. The movie shoots for light-hearted adventure but sinks like a leaden anchor.'
Scott Weinberg, *DVD Talk*, 2 June 2006.

5

SIXTEEN CANDLES (1984)

Channel Productions/Universal Pictures

Director: John Hughes
Producer: Hilton A. Green
Screenwriter: John Hughes

MAIN CAST

Molly Ringwald	-	Samantha Baker
Michael Schoeffling	-	Jake Ryan
Haviland Morris	-	Caroline Mulford
Gedde Watanabe	-	Long Duk Dong
Anthony Michael Hall	-	Farmer Ted/'The Geek'
Paul Dooley	-	Jim Baker
Carlin Glynn	-	Brenda Baker
Justin Henry	-	Mike Baker

Sixteen Candles was to mark John Hughes's debut as a film director, but it is also a feature which has become equally well known for making a star of Molly Ringwald, perhaps the actor who became most closely associated with Hughes's filmic output throughout the course of the 1980s.[1] It was this film which was to firmly establish the style and themes for which Hughes would become best known in subsequent years, and which was to mark the first of his many hugely successful entries in the teen movie genre.

Sixteen Candles was not only Hughes's earliest attempt at a teen movie, but it is now widely regarded as one of his most successful.[2] By the time of the early eighties, the teen film genre was in the process of changing out of all recognition. Although the modern American teen movie had been around in one form or another from at least the 1950s, with prominent entries including Marlon Brando's famous appearance in *The Wild One* (Laslo Benedek, 1953) and James Dean's iconic performance in *Rebel Without a Cause* (Nicholas Ray, 1955), the rapidly changing customs and fashions of subsequent generations naturally required the genre to adapt swiftly to changing social conditions. From *High School Confidential* (Jack Arnold, 1958) and *The Party Crashers* (Bernard Girard, 1958) to *American Graffiti* (George Lucas, 1973) and *Over the Edge* (Jonathan Kaplan, 1979), the teen movie has long been an interesting barometer of the period in which each particular entry in the genre has been produced. By the time of the eighties, teenagers had become sophisticated, savvy consumers, highly attuned to the commoditised, market-driven society in which they were growing up. *Times Square* (Allan Moyle, 1980), *Flashdance* (Adrian Lyne, 1983) and *The Outsiders* (Francis Ford Coppola, 1983) were all prominent early-eighties features which showcased uniquely different aspects of the teen consciousness of the new decade, and rang the changes around the now-dated genre films which had originated from the seventies.

Yet from the very onset of his engagement with the genre,

John Hughes seemed able to capture the voice of the eighties teenager with greater sensitivity than any of his peers at the time. Reflecting the social confidence of his characters without straying into youthful arrogance, and proving to be emotionally touching without ever being sentimental, *Sixteen Candles* was to mark the beginning of the most popular and critically successful period in Hughes's filmic career in the eighties.

It's Samantha Baker's (Molly Ringwald) sixteenth birthday, and it's fair to say that things could have gone better. Her parents and siblings have forgotten the significance of the date, largely because of the arrangements for the impending marriage of her older sister Ginny (Blanche Baker), which are overshadowing everything and anything else. To make matters worse, Samantha finds herself spending the day at school pining over hunky senior student Jake Ryan (Michael Schoeffling), her dream man whom she fruitlessly lusts after, but who is already in a steady relationship with the beautiful but shallow Caroline Mulford (Haviland Morris). Her gloom over his unavailability is only equalled by her determination to fight off the deeply unwelcome affections of the geeky 'Farmer' Ted (Anthony Michael Hall), a well-intentioned but hopelessly inept would-be lothario.

Samantha returns home to discover her bedroom is now occupied by visiting relatives, and – in an attempt to politely withdraw – comes face-to-face with Long Duk Dong (Gedde Watanabe), an eccentric, party-loving Asian exchange student who has been living with her grandparents during term-time. While the pompously vain Ginny prepares for her wedding, parents Jim and Brenda (Paul Dooley and Carlin Glynn) grit their teeth and prepare to meet the soon-to-be in-laws. Keen to avoid the ensuing turmoil, Samantha excuses herself in order to attend a high school dance. Unexpectedly, however, she finds herself with an unanticipated partner in the form of Long Duk when her grandparents 'volunteer' her services as a reluctant cultural tour guide for the evening.

Sadly the dance doesn't go well for Samantha either, as she

finds herself painfully reminded of Jake's lack of accessibility while simultaneously watching Long Duk quickly striking it lucky with bubbly, well-endowed classmate Marlene (Deborah Pollack). However, Samantha is completely unaware that Jake has now also become intrigued by her, and is secretly trying to discover more about her. He enlists the help of Ted, who has spent the evening hopelessly trying to impress Samantha with his ham-fisted attempts at dancing. Ted, in turn, finally manages to have a quiet heart-to-heart with a reluctant Samantha, and discovers the true depth of her feelings for Jake. Putting two and two together, he tries to convince Jake that his romantic interest in Samantha is in fact reciprocated.

The action moves to the home of Jake's parents, where a raucous party is taking place (largely, we are led to suspect, at Caroline's bidding). The house's interior undergoes a riotous demolition at the hands of its inebriated teenaged interlopers, but while Caroline and the others drink themselves into oblivion Jake remains wistful. He tries unsuccessfully to call up Samantha on her bedroom phone (leading to a memorably terse encounter with the curmudgeonly grandparents who are currently occupying her bed). His efforts frustrated, he then hatches a astute plan; tiring of Caroline's spitefulness and superficiality, he asks Ted (who has gatecrashed the party) to drive her home in his father's Rolls Royce. Ted, who is neither insured or licensed, readily agrees. Now drunk into a state of euphoric torpidity, Caroline proves to be a surprisingly genial travelling companion, and by the time night turns to dawn she and Ted discover that their encounter has led them to an entirely unexpected conclusion.

The morning finally brings Ginny's wedding, much to the relief of the Bakers who now are longing to see it over with. However, with the discovery of a catatonic Long Duk in the front yard (his evening being rather more of a success than he'd ever imagined) and the revelation that the bride has taken an overdose of muscle relaxant to deal with a rather sensitive health issue, the ceremony doesn't get off to the smoothest of starts (to put it mildly).

Jake, meanwhile, finds Ted and Caroline parked across from the church together and – taking his scheme to its planned conclusion – uses the apparent tryst as grounds to break up with her. However, he is surprised when Caroline appears unmoved by his severance of their relationship, as she now appears to be more interested in Ted instead (much to Ted's bemusement). Jake then wastes no time in racing for the church as the families head off after the vows have been exchanged. But will he be in time to present Samantha with her happy ending, and can his new-found devotion to her prove to be the best belated birthday gift that she could hope for?

The one thing that is immediately apparent about *Sixteen Candles* is that Hughes's directorial style closely matches the finesse of his writing skills. Scenes advance with slick efficiency; the camera does not linger unduly, nor does it ever treat its subjects cursorily. Indeed, Hughes's overriding respect – and talent – for characterisation are firmly at the forefront of *Sixteen Candles*, and the film was to establish many of the key themes of his teen movies early on. This includes his keen ear for the teenage idiom of the time, which is employed very skilfully, and also his capacity for subverting character archetypes in entertaining and unforeseen ways. In Long Duk Dong, for instance, Gedde Watanabe's energetic performance creates a memorable character who, though almost always amorous and often gleefully bizarre in his behaviour, is never less than congenial or charismatic. Neither Hughes nor Watanabe ever allow the character to descend into crude racial stereotyping. This is also true of Ginny's Italian-American in-laws-to-be; although Hughes generates humour from cultural differences, he does so in a droll manner rather than a distasteful one.

Likewise, the geeky Ted and his (often reluctant) entourage of nerdish friends are never delineated solely by way of well-worn clichés, and beneath their veneer of insecurity we are always made aware of the existence of very distinct personalities –

something which is never less than apparent from the sophisticated dialogic interplay which Hughes employs throughout the film. Even the most hackneyed of high school truisms, the shallow prom queen and the muscular, hero-worshipped senior, are subverted with great lightness of touch, both ultimately being developed into something far more substantial and three-dimensional than any initial summation would suggest. Hughes even plays this subversion to his advantage within the storyline of the film itself, given how much of the plot is centred around Samantha's assumption that Jake's lofty position in the high school social hierarchy is what isolates him from her, while she never really entertains the thought that his own individual feelings may supersede his purely peer-defined status. This was only the first time that Hughes would explore such social dynamics within high school culture, and he would return to the theme with even greater incisiveness as the decade progressed.

The film has many other laudable qualities, from Ira Newborn's energetic score (skilfully augmented by occasional themes from classic American television shows and films for a tongue-in-cheek comic effect) to Jackie Burch's inspired casting. Yet in terms of performance, *Sixteen Candles* belongs first and foremost to Molly Ringwald. Her remarkable rendering of Samantha is entirely convincing, and lends the film a strong sense of cohesion – particularly important given the generally chaotic nature of the action which unfolds with ever-greater momentum as the plot progresses. Although *Sixteen Candles* was not Ringwald's debut film performance – as well as television acting, she had previously appeared in the Shakespeare-influenced drama *Tempest* (Paul Mazursky, 1982) and science fiction fantasy *Spacehunter: Adventures in the Forbidden Zone* (Lamont Johnson, 1983) – it was Hughes's film which was to make her into a star, and indeed her performance as Samantha Baker remains one of her most fondly remembered by audiences. Ringwald's performance achieves a finely-attuned balance, depicting her character's anxiety, disappointment and emotional turmoil without ever straying into peevishness or petulance, and articulating Samantha's earnest affections for Jake while deftly avoiding any trace of mawkish sentimentality. Indeed, Ringwald's accomplishment in the role of Samantha provides the perfect demonstration of Hughes's absolute resolve to depict his teenage cast with respect and depth of character throughout.

Interestingly, Samantha's main counterpoint in the film is not her love interest Jake, but rather the hapless (and largely hopeless) Ted. Anthony Michael Hall pulls off a fascinating and convincing feat of character creation, presenting the audience with someone who is simultaneously an idiosyncratic geek and a strangely noble anti-hero. Ted's social awkwardness and general oddness of character are very effectively offset by his sympathetic qualities of compassion and his ability to listen, such that when he unexpectedly manages to achieve romantic success by the film's conclusion – albeit in a way that neither he nor the audience could have foreseen – he seems just as deserving of his amorous accomplishment as Samantha does. The role of Ted was a world away from the beleaguered Rusty Griswold of *National Lampoon's Vacation*, and Hall amply demonstrates a broad comic range even at this comparatively early stage in his career. This is particularly evident from the film's auto-shop sequence, where Ted manages in one short period of time to convert Samantha's revulsion towards him into a strained but amicable rapport. The eventual employment of his strangely potent capacity for persuasion, which allows him to convince Samantha to part with her underwear in order to let him win a wager, provides one of the *Sixteen Candles'* comedy high-points (and also gives Hall the opportunity to deliver the best line in the film).

Yet although *Sixteen Candles* is indisputably a film dominated by its teenage cast, there are almost as many stand-out performances by adult performers. These include the ever-watchable Paul Dooley as Samantha's father Jim. Active on American TV since the early 1960s, Dooley had become noted for appearances in films as diverse as *The Out of Towners* (Arthur Hiller, 1970), *Popeye*

(Robert Altman, 1980) and the splendidly bewildering comic fantasy *Strange Brew: The Adventures of Bob and Doug McKenzie* (Dave Thomas and Rick Moranis, 1983). He provides an interesting and congenial depiction of the harried Jim, a supportive father who is working hard to keep everyone happy (while knowing exactly how unlikely his success will be) as pre-wedding pandemonium sets in around his family. Dooley displays a real gift for comic timing when, following his realisation (a day too late) that he has forgotten Samantha's birthday, he apologetically visits his daughter late at night to deliver a ham-fisted apology. The discomfited sincerity of his regret, beautifully counterbalanced by Ringwald's sleepy bewilderment, makes for a memorable comic scene, and one which helps to accentuate another common characteristic of Hughes's teen movies: that the adult cast, while largely well-meaning, are usually consumed by their own everyday lives to the point that, more often than not, they find themselves unable to relate to (and connect with) the shrewdly perceptive modern youth around them.

Paul Dooley had been awarded a National Board of Review award in 1980 for his supporting performance in drama *Breaking Away* (Peter Yates, 1979), and would later go on to be nominated for Emmy Awards for his television work in 1994 and 2000. Yet he was not the only prominent award winner in the cast, as Blanche Baker had won an Emmy award for her performance in the harrowing television mini-series *Holocaust* (Marvin J. Chomsky, 1978), and Justin Henry had been nominated for an Academy Award for his supporting appearance in high-profile divorce drama *Kramer vs Kramer* (Robert Benton, 1979). *Sixteen Candles* also featured a number of noteworthy early appearances from young actors such as John and Joan Cusack, who would both later go on to achieve significant success in the film industry, and a welcome cameo appearance from the ever-popular character actor Brian Doyle-Murray.

Sixteen Candles performed well with the critics of the time, with many commentators considering the film to be a modern breath of fresh air into a sometimes hackneyed genre.[3] Some were to praise Hughes's intelligent, smartly-employed dialogue[4], while others put the strong performances by the film's mostly teenaged cast squarely at the forefront of their commentary.[5] More recent reviews have remained supportive of the film's merits, approving of the faithfully-rendered depiction of eighties life, music and fashions[6] as well as its nostalgic charm.[7] *Sixteen Candles* was also not to be overlooked at awards ceremonies, with both Molly Ringwald and Anthony Michael Hall winning Young Artist Awards in 1985 for their performances, while Jackie Burch was nominated for the Artios Award for Best Casting by the Casting Society of America in the same year.

With *Sixteen Candles*, Hughes was to achieve enormous popularity with audiences, and demonstrated that his talents were not restricted to his considerable aptitude for screenwriting. The relatable world that he creates, populated by embarrassing grand-parents, bickering siblings and the tongue-tied self-consciousness of first love, works so successfully on so many levels that it comes as no surprise to consider the shockwaves that the film would send through the teen movie genre. Seeming far removed in tone from rowdily popular entries in the genre at the time, such as *Meatballs* (Ivan Reitman, 1979) and *Porky's* (Bob Clark, 1982), *Sixteen Candles* was an intelligently written and socially aware break from tradition which would quickly become one of Hughes's best-loved features with audiences, and it remains so even today. Indeed, so great is the affection held for the film by aficionados of the genre that occasional talk surfaced, in the years prior to Hughes's death, of the possibility of a sequel being filmed, though no actual production was ultimately ever to surface.[8] Nonetheless, with the release of *Sixteen Candles* Hughes had made a decisive impact on the cinemagoing audience, and – now firmly on the map of American cinema – his next feature was to expand upon the themes he had begun to develop in his directorial debut and take them to entirely new levels.

Sixteen Candles made its debut in American cinemas on 4 May 1984. Also released on that day were a number of dramas including Amos Poe's *Alphabet City*, John Hanson's *Wildrose*, and Joel Silberg's dance-themed *Breakin'*. The same date was also to see the appearance of a number of historical dramas including Peter Ustinov's *Memed My Hawk*, Sidney J. Furie's wartime thriller *Purple Hearts* and Roger Donaldson's epic *The Bounty*, starring Mel Gibson and Anthony Hopkins. Comedy films were represented by Glenn Jordan's *The Buddy System* and Gian Luigi Polidoro's *Rent Control*. Phil Collins was topping the Billboard Charts that week with 'Against All Odds (Take a Look at Me Now)'. In the news at that time, a total of 1700 skiers in Sweden participated in a landmark alpine event, the United States and United Kingdom performed atomic test explosions at the Nevada Test Site, and the play *Sunday in the Park with George* premiered at the Booth Theater, New York City; it would eventually run for a total of 604 performances.

'It doesn't amount to much, and it's certainly not to be confused with a work of art or a work of any depth, but the young writer-director John Hughes has a knack for making you like the high-school age characters better each time you hear them talk.'
Pauline Kael, *The New Yorker*, 28 May 1984.

'Hughes has created a lovely heroine, Samantha (Molly Ringwald), and her treats her as delicately as he might a princess opening her first ball. His affection for her redeems the picture.'
David Denby, *New York*, 28 May 1984.

'Hughes, working from his own screenplay, does an expectedly stellar job of initially luring the viewer into the proceedings, as the filmmaker front-loads the picture with tremendously likable characters and an emphasis on scenes and sequences of an irresistibly engrossing nature.'
David Nusair, *Reel Film Reviews*, 13 February 2012.

6

THE BREAKFAST CLUB (1985)

A&M Films/Universal Pictures

Director: John Hughes
Producers: John Hughes and Ned Tanen
Screenwriter: John Hughes

MAIN CAST

Emilio Estevez	-	Andrew Clark
Anthony Michael Hall	-	Brian Johnson
Judd Nelson	-	John Bender
Molly Ringwald	-	Claire Standish
Ally Sheedy	-	Allison Reynolds
Paul Gleason	-	Principal Vernon
John Kapelos	-	Carl the Janitor
Ron Dean	-	Mr Clark

The Breakfast Club[1] is perhaps the most recognisable of all John Hughes's teen features, and is certainly among his most iconic. For many people, it is – even now – considered to be among the best-known of his entire filmography, given how skilfully and astutely it succeeds in its artistic purpose. *The Breakfast Club* was also to mark an even more deliberate break from pre-existing teen movie conventions than had been the case with *Sixteen Candles*, and so thorough was Hughes's shattering of generic shibboleths that this film, perhaps more than any of his films still to come, was to clearly establish his pioneering approach to the teen movie genre and the resultant redefinition of genre boundaries which were to result from it.

The Breakfast Club has also become well-known as one of the two films which were responsible for popularising the Brat Pack,[2] a loose designation attributed to a group of talented young American actors who would go on to considerable renown as the decade progressed. The other main film associated with the rise of the Brat Pack was Joel Schumacher's *St Elmo's Fire*, also released in 1985, and some of the cast members of that film would also appear in *The Breakfast Club*, meaning that the Brat Pack appellation encompassed a fairly extensive range of performers.[3] They included Anthony Michael Hall and Molly Ringwald (who starred in *The Breakfast Club*); Andrew McCarthy, Rob Lowe and Demi Moore (who appeared in *St Elmo's Fire*), and Emilio Estevez, Ally Sheedy and Judd Nelson (who performed in both films). The Brat Pack term is malleable enough to suggest the presence of numerous other actors under the same umbrella, but the above are generally regarded to be the core players associated with the term. Individual Brat Pack actors had appeared in earlier teen dramas, including *Class* (Lewis John Carlino, 1983) and *Oxford Blues* (Robert Boris, 1984), and would continue to perform in films with themes of youth and emergent adulthood until the turn of the decade, including features such as *Fresh Horses* (David Anspaugh, 1988) and *Betsy's Wedding* (Alan Alda, 1990).[4]

With *The Breakfast Club*, Hughes was to build upon several

themes that he had established in *Sixteen Candles*, including the subtle differentiation between teen anxieties that were specific to the decade and those which spanned generations, being more universal in nature. He was also to further explore the gulf that existed between the disillusioned, goal-driven world of adulthood and the increasingly sophisticated lives and views of the free-thinking generation which was cruising headlong towards it. As with *Sixteen Candles*, the traditional themes of the teen movie genre – such as the significance of peer pressure and the questioning of traditional authority – were only to mark the foundation of Hughes's line of rigorous social enquiry which were to take place throughout *The Breakfast Club*.

It's early Saturday morning at Shermer High School in Illinois. Five students who barely know each other have been summoned to a day of detention by the school's self-important principal, Richard Vernon (Paul Gleason). It quickly becomes apparent that each student is radically different in nature, coming from separate cliques within the school and having been landed in detention for wildly dissimilar reasons. Upright sports enthusiast Andrew Clark (Emilio Estevez) was caught taping a classmate's backside together in the school locker room in an ill-judged moment of waywardness. Smart-mouthed rebel John Bender (Judd Nelson) is found setting off a fire alarm, falsely triggering an evacuation of the school. The spoiled, upmarket Claire Standish (Molly Ringwald) was discovered truanting when skipping classes to spend time shopping. Bookish intellectual Brian Johnson (Anthony Michael Hall) is punished when a flare gun accidentally goes off inside his locker. And eccentric loner Allison Reynolds (Ally Sheedy) hasn't done anything to warrant being in detention, but having decided that she didn't have any better way of spending the weekend she elects to turn up anyway.

Vernon sets the students the task of composing an essay of at least a thousand words about who they are and, by extension, how they see themselves. Their boredom is only matched by the awkwardness that they feel at being trapped together; given the rigid social factionalism within the school, none of them would ordinarily mix with one another, let alone interact at length. But as they are alone in the school, save for Vernon and an affable janitor named Carl (John Kapelos), they soon discover that they need to work together to some degree in order to get through the day.

The social chasm which exists between the students soon becomes readily apparent. Bender, who has an unhappy home life, resents Claire's privileged snootiness. Andrew defends Claire from Bender's animosity, but finds himself at variance with Bender when his slavish conformity is mocked. Brian, who is meekly compliant and has difficulty relating to anyone outside of his own narrow peer group, finds that he has to fight the others' preconceptions about his geeky, anally-retentive persona. And Allison, with her natural reticence and kleptomaniac tendencies, seems almost as much at odds with herself as she is with the others.

As the day wears on, the students discover that they may indeed have far more in common with each other than any of them could have anticipated. All of them seem to be in dispute, to some degree, with their parents, often keen to fulfil expectations while simultaneously longing for a better way to relate to their mothers and fathers. Whilst recognising the irresistible lure of peer pressure, none of them are quite sure why they have each become so entwined by its influence – even Allison, whose facade is largely defined by being set at diametric odds with what is expected by the mainstream. By the time their detention session nears its conclusion, all of the group feel that they have learned something about each other, but moreover that they have discovered certain unavoidable truths about themselves. Only one question remains for the students – what exactly is the appropriate response to the question that Principal Vernon set in his essay assignment?

Just as the sensitively-rendered romance of *Sixteen Candles* had seemed a welcome contrast to the riotous revelry of other teen movies of the early eighties, so too was *The Breakfast Club* a significant break from the conventions of the traditional campus comedy – to say the least. That Hughes is able to sustain an entire motion picture from the interactions between half a dozen teenagers in a single location is noteworthy in itself; that he does so with such style and panache is nothing short of remarkable. His lively direction is continually augmented by many beautifully observed moments, from Bender's inventively booby-trapped locker to the group's tongue-in-cheek rendition of the 'Colonel Bogey March' popularised by *The Bridge on the River Kwai* (David Lean, 1957). The film has also become famous for featuring one of the most memorable soundtracks of the eighties, most especially the title track, Keith Forsey's 'Don't You Forget About Me', which was performed to great acclaim by Simple Minds (indeed, the track would later meet with great success in the singles charts on both sides of the Atlantic).

Central to the success of *The Breakfast Club*, of course, is the array of memorable performances from its ensemble cast. Both Molly Ringwald and Anthony Michael Hall had already become established in the psyche of the cinemagoing public for their roles in *Sixteen Candles*, and here give very different performances to meet the film's disparate demands. The supercilious but elegant Claire is a marked contrast from the appealing warmth and charm of Samantha from *Sixteen Candles*, while Brian's nerdy interjections and deep social insecurity form an interestingly complimentary study of high school geekdom when equated to the comparative flamboyance and self-doubting showmanship of 'Farmer' Ted. Emilio Estevez, who in later years would become an acclaimed director, had previously appeared in *The Outsiders* (Francis Ford Coppola, 1983) and *Repo Man* (Alex Cox, 1984), and his beautifully restrained performance as the energetic but earnest Andrew contrasts magnificently with the joyfully flippant noncompliance of Judd Nelson's Bender. Nelson, who would also subsequently become a writer and producer, was known to audiences of the time for his appearances in *Making the Grade* (Dorian Walker, 1984) and *Fandango* (Kevin Reynolds, 1985), and delivers a career-best performance as Bender, a teacher-baiting delinquent nightmare who absolutely refuses to back down in the face of authority, irrespective of the consequences. Rounding off the group is Ally Sheedy's Allison, the least conformist of all the students and one who is – in physical terms, at least – altered the most profoundly by the day's revelatory events. Sheedy had performed in a number of features throughout the early eighties, including *Bad Boys* (Rick Rosenthal, 1983) and *Oxford Blues* (Robert Boris, 1984), though she was perhaps best known at the time for her appearance in technological drama *WarGames* (John Badham, 1983), which had earned her a nomination at the Young Artist Awards for Best Young Motion Picture Actress in a Feature Film. Sheedy excels in peeling back the layers of the inscrutable Allison until the audience are able to consider the fact that, while they may not fully identify with the person that she is, they do at least have some understanding of how she sees life and why she has developed into the character that she has become.

Although the performances of the Brat Packers are absolutely pivotal to the success of the film, the sparse adult cast are also uniformly excellent. This is particularly true of Paul Gleason's tour-de-force rendering of the tragi-comic school principal, Richard 'Dick' Vernon.[5] A pompous, strutting authoritarian who is as disillusioned with his career as he is embittered by the disappointment of life in general, Gleason delivers a note-perfect interpretation of the sort of balefully malevolent teacher who is instantly recognisable to just about anyone who has ever attended high school. From his arrogant bearing to his ostentatious clothing, Vernon is presented as a kind of archetypal dis-approving teacher of the late-modern era in a manner effective enough to transcend generations. A veteran character actor, Paul Gleason had appeared widely on TV and in films such as *Fort Apache the Bronx* (Daniel Petrie, 1981) and *Trading Places* (John Landis, 1983), but he was rarely more memorable than in his appearance in *The Breakfast Club*. The students' constant (and highly successful) attempts to outwit, taunt and evade Vernon throughout the course of the day are as inspired as they are entertaining. Yet for all his spiteful despotism within the school, Principal Vernon is not simply a straightforward figure of fun. Given the film's message that everyone is a unique individual irrespective of any presupposition which may be generated by their place in the social order, Hughes emphasises that Vernon is no different in this regard and subtly applies an additional strata of characterisation to him as the film progresses, emphasising just how disenchanted and cynical the principal has become. For the students, we know that the punishment of detention lasts only for a Saturday, but Vernon, we are led to suspect, is similarly trapped in a lifelong commitment which is largely of his own making.

John Kapelos, who had previously played Rudy Ryszczyk in *Sixteen Candles*, also impresses as Carl the savvy school janitor. Carl is clearly almost as contemptuous of the self-important Vernon as the students are, though for entirely different reasons – he perceptively notes the way in which Vernon demands unconditional respect from the students while never affording them any consideration in return. Carl's rapport with the high school rebels forms a useful counterpoint to Vernon's heavy-handed condescension towards them. Kapelos had been a fairly prolific performer in the film world of the early eighties, and had also appeared in features including *Class* (Lewis John Carlino, 1983) and *The Naked Face* (Bryan Forbes, 1984). Other adult roles in *The Breakfast Club* are exclusively reserved for the very brief appearances of the students' various parents who drop them off at detention, and it is noteworthy that Hughes himself makes a rare uncredited cameo as Brian's father, seen only fleetingly at the film's climax when arriving to drive him home.

At the core of *The Breakfast Club* is a range of themes stemming from Hughes's deft exploration of the rigid social system which operates within high school, and the cliques which constitute the structure of this system. Andrew finds himself questioning why he is so acquiescent to mainstream expectations of him as an athlete, a student and a social individual. Conversely, Allison must examine the reasons why she so thoroughly subverts and rejects exactly this kind of passive social compliance. Brian, whose personality is initially almost buried by overwhelming parental and establishment pressure to keep his head down and ensure his future prospects, contrasts with the popular and ostensibly *laissez-faire* Claire, desperate to embrace her individuality whilst simultaneously enslaved to the opinions and attitudes of her peers. At odds with all of the others, at least initially, is the fiery Bender. Judd Nelson's high-energy performance is one of the film's most impressive features, and his rendering of the quick-witted, tenaciously intractable classroom rebel is most remarkable not because of his spontaneously droll exchanges or his entertainingly confrontational demeanour, but rather due to the simmering anger and burning resentment which lies just below the surface, threatening to erupt at any moment. Bender's relentless brinkmanship with Vernon becomes ever sharper as the day continues, and takes on a darker edge as Vernon finally starts to reach the end of his tether. Yet even when humiliated and faced with two months of additional detention due to his persistent defiance of Vernon's authority, the anarchic Bender is still unable to back down because he knows that every shred of his own self-respect now hinges on maintaining his opposing position to Vernon and, by extension, the establishment at large.

A common thread which runs through *The Breakfast Club* is the pressure that is placed on teenagers to conform to the preconceived notions not only of their peer group, but also of adults whose own obligations have led them to forget what it was like to be a teenager themselves. Thus the students' own individual expectations of life are coloured by the influences of their respective parents, whose experiences and misgivings have had a sobering effect on the views of their offspring. In turn, Hughes also deals with a perennially recurring motif in teen movies, that of the importance of belonging often being juxtaposed with the essential need to be an individual. This is proficiently considered in the short essay which Brian writes on behalf of the group, his reading of which both opens and closes the film. This essay has become one of *The Breakfast Club*'s most memorable features, and was so emblematic of the film's offbeat but insightful approach to its subject matter that it has been endlessly emulated and parodied ever since.

The sheer entertainment value arising from the colourful interplay between Hughes's characters amply demonstrates why *The Breakfast Club* has become, in the eyes of critics as well as audiences, one of the most memorable works in 1980s American popular film-making. Yet at the time of the film's release, its critical reception was uneven. Some commentators were sceptical but cautiously optimistic about Hughes's fresh approach to a well-worn genre,[6] whilst others were much less convinced of the film's merits.[7] However, *The Breakfast Club*'s subsequent cult status in eighties movie lore – and the significant nostalgia that it holds for audiences – has meant that recent analytical appraisals of the film have been much warmer in tone.[8]

So wide-ranging is the appeal of this groundbreaking and distinctively Hughesian take on high school rebellion that the film is still occasionally screened in cinemas today,[9] in addition to receiving regular airings on television.[10] Although the fashions may have changed and the music has inevitably dated, the film's overarching themes of youth rebellion and the desire to fit in without losing oneself still resonates with audiences even today. Like *Sixteen Candles*, there have even been occasional reports in recent years of potential interest in a sequel being produced in the future, though the untimely death of John Hughes has made the likelihood of such a project considerably less probable.[11]

The Breakfast Club was instrumental in profoundly energizing the American teen movie genre, reinventing it so intensely that the film's influence was to be felt for many years to come.[12] The seismic success of *The Breakfast Club* would inadvertently launch scores of imitations, and its lasting commercial success ensured that John Hughes was indisputably to become a name that was to stay on the lips and in the minds of cinematic commentators both in America and throughout the world.[13]

The Breakfast Club went on general release on 15 February 1985, alongside dramas such as Daniel Petrie's *The Bay Boy*, Uri Barbash's prison-themed *Me'Ahorei Hasoragim* (*Beyond the Walls*), and Sidney Poitier's musical dance feature *Fast Forward*. The same date saw the release of thrillers including John Landis's *Into the Night* and Phillip Borsos's psychologically suspenseful *The Mean Season*. Rounding off the releases were Harold Becker's romantic sports drama *Vision Quest*, Bob Clark's action comedy *Turk 182!*, and Albert Brooks's *Lost in America*. At number one in the Billboard Charts that week was 'I Want to Know What Love Is' by Foreigner. Appearing in current affairs that week, King Hussein of Jordan signed an accord with Palestinian leader Yasser Arafat, CNN reporter Jeremy Levin was released in Beirut after having been held hostage, and the World Chess Championship in Moscow between Anatoly Karpov and Garry Kasparov was abandoned with no result.

'*The Breakfast Club* doesn't need earthshaking revelations; it's about kids who grow willing to talk to one another, and it has a surprisingly good ear for the way they speak.'
Roger Ebert, *The Chicago Sun-Times*, 15 February 1985.

'There is nothing quite so depressing, for anyone but teenagers, as the average American movie directed towards the youth market. But John Hughes [...] has come up with something much more intelligent in *The Breakfast Club*.'
Derek Malcolm, *The Guardian*, 16 June 1985.

'Hughes has made funnier (*Ferris Bueller*) and better (*Pretty in Pink*), but this is the only one you could get away with calling iconic. Good and bad, it's still the definitive '80s teen movie – and, to paraphrase Simple Minds – don't you forget about it.'
Simon Crook, *Empire Online*, 4 February 2006.

7

NATIONAL LAMPOON'S
EUROPEAN VACATION (1985)

Warner Brothers

Director: Amy Heckerling
Producer: Matty Simmons
Screenwriter: John Hughes and Robert Klane, from a story by
John Hughes

MAIN CAST

Chevy Chase	-	Clark Griswold
Beverly D'Angelo	-	Ellen Griswold
Dana Hill	-	Audrey Griswold
Jason Lively	-	Russell 'Rusty' Griswold
John Astin	-	Kent Winkdale
Eric Idle	-	The Bike Rider
William Millowitsch	-	Fritz Spritz
Erica Wackernagel	-	Helga Spritz

John Hughes was to take a short break from the teen movie genre – and from directing – when he co-wrote the screenplay to *National Lampoon's European Vacation*, a sequel to Harold Ramis's popular original film in the *Vacation* series. Collaborating with Robert Klane, an award-winning veteran screenwriter for both television and film, Hughes also devised the story for this offbeat follow-up. *European Vacation* was directed by Amy Heckerling, known to audiences for having helmed crowd-pleasing films such as *Getting It Over With* (1977), *Fast Times at Ridgemont High* (1982) and *Johnny Dangerously* (1984), and who would later write and direct popular films including *Look Who's Talking* (1989) and *Clueless* (1995).

Reprising their roles as the hapless Clark and Ellen Griswold were Chevy Chase and Beverly D'Angelo. Chase's comic skills had remained firmly in the public eye thanks to critically successful appearances in films such as *Deal of the Century* (William Friedkin, 1983) and, more prominently, *Fletch* (Michael Ritchie, 1985). D'Angelo had also earned further critical success due to performances in films including *Finders Keepers* (Richard Lester, 1984) and *Get Out of My Room* (Cheech Marin, 1985). She had also appeared, to great acclaim, as Stella DuBois Kowalski in John Erman's television presentation of *A Streetcar Named Desire* (Tennessee Williams, 1984), a performance which subsequently earned her an Emmy nomination for Outstanding Supporting Actress. (Additionally, *A Streetcar Named Desire* would reunite D'Angelo onscreen with Randy Quaid – *Vacation*'s Cousin Eddie – who also received a nomination at that year's Emmy Awards due to his supporting performance as Harold Mitchell.)

Anthony Michael Hall and Dana Barron, who had portrayed the Griswolds' long-suffering children Rusty and Audrey, were succeeded in the sequel by actors Jason Lively and Dana Hill. Lively had appeared on TV and in the film *Brainstorm* (Douglas Trumbull, 1983) prior to *European Vacation*, while Hill – who was also known for her prolific television work since the late seventies – had performed in films including *Shoot the Moon* (Alan Parker,

1981) and *Cross Creek* (Martin Ritt, 1983). This change of cast was to begin a long-running gag amongst fans that the appearances of the Griswold kids were always altered from film to film, remaining perennially youthful while their parents aged normally. This culminated in a droll line in the series' final instalment – *Vegas Vacation* (Stephen Kessler, 1997) – which confirmed the fact that Clark himself is hardly able to recognise them.

For once in their lives, the Griswold family has benefited from some good fortune. More by luck than design, they have won the top prize on a TV game show – a two week vacation around Europe. Clark is elated; not only will he have the opportunity to catch up with distant German relatives, but he'll also be able to make use of his new video camera (which, being an early eighties model, is about the same size as a breeze-block). Clark's camera has so far been relegated to shooting home movies and an amateur song and dance routine by his wife Ellen which has become, to put it mildly, rather close to his heart. For her part, Ellen is quietly resigned to the prospect of a couple of weeks travelling across a foreign continent with Clark, though she surreptitiously hopes that there will be time for the two of them to rediscover their marital passion against the romantic backdrop of Europe. Their children Rusty and Audrey, however, are less than enamoured at the prospect of the vacation. Rusty senses the potential for endless dull trips around heritage sites, while Audrey can't bear the thought of being away from her new boyfriend Jack (William Zabka).

The first stop on the Griswolds' tour is London, which – in spite of their grand expectations (Ellen dreams of meeting the Royal family) – turns out to be rather more pedestrian than they'd anticipated. Their grandiose-sounding hotel is disappointingly cramped and run-down, and – even worse – they can only find four channels on their room's television set. Following a few motoring mishaps due to Clark discovering – a bit too late – that the British drive on the opposite side of the road than he's used to, the family end up trapped on the Lambeth Bridge roundabout, endlessly circling next to Whitehall as Clark tries his best to find an exit (and fails). Thus they see a great deal of the exterior of Big Ben and the Palace of Westminster, but little else. They do, however, manage to resume their sightseeing just before leaving the country, when a short visit to Stonehenge has an unexpected outcome.

Next they move on to Paris, where Clark is determined to enjoy the unique cultural experiences on offer at any cost (including a high-speed visit to the Louvre; the family manage to race around its galleries within fifteen minutes of arriving). Rusty is annoyed when his chances of romance at the Eiffel Tower are thwarted by an embarrassing personalised beret that Clark has made him wear, while Audrey is incensed when she receives an airmail letter from her boyfriend and discovers that one of her best friends has made a move on him in her absence. Clark, meanwhile, is more concerned by the fact that his video camera has been stolen – particularly as his private footage of Ellen's dance routine had been recorded on the same tape that was in the camera at the time.

A quick side-trip has then been planned by Clark so that he can visit the family's relations in rural Germany, the Spritzes (William Millowitsch and Erica Wackernagel). There's only one drawback to Clark's plan: although he and Ellen have corresponded with the Spritzes by letter, they haven't a clue what the couple actually look like. The language barrier fortunately masks an unfortunate error of mistaken identity, but an even worse blunder awaits them when Clark accidentally starts a fight during a traditional German folk dance, leading the family to race frantically from a pursuing mob of angry villagers. This is particularly disappointing for Rusty, who once again finds his romantic ambitions thwarted by Clark's mishaps. After the Griswolds manage to make good their escape, it's on to the final destination of their journey: Rome.

Upon arrival in Italy, Clark and Ellen unwittingly become ensnared in a robbery plot devised by two criminals (Victor

Lanoux and Massimo Sarchielli), whose interrupted hold-up of a Bureau de Change forces them to conceal the store's manager (Jorge Krimer) in the locked boot of a car. Clark, in search of Traveller's Cheques, finds himself being handed the keys to the car by one the criminals, in the guise of it being a rental vehicle. He thus inadvertently removes the evidence from the crime scene but, being obsessed as ever with sightseeing, is oblivious to any of these internecine goings-on.

Ellen is crushed when she discovers herself on a billboard poster advertising a pornographic film – it seems that Clark's stolen video camera footage has been put to less than savoury uses. Storming back to the hotel, she is kidnapped by one of the crooks when his attempt to retrieve the bound-and-gagged manager from the Griswolds' car is thwarted. This then culminates in a frantic chase through Rome with Clark and the kids, as well as a beautiful Californian (Moon Zappa)[1] whom Rusty has befriended in the city. Can Clark win the day and retrieve Ellen in time, avoiding a tragic end to their vacation?

It could be argued that Hughes and Klane's screenplay for *National Lampoon's European Vacation* suffers to some extent from the fact that (by necessity) it presents a less familiar experience to American viewers than the knowing cross-country chaos of the original *Vacation*, set entirely within the confines of the United States. However, what the film's situations lack in domestic cultural satire and parodying of American traditions is compensated for by the entertaining interpretation (and occasional sly subversion) of European national stereotypes. The sharpness of the original film's observant social commentary has been blunted in the sequel, but the Griswolds' wide-eyed, fish-out-of-water artlessness is firmly retained as they meander through a journey that is much more pliable than the focused 'quest' structure of the first *Vacation*. Indeed, Clark is so good-natured and ingenuous that he appears an even more sympathetic character this time around, still desperate for everyone to enjoy their holiday experience at absolutely any cost. Hughes's quick eye for sardonic caricature is evident in his treatment of the tourist trade throughout the film; when Clark orders food at a Parisian restaurant, clearly revelling in the French reputation for fine cuisine, the viewer is treated to footage of a bored chef gracelessly splattering a microwaveable meal onto a plate. Although the film at times presents the viewer with some exaggerated cultural clichés – a London full of ultra-polite eccentrics and Cockney rhyming slang, or a Paris replete with rude waiters and condescending hotel staff – everything is handled with a general air of knowing light-heartedness, and the audience is left with the abiding impression that Europe falls foul of the Griswolds rather than the opposite being the case.

The film has many nicely-observed sight gags and decent character moments. Clark wears a sweater emblazoned with the Walley World logo, harkening back to the original film, while we soon discover that Rusty has transformed from a subdued adolescent voice of reason into a hormonally-charged teenager, his every attempt at romantic conquest thwarted (both intentionally and accidentally) by Clark at every turn. The longing look on Lively's face as Rusty ogles a besotted honeymooning couple in Paris speaks volumes about the character's constantly frustrated romantic motivations. The subplot concerning Audrey's unfaithful boyfriend sometimes appears overly obtrusive, but is played out so wittily by Hill that it never strains the viewer's patience. Likewise, D'Angelo builds upon the reserved, self-possessed take on the long-suffering Ellen that she began in *Vacation*, which contrasts nicely with Chase's madcap, larger-than-life perform-ance. His gift for physical comedy is even more evident this time around, most especially in the unexpectedly (and amusingly) violent folk dance in Germany, and then again in his beautifully-observed truculence during the sulky, near-silent train journey to Rome.

The supporting cast are uniformly excellent, even although their appearances tend only to be brief. John Astin, affectionately remembered as Gomez Addams in *The Addams Family* (1965-66), is particularly amusing as amorous game-show host Kent

Winkdale. The trip to Britain brings fleeting but memorable appearances from director and character actor Mel Smith, stage and screen star Maureen Lipman, actor and comedian Robbie Coltrane, and also Ballard Berkeley, known best to international audiences for his role as Major Gowen on British television's much-loved situation comedy *Fawlty Towers* (1975-79). Writer and director Eric Idle, of *Monty Python's Flying Circus* fame, gives an especially funny recurring performance as an accident-prone cyclist whom Clark injures in London, and who then unexpectedly (and somewhat unluckily) continues to bump into the Griswolds later in their vacation. William Millowitsch and Erica Wackernagel are similarly comical as the genial but perpetually baffled Fritz and Helga Spritz, while Victor Lanoux is smoothly charming as the shady career criminal who tries (and fails) to win Ellen's affections.

European Vacation is not without its drawbacks, most notably the awkward pacing as the film lurches from a series of interconnected humorous set pieces into an elaborate mini-crime caper at the beginning of the third act. Though Amy Heckerling's direction was considered in some quarters to be rather uneven in places,[2] she does undeniably make good use of many prominent European landmarks, including Buckingham Palace, the Eiffel Tower, the Colosseum, and the Cathedral of Notre Dame de Paris. These visual attractions provide the backdrop for many of the film's sight gags, ranging from the inspired (the observation level of the Eiffel Tower) to the achingly clichéd (Stonehenge). The score by Charles Fox is both energetic and efficient, successfully punctuated by a number of contemporary tracks from artists which included Plastic Bertrand, Power Station and Danger Zone. The film also features the welcome return of Lindsey Buckingham's foot-tapping 'Holiday Road', which by now had more or less become the Griswolds' unofficial vacation anthem.

Ultimately *European Vacation* did not fare as well at the box-office as its predecessor, nor was it as favourably received by the critics. Commentators' views were to range from the merely lukewarm[3] through to the unenthusiastic but vaguely appreciative.[4] Interestingly, retrospective reviews in recent years have remained unconvinced of the film's merits, with nostalgia doing little to soften the tone of critical analysis.[5] Yet in spite of this, *European Vacation* was not forgotten at awards ceremonies of the time, with Charles Fox's original score winning a BMI Film Music Award, and Jason Lively being nominated for Best Starring Performance by a Young Actor at the Young Artist Awards.

With *National Lampoon's European Vacation*, Hughes had taken a short side-step from his innovative work in the teen movie genre, and indeed the success of the films which surround *European Vacation* have meant that his contribution to its screenplay has become one of his lesser-known works. Today, it is considered by many to be the least successful of the four Chevy Chase *Vacation* films,[6] although for many it still remains an entertaining diversion with considerable reminiscence value. For his next feature, however, Hughes would return to the teen movie once again – and to the director's chair – with yet another new approach up his sleeve.

National Lampoon's European Vacation first hit the big screen in America on 26 July 1985. Also on that day, two foreign dramas were making their debut in the United States – Francis Veber's *La Chèvre* (*The Goat*), starring Gerard Depardieu, and Mira Recanati's *Elef Nishikot K'tanot* (*A Thousand Little Kisses*). Both of these films were receiving their first screenings in America following original 1981 release dates in their countries of origin. Also newly on release were Cary Medoway's supernatural romantic comedy *The Heavenly Kid* and Tim Burton's family adventure *Pee-Wee's Big Adventure*, with Paul Reubens in the title role. But perhaps the most prominent release on that date was Hector Babenco's complex drama *Kiss of the Spider Woman*, starring William Hurt and Raul Julia, which went on to win an Academy Award for Hurt's performance and receive nominations for four other Oscars. Topping the Billboard Charts that week was 'A View to a Kill' by Duran Duran, the title song from the eponymous fourteenth film in Eon Productions' James Bond series. In current affairs at that time, Alan García was sworn in as Peru's President, the Punjab Accord was signed between Indian Prime Minister Rajiv Gandhi and Akali Dal President Harcharan Singh Longowal, and a team of deep-sea divers led by Mel Fisher discovered the wreck of the Spanish galleon Nuestra Señora de Atocha.

Representative Critical Opinion

'[*National Lampoon's European Vacation*] has a jokey, loose-jointed comic style. While it's very much a retread, it succeeds in following up the first film's humor with more in a similar vein.'
Janet Maslin, *The New York Times*, 27 July 1985.

'Story (by John Hughes) of a frenetic, chaotic tour of the Old World, with Chevy Chase and Beverly D'Angelo reprising their roles as determined vacationers, is graceless and only inter-mittently lit up by lunacy and satire.'
Variety Staff, *Variety*, 9 August 1985.

'John Hughes once again pens the screenplay, but it feels disjointed and oddly meandering for a Hughes script.'
Patrick Naugle, *DVD Verdict*, 10 August 2010.

8

WEIRD SCIENCE (1985)

Universal Pictures

Director: John Hughes
Producer: Joel Silver
Screenwriter: John Hughes

MAIN CAST
Anthony Michael Hall	-	Gary Wallace
Kelly LeBrock	-	Lisa
Ilan Mitchell-Smith	-	Wyatt Donnelly
Bill Paxton	-	Chet Donnelly
Suzanne Snyder	-	Deb
Judie Aronson	-	Hilly
Robert Downey	-	Ian
Robert Rusler	-	Max

With *Weird Science*, John Hughes was to attempt an interesting and typically brave cross-pollination of the teen movie and the science fiction genre. Emblematic of his pioneering artistic determination in the eighties, the result would prove to be a refreshingly energetic escapade which presented audiences with something quite new, whilst balancing generic reinvention with long-held conventions that stemmed from the respective histories of both genres.

Science fiction was big business in the film industry of the mid-1980s. Although it was a genre that had a long and established history with the cinema, reaching as far back as *Charcuterie Méchanique* (Louis Lumière, 1895) and *Le Voyage dans la Lune* (Georges Méliès, 1902), filmic science fiction went through a golden age of popularity during the fifties and sixties, finding great favour with the public. However, the genre was to reach even greater heights in the 1970s thanks to a succession of critically and commercially successful blockbusters including *Star Wars* (George Lucas, 1977), *Close Encounters of the Third Kind* (Steven Spielberg, 1977), *Alien* (Ridley Scott, 1979) and *Star Trek: The Motion Picture* (Robert Wise, 1979). By the time of *Weird Science*'s release, some of the most lucrative films at the eighties box-office had been science fiction features, including *E.T.: The Extra-Terrestrial* (Steven Spielberg, 1982), *Blade Runner* (Ridley Scott, 1982), *The Terminator* (James Cameron, 1984), and perhaps most notably the two top-grossing *Star Wars* sequels, *The Empire Strikes Back* (Irvin Kershner, 1980) and *Return of the Jedi* (Richard Marquand, 1983). Thus by midway through the decade, there was unmistakeable interest in science fiction among the cinema-going public, and by engaging directly with the field of contemporary fantasy Hughes was to tap specifically into growing interest in the new home computer technology which was beginning to make its way into the lives of people right across America. This theme had been picked up very effectively by technologically-focused Cold War thriller *WarGames* (John Badham, 1983) and whimsical comedies like *Electric Dreams* (Steve Barron, 1984), and Hughes was to follow in this tradition by harnessing the developing audience familiarity with the increasing role of computers in modern life, while also adding a youth culture spin to conventional expectations of the sci-fi genre. The distinctive result would indisputably prove to be *Weird Science*.[1]

Best friends Wyatt Donnelly (Ilan Mitchell-Smith) and Gary Wallace (Anthony Michael Hall) are rapidly becoming sick and tired of their geeky self-image. Their nerdish traits and lack of social confidence mean that, in spite of their best efforts, they are both approaching sixteen with no hope of a date in sight. Wildly unpopular at Shermer High School, they find themselves frenetically trying to devise some new way of gaining credibility for themselves amongst their peers.

With Wyatt's parents (Doug MacHugh and Pamela Gordon) out of the town for the weekend, Gary is invited for a sleep-over – an opportunity for the pair to lament the embarrassment of an unfortunate incident that took place in front of the school's female gymnastics team earlier in the day. However, during a late-night TV screening of *The Bride of Frankenstein* (James Whale, 1935), Gary has a plan. If the pair can't find a woman who is willing to date them, they'll have to build one for themselves. A reluctant Wyatt is persuaded to use his computer to simulate their shared idea of the perfect female form, though he reminds Gary that it is, after all, only an image – nothing more. However, after hacking into a government installation in order to 'borrow' some additional processing power, things take an unexpected turn. They begin to feed the computer additional data about their simulated subject – not only physical characteristics, but also mental prowess and qualities of personality. With the machine now running haywire (even pulling the plug from the wall can't slow down the process, much less stop it), an opportune bolt of lightning strikes the house, astonishing the pair as Wyatt's simulation manifests itself in stunning physical reality.

The end result of this perplexing process is Lisa (Kelly LeBrock), a beautiful woman who – ostensibly, at least – appears to be in her mid-twenties. With an expansive intelligence and knowing wit to match her physical flawlessness, she is everything that Wyatt and Gary could possibly dream of in a partner. There's only one problem; now that they've created her, they haven't a clue what to do next. Thus Lisa finds herself forced to take matters into her own hands. Conjuring up a flash car and some well-tailored outfits for the pair, she takes them on a mystery tour into the city, eventually settling on a visit to the eclectic Candy Bar. Her aim is to get both of the boys to loosen up a little within a relaxed social setting, but she is only marginally successful; Gary gets blind drunk on bourbon and starts speaking in a bizarre strain of cod-bluesy vernacular, while Wyatt lives in dread of the hostile reception he will face from his obnoxious older brother Chet (Bill Paxton), who is minding the house during his parents' absence.

The two awaken in the morning to discover that the aftermath of the previous night's chaos appears to have been completely eliminated, thanks to Lisa's enigmatic powers. After managing to evade the oppressive Chet, Wyatt and Gary head for a local mall to buy Lisa perfume and some other supplies. However, their new-found sense of self-esteem doesn't last long before they are publicly humiliated by arrogant party jocks Ian and Max (Robert Downey and Robert Rusler), who are attempting – unsuccessfully – to impress their girlfriends Deb and Hilly (Suzanne Snyder and Judie Aronson). Max and Ian's interest is greatly piqued when they briefly catch sight of Lisa, though they are bewildered when they eventually discover that she is with their two geeky nemeses. Lisa then stuns everyone when she invites the antagonistic pair to a party being held at Wyatt's house – a fact that particularly astonishes Wyatt, given that it's the first that he's heard of it.

Determined that Gary and Wyatt are going to have a good time, Lisa has left no stone unturned in preparing the house for a raucous bash. However, when a vast number of teenagers arrive out of the blue – most of whom the pair have never seen before in their lives – Gary and Wyatt retreat to the bathroom while the party starts to gain momentum downstairs. There, they find themselves interrupted by Deb and Hilly, with whom (after a few awkward false starts) they eventually manage to strike up a friendly rapport. Wyatt and Gary have both admired the girls from afar at school, but this has been their first opportunity to actually interact with them. To their amazement, they find that their interest is actually reciprocated.

Ian and Max, meanwhile, are busily trying to flirt with Lisa, but to no avail. Frustrated, they give up and ask Wyatt and Gary's permission to have 'access' to her. The pair are reluctant, but eventually – against their better judgement – agree to re-engineer Lisa on their computer. Pandemonium ensues as the outlandish conditions of their earlier experiment are repeated, but Gary and Wyatt's lack of attention to detail this time around mean that Ian and Max's lust ultimately goes unfulfilled. Deb and Hilly are less than happy with their boyfriends' actions, and begin to consider moving on in life without them.

As the party becomes wilder and more raucous, the boys have to cope with the unexpected arrival of Wyatt's well-intentioned but strait-laced grandparents Henry and Carmen (Ivor Barry and Anne Bernadette Coyle) and, only slightly more worryingly, witnessing part of the house turning into a silo for a Pershing II missile. But it's the unwelcome entrance of a gang of motorbike-mounted gatecrashers, led by the formidable Lord General (Vernon Wells), which really ups the ante. Forced out of their usual passive roles for once in their lives, can Wyatt and Gary face up to the intruders and win the hearts of Deb and Hilly once and for all? If they manage to survive the party, will they still be able to endure the inevitable face-off with Chet and Wyatt's parents? And what exactly will be the culmination of Lisa's covert master-plan?

Weird Science was John Hughes's only entry in the science fiction genre in the eighties, and although he would deal with fantastical subject matter again in later years – particularly in films such as *Miracle on 34th Street* (Les Mayfield, 1994) and *Flubber* (Les Mayfield, 1997) – *Weird Science* is considered by many to be his best-known effort within the sci-fi discipline to date. However, given the film's broad range of comedic situations it is only fair to note that Hughes's approach to science fiction firmly veers more towards fiction than science. The narrative's gleefully far-fetched technology and perceptive (if only sporadic) exploration of male desire – specifically the fantasies of teenaged youth – lend the film a whimsical sense of breezy light-heartedness. There is considerable tongue-in-cheek enjoyment to be had in watching Wyatt's very eighties Memotech MX512 microcomputer, hooked up to a government facility full of anachronistic spinning tape-reels, managing somehow to generate the perfect woman out of thin air.

Likewise, Hughes manages to steer the film away from the kind of barefaced sexism that such a situation might suggest. Lisa may be the unanticipated creation of Wyatt and Gary's outlandish experiments, but she is always far from seeming to be their 'property'; indeed, given the mentoring role that she ultimately assumes, quite the opposite seems true. Kelly LeBrock brings a cheerful, confident independence to the role, clearly revelling in the character's embodiment of male desires while never allowing her to be conventionally objectified. Lisa is never less than the arbiter of her own free destiny, even deciding to withdraw from the lives of her 'creators' at a time of her own choosing. LeBrock builds very effectively upon the portrayal of the knowing temptress that she had created so memorably the previous year in *The Woman in Red* (Gene Wilder, 1984), and if *Weird Science* belongs to anyone, it is her.[2]

Hughes's artistic decision to focus on Lisa's role in altering and improving the lives of her accidental creators was contentious in some quarters, due to the resultant hesitance in directly addressing the film's most fundamental premise – exploring the way in which the two protagonists deal with the nature of their specifically teenage male desires which, through their technological instigation, have become embodied in Lisa. It is interesting to compare the process of Lisa's creation with the manner in which similar concepts are handled elsewhere in cinematic science fiction. *The Rocky Horror Picture Show* (Jim Sharman, 1975), for instance, toys with the invention of a self-aware being, both highly sexualised and psychologically vulnerable, but situated within a parody of 1950s 'creature features' and stereotypical haunted house stories which had become common to the horror genre. Hughes seems less interested in explicitly satirising particular genre characteristics, which was key to the success of *Rocky Horror*, but eager instead to employ the fantastic as a means to explore notions of empowerment and self-perception in ways that would have seemed less striking if set against a realistic backdrop of the everyday and the mundane. Though his engagement with the intensity of desire is only intermittent throughout the film, it is quite amusingly typified by early sequences which see Wyatt and Gary showering – more or less fully clothed – with their new creation, still so awestruck by her very existence that they are unable even to converse with her. But as Lisa's character begins to develop surrogate maternal qualities of protectiveness and benevolent compassion towards her two ostensible designers, so too does Hughes lead the audience towards the revelation that the boys' two contemporaries Deb and Hilly – both authentic individuals who stand apart from the artificially manufactured Lisa and her improbable powers of invention – have the ability to provide them with the potential for a more structured and meaningful relationship than Lisa's attractive charms or charismatic enchantment.

Performances throughout the film are solid, particularly in the case of Anthony Michael Hall who manages to discover yet another dimension to geekdom in his portrayal of Gary. Less insecure than 'Farmer' Ted of *Sixteen Candles*, yet savvier than *The Breakfast Club*'s Brian, Gary is a likeable nerd with a heart whose qualities of loyalty and courage eventually win through, to his lasting benefit. Ilan Mitchell-Smith likewise gives a strong performance as Wyatt. Having previously appeared in *Daniel* (Sidney Lumet, 1983) and *The Wild Life* (Art Linson, 1984), Mitchell-Smith brings a genial air of amiability to the spectacularly anxious Wyatt, watching in stupefied bafflement as his world is turned upside-down and inside-out. The film also featured an early appearance from future Academy Award nominee and Golden Globe winner Robert Downey Jr as the smug but ultimately craven Ian, and Suzanne Snyder and Judie Aronson both deliver appealing performances as the likeable friends Deb and Hilly. But of all the supporting cast, it is Bill Paxton who comes closest to stealing the show as the repellent, militaristic Chet. Obviously relishing every ounce of the extortionist elder brother's studied obnoxiousness, Paxton's performance is a master-class in delivering an entertaining and humorous depiction of a thoroughly unsympathetic character. From Chet's sneeringly exaggerated facial expressions to his distinctive wannabe armed forces hairstyle, Paxton's portrayal is perfectly pitched to represent the nominal antagonist of the piece, and the character's transformation into quite literally a new man at the film's conclusion is both inspired and perfectly in keeping with the general tone of the film. Paxton had earlier given performances in films including *Streets of Fire* (Walter Hill, 1984), *Impulse* (Graham Baker, 1984) and *Commando* (Mark L. Lester, 1985), and he would go on to considerable acclaim the following year for his appearance as Private Hudson in science fiction horror sequel *Aliens* (James Cameron, 1986).

Although very different in tone from *The Breakfast Club*, Hughes was to use *Weird Science* to pick up on a number of the same themes that had been discussed in the previous film, most notably the effects of parental expectation on, and desire for familial communication by, teenagers. This is best exemplified by Gary's disaffected parents Al and Lucy (Britt Leach and Barbara Lang), whose apoplectic rage at Lisa's party plans eventually force her to wipe their memories of the event – and also, accidentally, of Gary's very existence. Wyatt's embarrassing but ultimately well-meaning grandparents, on the other hand, clearly hearken back to *Sixteen Candles*. Of similar note, the action of *Weird Science* takes place in fictional Shermer, Illinois, including scenes set at Shermer High School – the same school which had housed the events of *The Breakfast Club*. Likewise, Gary claims to have an (entirely fabricated) girlfriend in Canada, just as Brian had done in the earlier film, while John Kapelos – *The Breakfast Club*'s Carl the Janitor – makes a welcome cameo as Dino, one of the unconventional patrons of the Candy Bar.

Hughes makes good use of *Weird Science*'s special effects, which are skilfully and sparingly employed throughout. This is particularly true during the freak events resulting from the ever more intense mayhem of the film's climactic party sequence. Yet for a teen movie so firmly wedded to the appeal of the fantastic, it seems strangely contrary to note that some of the most effective humour is generated from distinctly low-tech sources, such as Gary and Wyatt's inexplicable brassiere headgear during the course of their scientific experimentation, or memorable character moments such as the hilariously forced politeness of the mutant bikers during their embarrassed withdrawal from Lisa's party. Ira Newborn's score is also highly complementary to the film's frenetic action, as is Oingo Boingo's inimitable title track 'Weird Science'.

Perhaps because of the film's bold and unconventional amalgam of teen movie exploits and the genre apparatus of science fiction, the critical reception of *Weird Science* was decidedly mixed at the time of its release. While some disapproved of the film's perceived propensity for excess and gimmickry,[3] others were to commend the film for its agreeable sense of fun and mischievous subversion of pre-existing genre conventions.[4] More recent analysis of *Weird Science* has remained generally supportive of the film,[5] particularly given the film's nostalgic charm and now-hopelessly dated technology and fashion.[6] Some reviewers also noted that in spite of some earlier critical comparisons, the film's main subject actually owed less to *Frankenstein* (James Whale, 1931) and more to the science fiction magnum opus that was *Metropolis* (Fritz Lang, 1926), drawing comparisons between Hughes's sensitive, intellectually adept Lisa and Lang's angelic Maria.[7]

Weird Science gained Ilan Mitchell-Smith a nomination for a Saturn Award for Best Performance by a Younger Actor at the 1986 Academy of Science Fiction, Fantasy and Horror Films Awards. However, perhaps the film's more enduring legacy was to be the creation of a long-running television series of the same name which launched almost a decade later. *Weird Science* (1994-97) ran for 88 episodes over the course of five seasons, and starred Vanessa Angel as Lisa, John Mallory Asher as Gary and Michael Manasseri as Wyatt. The series proved the versatility of the format which Hughes had established in his film, whilst updating the fashion styles and commentary on popular culture for the America of the nineties.

With *Weird Science*, Hughes had again proven his willingness to experiment both as a writer and a director, pushing against genre boundaries and challenging mainstream expectations of science fiction, comedy and the teen movie. All of the trademark aspects of a Hughes film were in evidence, from dryly-delineated character observation to snappy and wittily-rendered dialogue, but this time placed against a dynamic backdrop of the bizarre and the eccentric. With considerable panache, Hughes had turned his established studies of middle-class American life on their head by unleashing the fantastic into a well-ordered and unsuspecting section of the Midwest. But for his next feature, he would return to the sensitive characterisation and social commentary for which he had become best known, in order to create what – for many – has become one of his defining works.

Weird Science made its first appearance in American cinemas on 2 August 1985. Perhaps the most noteworthy other film being released on that date was Nicolas Roeg's complex comedy-drama *Insignificance*, starring Tony Curtis and Theresa Russell. There was a wide range of other features also making their debut that day, including Tom Holland's tongue-in-cheek horror *Fright Night*, Dario Argento's fantasy mystery *Phenomena*, Michel Deville's challenging thriller *Péril en la Demeure* (*Peril*), and family entertainment from the Children's Television Workshop with Ken Kwapis's *Sesame Street Presents Follow That Bird*. At the number one spot on the Billboard Charts was 'Everytime You Go Away' by Paul Young. Appearing in that week's news, the Rock and Roll Hall of Fame was established, thirty-five people were killed in a train crash occurring at Flaujac in France, and NASA's Space Shuttle *Challenger* launched on Mission STS-51-F carrying the *Igloo* pressurised module for the Spacelab laboratory.

'Forty-seventh, or so it seems, in writer-director John Hughes' illustrated teen-age daydreams, *Weird Science* divides its audience irrevocably: this time it's truly them or us. The crossover audience is maybe the 16-year-olds, if they aren't yet too fussy.'

Sheila Benson, *The Los Angeles Times*, 2 August 1985.

'Mr Hughes shows that he can share the kind of dumb joke that only a 14-year-old boy could love. There are enough moviegoing 14-year-old boys to make a hit out of *Weird Science*, of course, but for the rest of the population, its pandering is strenuous enough to be cause for alarm.'

Janet Maslin, *The New York Times*, 2 August 1985.

'Surely it's the least profound film Hughes ever made, but for sheer laughs, it's one of his strongest efforts. Throw in an infectious Oingo Boingo title tune, LeBrock in the finest fashions the Reagan-era could offer, and intoxicated tales of large-chested, knee-happy ex-girlfriends, and you have yourself one delectable adolescent comedy.'

Brian Orndorf, *DVD Talk*, 16 September 2008.

9

PRETTY IN PINK (1986)

Paramount Pictures

Director: Howard Deutch
Producer: Lauren Shuler
Screenwriter: John Hughes

MAIN CAST

Molly Ringwald	-	Andie Walsh
Harry Dean Stanton	-	Jack Walsh
Jon Cryer	-	Phil 'Duckie' Dale
Annie Potts	-	Iona
James Spader	-	Steff McKee
Andrew McCarthy	-	Blane McDonnagh
Kate Vernon	-	Benny Hanson
Alexa Kenin	-	Jena Hoeman

Pretty in Pink was to prove something of a transitional film for John Hughes. It marked the last time that he would work with the popular Molly Ringwald, but also the beginning of his professional relationship with Howard Deutch, who was to direct a number of Hughes's screenplays throughout the course of the late eighties. Although it was to be one of the few teen movies in his canon that Hughes did not personally direct, the screenplay that he created was so distinctively evocative of teenage life – and his return to the issue of high school social order was so effective – that for many people it has become the quintessential John Hughes take on class politics in eighties American youth.

Already an accomplished director of music videos, *Pretty in Pink* was Howard Deutch's debut as a motion picture director, and indeed the first three films that he was to helm in the eighties would be in collaboration with Hughes.[1] This was to form the foundation for a successful career in directing not only within the film industry, but also episodes of many long-running American television series. Later to direct films as diverse as *Article 99* (1992), *Grumpier Old Men* (1995), *Family Affair* (2000), *The Replacements* (2000) and *The Whole Ten Yards* (2004), Deutch was nominated for a prestigious Directors Guild of America Award in 2003 for his work on *Gleason* (2002), a well-regarded televised account of the life of popular actor and comedian Jackie Gleason (1916-87).

With *Pretty in Pink*, Hughes was to move beyond the fantastical excesses of *Weird Science* and return to the shrewdly-drawn, compassionately rendered characterisation which had distinguished *Sixteen Candles* and *The Breakfast Club* in the eyes of critics. It was also to provide him with the opportunity to both widen and refine a key theme that he had established in the two earlier films: that of the complex and implicit hierarchical structure which governed social interaction between high school students, and the profound way in which it was to influence and shape the course of their young lives.

Andie Walsh (Molly Ringwald) is a hard-working high school

student in her late teens, who lives with her father Jack (Harry Dean Stanton). Jack is a loving but directionless parent, struggling to cope with life after the departure of Andie's mother some years previously, and he has difficulty motivating himself to seek employment. However, Andie's optimism and deeply practical approach to life keeps him struggling onward from day to day.

Andie attends the community's high school, where there is a sharp division between students from affluent families and everyone else. The former treat the latter with snooty disdain, forever criticising their fashions or lack of expensive luxury goods; in retaliation, the rich kids are handled with thinly-veiled contempt, and withering insults are traded with regularity between the two groups. Against this rarefied background, Andie finds herself developing an attraction to Blane McDonnagh (Andrew McCarthy), who comes from a highly prosperous background and is the heir to his family's lucrative electronics business. She is stunned when he later reveals that he reciprocates her affections, though given the social rift that exists between them, she finds herself unsure about how to proceed for the best.

There is justification for Andie's unease, however, as Blane's wealthy friend Steff McKee (James Spader) discovers the attraction between the pair and is appalled at the notion of his friend dating someone who he considers to be beneath their social stature. Secretly, however, Steff is incensed that Andie has never shown any interest in him, despite his numerous attempts to catch her eye in the past. Thus he quietly resolves to do his best to poison any chance of a romance between Blane and Andie.

Seeking advice from her friend Iona (Annie Potts), the manager of the record store named Trax where she works part-time, Andie finds the confidence to follow her heart and see where her attraction to Blane will lead. However, this does not sit at all well with her best friend Phil Dale (Jon Cryer) – better known as 'Duckie' – who has known Andie since childhood and has secretly been building himself up to ask her out on a date. Sadly for Duckie, he discovers that his big chance has been blown when Blane arrives at Iona's store to whisk Andie away for the evening.

Andie and Blane's first destination is a party being held by one of his prosperous friends. They arrive some way into the proceedings, when most of the partygoers have already had more than a fair amount to drink, and it soon becomes abundantly clear that Andie's presence there is far from welcome. A run-in with Steff and his partner for the evening, the repugnant Benny Hanson (Kate Vernon), mean that the pair are forced to beat a hasty retreat. Unfortunately, their next destination is just as ill-starred, as they arrive at a cabaret bar to discover a crestfallen Duckie drowning his sorrows with a sympathetic but puzzled Iona. Andie attempts to pour oil on troubled waters, but Duckie is having none of it. With his dreams of romance now shattered, he pours scorn on Blane until they he and Andie are again persuaded to withdraw. In spite of Blane's good-natured attempts to salvage some kind of a good time from what remains of the date, Andie decides to draw a line under the evening. She panics when he offers to drive her home, as she desperately wants to conceal her modest accommodation from him, but relaxes when he compromises and agrees to drop her off nearby instead. Against all odds, the disastrous evening even ends on something of a high point when Blane asks Andie to the school prom – something that she had dreamed of but never dared wish for.

Regrettably the path to the prom is far from a smooth one, with Steff intensifying his efforts to thwart Blane's feelings towards Andie. After a concerted attempt to convince Blane that he is terminally crippling his social standing by pursuing a romance with Andie, Steff eventually succeeds in making the relationship lose momentum. When Andie confronts Blane at school, he is decidedly uncomfortable and tries to weasel his way out of taking her to the prom, backtracking on his earlier promise. Andie is distraught by this highly personal emotional betrayal, though no less than Blane seems to be at his weakness in the face of the influence of his peers. Duckie, incensed at the treatment of his friend, spots a gloating Steff on the sidelines of the argument and furiously attacks him. Steff, for once in his pampered life, genuinely doesn't seem to know what has hit him.

The prom night arrives, and Andie decides to attend the event even without a date to accompany her. Sporting a new dress that she has made for the evening, she arrives with very low expectations, but is nonetheless desperate not to lose face. However, with the support of her true friends, will she be able to turn the prom's potential for catastrophe into to a happy ending, or are the prejudices of the school's elitist snobs destined to win the day instead?

The most immediately recognisable factor of *Pretty in Pink* is that it seems much more sedate in tone and pace (indeed, almost staid at times) than any of the Hughes teen movies which had preceded it. Whereas *Sixteen Candles* and *Weird Science* had both derived their humour from unexpected or outlandish situations – albeit in very different ways – *The Breakfast Club* had used a clash of personalities to drive forward its comedic objectives while simultaneously delivering a serious commentary about how teenagers see themselves, and each other. Although *Pretty in Pink* is not without its own humour – indeed, the comically-talented supporting cast have become one of its most celebrated features – the depth of the film's underlying themes are such that Hughes judiciously made a decision to scale back the quotient of overt comedy situations evident in his previous films, whilst retaining (and enhancing) his hallmark sensitivity of characterisation.

There are two major thematic threads which underpin *Pretty in Pink*; one which concerns strained relations between social classes, and another which examines the potency of unrequited love. Both themes are interlinked in unusual and rewarding ways. For instance, the dichotomy between rich and poor is most obviously represented by the faltering first steps down the road of romance for Andie and Blane, but the tension between the town's affluent denizens and the less well-off is explored in many other ways. The non-stop tirade of bitchery from the prosperous seniors towards Andie is mirrored in the wary hostility which greets Blane as he works his way through the exterior of the school campus on his way to meet Andie, obviously resented because of the attitude of his rich peers. And Duckie, who has his own reasons to keep Andie and Blane apart, proves that preconceptions about class characteristics are far from being purely a one-way street. Likewise, Duckie's strong feelings for Andie have their own parallel in Jack's painful and hopeless love for his absent wife, silently craving for her return from her self-imposed exile whilst knowing deep-down that they will almost certainly never be reunited. It is much to Hughes's credit that he is able to counterbalance these two themes sympathetically, without ever resorting to cliché in his exploration of class, or sentimentalism when dealing with issues of unreciprocated romance. And although it is true that the tone of the script is much more critical towards the film's wealthier characters – particularly the sneeringly vindictive Steff – Hughes is quick to avoid any kind of inverse snobbery, instead stressing the point that an individual's quality of character must always be the paramount consideration, rather than the question of how rich (or not) their parents happen to be.

The film's two leads are crucial to its success, and both deliver admirable performances which somehow manage never to stray onto any familiar territory that Hughes had previously demarcated in his earlier teen movies. Molly Ringwald's appearance impresses without ever evoking memories of her two preceding performances in Hughes's films, and her rendering of the independent, free-thinking Andie is typically skilled and well-balanced – particularly given the different ways in which the character's self-determination is challenged by the intense social pressures working around her. What is particularly noteworthy is the way in which Ringwald's performance – and indeed Hughes's script – differentiates between the kind of 'popularity gulf' that Samantha Baker must overcome in *Sixteen Candles*, and the more explicitly class-based social segregation which takes place throughout *Pretty in Pink*. (It is also significant to note that Andie is, in social terms, the diametric opposite of *The Breakfast Club*'s affluent Claire Standish.) As Blane, Andrew McCarthy gives a carefully rendered depiction of a generally decent teenager who finds himself caught between two inescapable but equally powerful forces – that of strong romantic attraction, and the other of intense peer pressure. His on-screen chemistry with Ringwald works very effectively due to the obvious thoughtfulness that he invests in the character, always emphasising a depth to Blane that was rarely to be found in the male lead of most eighties teen movies, outside of Hughes's own canon. McCarthy had been active in a variety of youth-themed films throughout the early eighties, including *Class* (Lewis John Carlino, 1983) and *Heaven Help Us* (Michael Dinner, 1985) as well as the famous Brat Pack mainstay, *St Elmo's Fire* (Joel Schumacher, 1985). He would go on to further commercial success as the decade progressed in films such as *Mannequin* (Michael Gottlieb, 1987), *Weekend at Bernie's* (Ted Kotcheff, 1989), and also *Fresh Horses* (David Anspaugh, 1988), which would see him reunited on-screen with Molly Ringwald.

Like *Sixteen Candles* before it, *Pretty in Pink* is indisputably Ringwald's film, but this should in no way distract the audience from the superb supporting cast which greatly enhance the viewing experience. Top of this list of talent is the inimitable Jon Cryer, who puts in one of the best-known performances of his career as Duckie Dale. Cryer's highly dexterous approach to this most offbeat of characters has made Duckie one of Hughes's most instantly memorable characters, replete with his rapid-fire dialogue, outlandish fashions and hyperactive physicality. His wild song and dance routine in Iona's record store, frantically lip-synching in time to Otis Redding, is one of the film's comedy high-points. (Duckie has become a character who has split reviewers deeply over the years; depending entirely upon personal opinion, he can be seen as a lovable attention-seeking eccentric[2] or a vague mass of insecurities with mildly obsessive stalker tendencies.[3]) However audiences came to receive Duckie's highly distinctive personality, Cryer achieved a great deal in constructing a sympathetic (if markedly alternative) character imbued with genuine pathos, who is forced to undergo the loss of his one great love in order to retain his best friend. Cryer was known to audiences of the time for his appearances on television and in films such as *No Small Affair* (Jerry Schatzberg, 1984) and *O.C. and Stiggs* (Robert Altman, 1985), and later in the decade would go on to appear in features including *Dudes* (Penelope Spheeris, 1987), *Hiding Out* (Bob Giraldi, 1987) and, in a high-profile role, as Lenny Luthor in *Superman IV: The Quest for Peace* (Sidney J. Furie, 1987). In subsequent years he has worked as a writer, producer and director, as well as making a prolific number of television appearances which have earned him no less than three Emmy nominations.

The adult supporting cast were no less impressive, with Harry Dean Stanton's appearance as Andie's father Jack being particularly touching. Stanton had been a veteran screen actor of many years standing, having appeared on television since the mid-1950s and being recognisable to the public of the time for high-profile appearances in films including *Alien* (Ridley Scott, 1979), *Escape from New York* (John Carpenter, 1981) and *Paris, Texas* (Wim Wenders, 1984). Although his roles had been wide-ranging over the years, rarely had he delivered such a touching and highly sensitive portrayal as he did with the silently grieving, self-pitying Jack Walsh, and his on-screen paternal dynamic with Molly Ringwald is highly effective throughout the film. Annie Potts, forever remembered as the feisty Janine Melnitz in *Ghostbusters* (Ivan Reitman, 1984), both impresses and amuses as the highly unconventional but wise Iona, whose constantly shifting guises and joyful embrace of nostalgic tastes in music and fashion make her an appealing character who is always easy to like. Multiple Emmy winner and Golden Globe nominee James Spader also puts in a fine performance as the spiteful, snobbish Steff. Spader's impeccable restraint in the part means that the

Iago-like Steff's bitterness and wounded pride are articulated very skilfully throughout the course of the film, and it is easy to see why Spader would go on to such acclaim in later years for his performances in films including *Sex, Lies and Videotape* (Steven Soderbergh, 1989) and *Wolf* (Mike Nichols, 1994).

Howard Deutch's direction throughout his debut feature is assured, and his years of experience in the music video industry were apparent in his eye for (and deft management of) the many cutting-edge fashions and styles on display. Special mention is also more than due to the sets created by Jennifer Polito and Bruce Weintraub; from the authentic titles lining the shelves of Trax, Iona's record store, to the interior of Steff's family's palatial study, there are some genuinely sumptuous pieces of design work on display throughout the course of the film. Michael Gore's original soundtrack is also highly effective, both lively and evocative as appropriate, and would win him a BMI Film Music Award later in 1987. The Psychadelic Furs' title song, 'Pretty in Pink', was also well received by many.[4]

The critics were generally receptive to *Pretty in Pink* on its release, with commentators praising Molly Ringwald for her assured performance,[5] Hughes's script for its sensitivity to youth issues,[6] and the film's intelligent and emotionally-astute take on its key themes.[7] However, retrospective appraisals of *Pretty in Pink* have become increasingly divided in more recent years. Some continue to praise the film for the veracity of its artistic intentions[8] and the considerable depth given to its subject matter,[9] while others have begun to feel that the passing years have numbed the potency of Hughes's engagement with class-related issues,[10] and also that the film suffers from audience over-exposure to the motor-mouthed Duckie – a definite love-him-or-hate-him character if ever there was one.[11]

Pretty in Pink has become well-known as the final film in what had formed – along with *Sixteen Candles* and *The Breakfast Club* – a loose trilogy of teen movie collaborations between Molly Ringwald and John Hughes.[12] Ringwald has continued to prove herself a prolific performer across many genres, including issue-based drama such as *For Keeps* (John G. Avildsen, 1988), ensemble comedies including *Betsy's Wedding* (Alan Alda, 1990) and even horror features like *Office Killer* (Cindy Sherman, 1997). Still very active in film and on television, Ringwald had noted in recent years that she would not rule out the possibility of working with Hughes again – an opportunity which sadly will no longer be achievable following his sudden and tragic death in 2009.[13]

Pretty in Pink formed an interesting difference in approach for Hughes. Although it intentionally lacks the spontaneous wit of the other films in the Hughes teen canon, it also offered a slightly darker, more mature take on the teen movie. With its willingness to explore issues of class division and emotional needs in a way that was expressively meaningful and never exploitative, the film was another example of Hughes's eagerness to explore every corner of the teen movie genre, and thus to demonstrate the considerable aptitude that it had for exploring important social, cultural and emotional issues in a manner that was both relevant and vital to modern audiences.

Historical Context

Pretty in Pink was released in America on 28 February 1986 against a wide range of other features which crossed a number of genres, including Penelope Spheeris's challenging drama *Hollywood Vice Squad*, Steve Miner's popular cult horror *House*, Valeriu Jereghi and Aleksandar Petkovic's wartime drama *Dikiy Veter* (*Wild Wind*), and Joyce Chopra's psychological thriler *Smooth Talk*. Perhaps the most significant other film release that week was Oliver Stone's Oscar-nominated political drama *Salvador*, which starred James Woods. Whitney Houston was at the top of the Billboard Charts at the time with her hit song 'How Will I Know?'. In that week's current affairs, Texas Air purchased the Eastern Airlines company for $676 million, NASA's Voyager II space probe completed its first flyby of the planet Uranus, and the European Economic Community signed into force a Special Act for European free trade.

Representative Critical Opinion

'*Pretty in Pink* is evidence, I suppose, that there must be a reason why certain old stories never seem to die. We know all the clichés, we can predict half of the developments. But at the end, when this boy and this girl, who are so obviously intended for one another, finally get together, there is great satisfaction.'
Roger Ebert, *The Chicago Sun-Times*, 28 February 1986.

'In summoning up the characters' rawest feelings about snobbishness and conformity, the film sometimes strikes what for Mr Hughes is an unusually serious note.'
Janet Maslin, *The New York Times*, 28 February 1986.

'There is nothing new in the story of a rich kid falling for a girl from the wrong side of the tracks, but when John Hughes writes it, you know people are going to sit up and take notice.'
John J. Puccio, *DVD Town*, 12 August 2008.

10

FERRIS BUELLER'S DAY OFF (1986)

Paramount Pictures

Director: John Hughes
Producers: John Hughes and Tom Jacobson
Screenwriter: John Hughes

MAIN CAST

Matthew Broderick	-	Ferris Bueller
Alan Ruck	-	Cameron Frye
Mia Sara	-	Sloane Peterson
Jeffrey Jones	-	Ed Rooney
Jennifer Grey	-	Jeanie Bueller
Cindy Pickett	-	Katie Bueller
Lyman Ward	-	Tom Bueller
Edie McClurg	-	Grace

Ferris Bueller's Day Off is one of John Hughes's most offbeat teen films, and certainly among the most overtly humorous of his canon. Contrasting perfectly with the more serious, issue-based tone of *Pretty in Pink* which immediately preceded it,[1] Hughes's wittily incisive dialogue was never as razor-sharp as when delivered by the smart-mouthed high school slacker Ferris Bueller. Cool as ice, massively popular with everyone and impossible to outsmart, Ferris was the teenager with all the answers; the person that everyone growing up in an eighties high school wanted to be.

Hughes was to return to the director's chair for *Ferris Bueller's Day Off*, and was also to assume production and scriptwriting responsibilities for the film. Cast in the title role was the talented Matthew Broderick, who had been enjoying critical and commercial success thanks to his performances in features including *WarGames* (John Badham, 1983), *Max Dugan Returns* (Herbert Ross, 1983), and *Ladyhawke* (Richard Donner, 1985). His unforgettable appearance as Hughes's eponymous hero was to ensure that Ferris Bueller would become one of Broderick's best-known performances, and indeed it remains one of his most fondly-remembered amongst audiences even today.

Ferris Bueller (Matthew Broderick) is a student in his final year of high school in Illinois. With finals beckoning and the prospect of college just around the corner, Ferris knows that hard work and dedication to study are the order of the day... which is precisely why he is absolutely determined to do nothing of the sort. Instead, resolved to make the most of life before being forced to take up the responsibilities of adulthood, the self-determined Ferris isn't about to let school attendance get in the way of his free-wheeling attitude. He has turned faking illness into an art-form, and manages to dupe his well-meaning parents (Cindy Pickett and Lyman Ward) into believing that he is suffering from a collection of indistinct ailments in order to dodge school. After all, who wants to contemplate a class test in European socialism when the sun is shining and a magnificent day of freedom beckons?

Ferris's apparent sickness has become the stuff of legend in the area, and his popularity has meant that news of his 'plight' has spread far beyond the high school and into the wider community, who have rallied around him with collections of cash donations and regular deliveries of 'get well soon' gifts to his home. However, his subversion of the rules – to say nothing of his deception of his peers – infuriates his sister Jeanie (Jennifer Grey), who is incensed at Ferris's ability to effortlessly hoodwink their parents and the school authorities. What Jeanie doesn't realise is that Ocean Park High School's dean of students, Edward R. Rooney (Jeffrey Jones), is pursuing Ferris's case with a vengeance. With nine absences since the beginning of the semester, Rooney dreams of forcing Ferris into a humiliating repeat of his final year of high school. But as he has so far been unable to prove Ferris's deceit, Rooney has become obsessed with providing evidence of his truancy – particularly as he has become increasingly irate about Ferris's ability to outwit him at every turn (to say nothing of his perceived contempt for authority in general).

Meanwhile, Ferris is keen to take full advantage of the glorious day ahead. He calls up his best friend Cameron Frye (Alan Ruck), who is genuinely ill, and after much persuasion manages to coax him out of his sick-bed in order to pick him up. (Ferris's lack of his own car is, we soon learn, a particular running sore for him, as he continually needs to cadge a lift from family and acquaintances.) Next, he hatches an elaborate plan to pull his girlfriend Sloane Peterson (Mia Sara) out of school, quite literally right under the nose of Rooney. Informed of the death of Sloane's grandmother – one of Ferris's carefully prearranged scams – the school have no choice but to release Sloane from class. In order to look the part, Ferris convinces Cameron (after much effort) to allow him to pick Sloane up in his father's immaculately conditioned vintage Ferrari. Cameron lives in abject terror of his dictatorial father, who clearly cares more about the car than his own son, but eventually relents in the face of Ferris's irresistible persuasion. With Sloane safely ensconced in the passenger seat, a heavily disguised Ferris speeds away from the school, leaving a now-chronically confused Rooney in his wake.

Ignoring Cameron's fevered pleas to return the Ferrari to his father's garage before it is damaged or its mileage is noticeably increased, Ferris wastes no time in driving into Chicago instead. They leave the Ferrari at an inner-city car park, where (unknown to them) a couple of parking attendants take it on a joyride. Ferris then makes good on his promise to make the most of the day, taking his friends to an expensive restaurant (where he narrowly avoids encountering his own father, there on a business meeting), and then on to many of the city's attractions including the Chicago Board of Trade, the observation level of the Sears Tower, and the Art Institute of Chicago.

Back at the school, Rooney remains deeply puzzled by the recent goings-on. Sensing foul play, and unable to reach Sloane's family by phone, he decides to take the bull by the horns. After a fruitless search of local hangouts in an attempt to catch Ferris out, he eventually visits the Bueller family home. Finding the house empty, his rather imprudent attempts to enter illegally are impeded by the Buellers' fierce guard-dog. Eventually, Jeanie returns home early from school, and Rooney – believing that Ferris has come back instead – senses his chance. Breaking into the house, he sneaks around in search of the elusive Ferris, but is knocked unconscious when Jeanie – unaware of his identity – attacks him in the belief that he is an unknown intruder. She calls the police, but Rooney manages to recover consciousness and leave the house before they arrive. With no obvious assailant present when they eventually respond to Jeanie's request for aid, the police come to the conclusion that she has made a prank call and take her back to the station for questioning.

In Chicago, Ferris, Cameron and Sloane have been enjoying a baseball game at Wrigley Field, and even attend a lively parade on Dearborn Street, where Ferris manages to talk his way onto one of the floats and regales the crowd with a number of songs including (most memorably) 'Twist and Shout'. However, their high spirits are quickly extinguished when they make their way back to the garage and Ferris notices that the figures on the Ferrari's odometer have increased dramatically since they dropped it off. Cameron takes this news particularly badly, and is so racked with anxiety at the prospect of his father's retribution that he enters a kind of comatose state.

Waiting at the police station, Jeanie finds herself striking up an unlikely conversation with a philosophical teenaged law-breaker (Charlie Sheen), who sees through her anger and persuades her that she needs to look beyond the injustice she perceives in Ferris's recklessly individualistic behaviour and concentrate on the importance of her own life instead. Jeanie's mother eventually arrives, furious at having been called away from her office (particularly as she inadvertently lost a lucrative contract in the process), and after resolving the situation with the police insists that Jeanie drive her home.

Ferris and Sloane eventually manage to snap Cameron out of his semi-catatonic condition, and after returning the Ferrari to the Frye family garage they try running the stationary car in reverse in an optimistic but foolhardy attempt to turn the odometer backwards. When this is not successful, Cameron's fury towards his father finally boils over. Causing superficial damage by repeatedly kicking the Ferrari, he resolves to punish his father for lavishing all of his affection on the vintage car whilst virtually ignoring his own son. However, as the Ferrari is still fixed in reverse gear, the battering causes it to slip its restraints and lurch out of the garage's glazed back wall, plunging several feet to the ground below. The car now thoroughly wrecked, Cameron calmly decides that he will have no choice but to face his father when he returns later, and indeed the older man will finally be forced to respond to his son on Cameron's terms for once in his life.

As late afternoon becomes early evening, Ferris realises that he is rapidly running out of time. Dropping Sloane off at her house, he races home on foot in a mad dash to evade both of his parents, who are separately returning from work by car. However, Jeanie spots him and deliberately increases her speed in the hope of outrunning him. Ferris only just succeeds in reaching his back door before his parents draw up at the front of the house. But before he can find a key to allow him entry, he is confronted in the back yard by a livid Ed Rooney, who is still in the area due to his car having been towed away during his earlier stakeout. Has Ferris finally been caught out, or can his incredible good fortune still somehow win the day?

Ferris Bueller's Day Off is a film of many skilfully-employed contradictions. It is a movie about high school students which only rarely features high school, and features a dense narrative that celebrates the family whilst emphasising the harm that can be caused by domestic tensions. Yet following the comparatively staid approach of *Pretty in Pink*, Hughes never allows issue-based drama to subordinate the film's humour, leaving the audience in no doubt that *Ferris Bueller's Day Off* signalled a return to comedy both sophisticated and farcical. From Ferris's urbane wisecracks to Ed Rooney's outrageous pratfalls, the film employs a wide variety of comedic approaches with a high degree of success throughout.

Matthew Broderick delivers a superb performance as Ferris, and indeed his handling of the cool-as-ice protagonist is vastly to his credit. Given the character's deviously manipulative nature and vaguely conceited manner, it may seem easy for the viewer to quickly develop contempt for Ferris, but in the hands of Broderick and Hughes he instead becomes a kind of champion for eighties youth, his life-affirming attitudes making him almost impossible to dislike. Ferris's deft subversion of his parents – and, by extension, the authorities in general – has made him a hero amongst his peers, while news of his ersatz illnesses has been so convincingly propagated around the community that everyone from his school teachers to the emergency services are rooting for his recovery. (A running joke in the film features endless floral arrangements being delivered to the Bueller house from well-wishers, and non-stop local media coverage of Ferris's 'plight'.)

Yet for all of his slacker genius and graceful sleight of hand in dealing with the adult world, Ferris is not without his deeper side.[2] Hughes uses admirable restraint in sketching out Ferris's concern for his uptight best friend Cameron, whom he worries is in danger of sleepwalking into a miserable adulthood due to his discontented upbringing by aloof, dysfunctional parents. (Alan Ruck's performance as the anxious Cameron is all the more remarkable given that, far from being a teenager himself, he was actually in his late twenties at the time of filming.) Hughes is equally understated in his exploration of Ferris's affection for his beautiful and astute girlfriend Sloane. The dichotomy between the characters' shared fondness for each other, and the knowledge that college and adulthood may well force them to drift apart, is delineated with considerable care, and is equally well-played by Mia Sara.

Another reason for the success of *Ferris Bueller's Day Off* is its exceptional supporting cast; there is no weak link in a flawless roll-call of performers, all of whom bring something of value to the film. Most prominent among them is Jeffrey Jones, who steals every scene he appears in as the self-important, authoritarian Ed Rooney. Surely a spiritual cousin of *The Breakfast Club*'s similarly dictatorial Principal Vernon, Rooney is one of the film's standout characters, and Jones delivers a performance of comic genius in his depiction of the increasingly unhinged dean of students. As Ferris outwits the boggling grotesque at every turn, Rooney grows ever more desperate in his attempts to expose his scheming and bunking off – a path which eventually leads Rooney to unabashed criminality such as stalking and housebreaking, with some major animal cruelty along the way. Active in television and film since the early 1970s, at the time of *Ferris Bueller's Day Off* Jones was perhaps best-known for his Golden Globe-nominated performance as Emperor Joseph II in historical drama *Amadeus* (Milos Forman, 1984), and he brings all of his considerable comedic talents to bear on the slow disintegration of Rooney's dignity (and, quite possibly, his sanity). From his frustrated interactions with his hopeless secretary Grace (a brilliantly pitched turn by Edie McClurg) to his magnificently tongue-tied telephone conversation with Sloane's grieving but assertive father (actually Cameron, disguising his voice), Jones's superb performance ensured that Rooney was to become one of the most memorable of all of John Hughes's characters. He even makes the end credits sequence worth watching, as the reactions of the bruised and humiliated Rooney – forced to hitch a ride on the school bus – are absolutely priceless.

Ferris's hard-working but ultimately gullible parents are both well portrayed by Lyman Ward and Cindy Pickett, who effectively combine their concern for their 'gravely ill' son with an assiduous dedication to their respective jobs, making them among the most sympathetically rendered parents to feature in any of Hughes's teen movies. But the trademark Hughesian portrait of distant adults who have difficulty relating to modern youth is still expertly articulated in the film thanks to Jonathan Schmock's marvellously condescending maitre d' of the upmarket Chez Quis restaurant, and most especially Ben Stein's monotonously droning economics teacher, whose teaching style is so dull that it verges on the hypnotic, reminding us of just why Ferris is so desperate to skip school in the first place.

Yet the film works even more effectively when it focuses on its young cast of actors, and Broderick is ably supported by Alan Ruck and Mia Sara as Ferris's two partners in crime. Ruck, who had appeared in a variety of prominent youth features in the early eighties including *Class* (Lewis John Carlino, 1983) and *Bad Boys* (Rick Rosenthal, 1983), puts in an admirably multifaceted performance as the twitchily neurotic Cameron, who finds himself overcoming long-held phobias as the day progresses until he is forced to confront his demons – and, indeed, his father. Although exploring the theme of familial friction in an otherwise light-hearted film may, in lesser hands, have seemed overwrought and awkward, Hughes makes Cameron's emotional journey a believable and touching one which fits perfectly into the narrative of the film. Indeed, Cameron's journey from melancholy into psychological enlightenment contrasts very skilfully with Rooney's concurrent descent from despotic primacy into humiliation and oblivion. Mia Sara, best-known at the time for her appearance in *Legend* (Ridley Scott, 1985), is also very effective in the role of Ferris's knowing and resourceful girlfriend Sloane. The character seems full of admiration for Ferris's underlying good nature, even when gleefully rewriting everyone's rules, and Sara's onscreen chemistry with Broderick is convincing throughout. Jennifer Grey also impresses as Ferris's resentful sister Jeanie, who begrudges her brother's endless scheming for his own benefit while she, conversely, seems incapable of getting away with anything. Grey had appeared in a variety of films including *Red Dawn* (John Milius, 1984) and *The Cotton Club* (Francis Ford Coppola, 1984), and would later go on to huge success in one of the eighties' most memorable box-office hits – *Dirty Dancing* (Emile Ardolino, 1987) – where her performance as Frances 'Baby' Houseman was to earn her a nomination for a Golden Globe award.

Ferris Bueller's Day Off was one of Hughes's most accomplished and fully-rounded works as director, and his skilful location shooting makes the most of everything that Illinois has to offer. From striking shots of Chicago's famously iconic skyscrapers to a whistle-stop travelogue of the city's landmarks and vibrant cultural identity, and from leafy Illinois suburbs to the dismal corridors of Ocean Park High School, the film is never less than a treat of visual variety. Jennifer Polito's excellent set design is also worthy of mention – especially in the case of Ferris's typically idiosyncratic room, a veritable masterpiece of top-flight teen paraphernalia and cutting edge eighties accoutrements. The film also marked an interesting side-step for Hughes in its appealing device of having Ferris addressing the audience directly, breaking the fourth wall with much aplomb as his offbeat protagonist frankly discusses his thoughts on the action throughout the course of the film.

Ferris Bueller's Day Off proved to be one of the most critically successful of all Hughes's 1980s films, with commentators of the time praising it for its easy-going charm,[3] the engaging charisma of its central character,[4] and aptitude for skilfully implemented comedy situations.[5] The few dissenting critical voices were disparaging of what they perceived to be a jarring break from the realism of most (though not all) of Hughes's earlier teen movies,[6] and – on the other hand – an inability to take full advantage of the film's anarchic central premise.[7] However, negative criticism was largely in the minority, and the generally affirmative attitude towards *Ferris Bueller's Day Off* has continued into the present day. Recent appraisals of the film have been upbeat and constructive, with reviewers approving of its highly proficient pacing,[8] considerable hidden depths of characterisation,[9] and the fact that Ferris's affability and unshakeable slacker credentials have managed to stand the test of time.[10]

His starring role as Ferris Bueller was to see Matthew Broderick nominated for a Golden Globe award for Best Performance by an Actor in a Motion Picture (Comedy/Musical) in 1987, and indeed it remains one of his most instantly recognisable roles of the eighties, even taking into account many other high-profile film performances later in the decade which included *Project X* (Jonathan Kaplan, 1987), *Biloxi Blues* (Mike Nichols, 1988) and *Torch Song Trilogy* (Paul Bogart, 1988). The film's popularity also led to the creation of a short-lived television series, *Ferris Bueller*, which was broadcast on NBC between 1990 and 1991. The series starred Charlie Schlatter as Ferris, and shifted the action from Illinois to California. Many of the film's main characters were to feature in the televised situation comedy, though all were played by different actors, and the events depicted in Hughes's film were not referenced in the series. In spite of an able ensemble cast which included Jennifer Aniston as Jeanie, Brandon Douglas as Cameron, Ami Dolenz as Sloane and Richard Riehle as Ed Rooney, the series lasted for only thirteen episodes before being cancelled, and unlike the film which originated it, the TV series has become an obscure curiosity which is little-known today.

Ferris Bueller's Day Off is not only one of Hughes's best-regarded teen movies, but has also become one of the most critically and commercially successful comedies in his entire filmography. With enough wit and style to win over audiences of all ages, *Ferris Bueller's Day Off* tapped into the eighties zeitgeist so effectively that it quickly established itself as one of the most fondly-remembered comedies of the decade amongst many commentators and Hughes fans alike. Indeed, the film's energy and nostalgic charm has led to its repeated re-release on video and DVD over the years since its original cinematic release. Its continued popularity with audiences even today proves that the themes of liberation and self-determination presented by Hughes remain as universal and as relevant in the twenty-first century as they did in the eighties.

Historical Context

Ferris Bueller's Day Off went on general release in America on 11 June 1986. The only other film making its debut in the United States that day was Gabriel Auer's drama *Les Yeux des Oiseaux* (*The Eyes of the Birds*), starring Roland Amstutz and Carlos Andreu, following its initial 1983 release in France. Headlining the Billboard Charts that week was 'Live to Tell' by Madonna. In the news that week, Kurt Waldheim was elected President of Austria, the results of the Rogers Commission report into the *Challenger* space shuttle disaster were announced, South African President P.W. Botha declared a state of national emergency.

'The sheer entertainment value of Ferris Bueller, which is considerable, [is] mostly thanks to the combination of Hughes' knack for verbal humor and Broderick's seamless delivery. It is the most surreal Hughes movie yet, and thus the most disjointed, but there are some truly memorable comic moments buried here.'

Rob Salem, *The Toronto Star*, 13 June 1986.

'At the expense of sounding like Norman Podhoretz (and that's a high price to pay), the unavoidable conclusion is that all those crabby cultural conservatives who bemoaned the '60s were right – the tyranny of youth has proven a nearly unmitigated disaster for American movies.'

Paul Attanasio, *The Washington Post*, 12 June 1986.

'I can't think of a single comedy film that (barring one minor slump) is such an end-to-end joy as *Ferris Bueller's Day Off*, hitting the mark word for word, scene after scene, with such note perfect characters, situations and performances.'

Noel Megahey, *DVD Times*, 29 March 2006.

11

SOME KIND OF WONDERFUL (1987)

Hughes Entertainment/Paramount Pictures

Director: Howard Deutch
Producer: John Hughes
Screenwriter: John Hughes

MAIN CAST

Eric Stoltz	-	Keith Nelson
Mary Stuart Masterson	-	Watts
Lea Thompson	-	Amanda Jones
Craig Sheffer	-	Hardy Jenns
John Ashton	-	Cliff Nelson
Elias Koteas	-	Duncan
Molly Hagan	-	Shayne
Maddie Corman	-	Laura Nelson

Some Kind of Wonderful was Hughes's final teen movie of the 1980s, completing the celebrated cycle that had begun with *Sixteen Candles*. The film marked another change in tone for him, moving away from the sophisticated satirical comedy of *Ferris Bueller's Day Off* and presenting themes of youth drama in an even more mature and thoughtful manner than had been the case in *Pretty in Pink*. Hughes's second collaboration with director Howard Deutch, *Some Kind of Wonderful* was also to signal an important transition between the established themes of his previous teen films and the issues of adulthood and responsibility that were to come later in the decade.

The protagonists of *Some Kind of Wonderful* were nearing the end of their teenage years, ever so slightly older than the central characters of previous Hughes features in the genre. College-bound, sexually active and coming to terms with the inevitable shift from youth into the duties and accountability that come with adult life, there is a thoughtfulness and subtle sense of melancholy evident in *Some Kind of Wonderful* that marks it out from Hughes's earlier teen movies, signalling with considerable refinement and restraint the end of his engagement with the genre in the 1980s.

Keith Nelson (Eric Stoltz) is far from a conventional teenager. Quiet and intense, he spends his time on artistic pursuits as well as sharing a passion for music with Watts (Mary Stuart Masterson), his best friend since childhood. Watts is a talented drummer who favours tomboyish fashions and, fully in touch with Keith's quirky approach to life, is equally distant from the conformist expectations of their judgmental peers in high school.

Keith's father Cliff (John Ashton) despairs of his son's wilfulness, as well as his single-minded focus on his creative tendencies. Although he cannot deny that Keith is a gifted artist, Cliff is determined to ensure that his son is the first Nelson to achieve a college education. As the end of high school is now looming ever closer, Cliff is taking a more than active interest in ensuring that Keith considers the full range of colleges to apply for. He also makes sure that every cent that Keith earns from his part-time job at a gas station is assiduously squirreled away in preparation for his anticipated shift into further education.

In spite of Cliff's well-intentioned parental concerns, Keith has other plans. Whereas Cliff is determined that his son should study a business-related subject with practical applications, Keith is far more interested in honing his artistic talents still further, and even questions whether attending college is really the best thing for his future. Yet although he is willing to risk the potential of long-term financial security in order to follow his dreams, Keith is not oblivious to the huge social gulf that exists at his school. Despite the fact that his hard-working family are far from under-privileged, he is constantly reminded of the pretensions of the affluent, high-flying students who constantly run roughshod over the lives and feelings of those less wealthy than themselves. Most prominent among this condescending elite is Hardy Jenns (Craig Sheffer), an arrogant snob who delights in ruffling the feathers of anyone he considers to be unworthy of his consideration (which, as it happens, is almost everyone that he encounters).

Hardy's comprehensive lack of respect extends even to his beautiful girlfriend, Amanda Jones (Lea Thompson), one of the most popular students at the school. Although respected among her peers, Amanda is not nearly as prosperous as her circle of friends, and Hardy derives great satisfaction from humiliating her by regularly arranging flings with other attractive women – even when he knows that she is fully aware of his licentious intent.

Amanda is unaware that Keith, who lives close to her home, is secretly attracted to her. Although he is more than aware of the difficulties that peer pressure will place on his chances of successfully courting her affections, he nonetheless tries hard to capture her attention. When Amanda is assigned to detention, Keith deliberately seeks a similar punishment in order to spend time with her. However, his plan is derailed when Amanda manages to sweet-talk her way out of the reprimand at the last minute. Keith then finds himself left in the company of a rag-tag assortment of teen rebels, ostensibly led by an eccentric skinhead named Duncan (Elias Koteas), while the unwitting object of his affections walks free.

Things unexpectedly fall into place, however, when Amanda finally suffers one embarrassment too many at Hardy's hands and publicly splits from him. Sensing that his chance has come at last, Keith asks her out on a date. Amanda senses a chance to further humble Hardy, and readily accepts – much to the astonishment and distaste of her genteel friends. Yet they are not the only ones to be dismayed by this development; Watts is deeply hurt by Keith's intense interest in Amanda, as she has begun to find herself feeling attracted to her old friend. Keith, however, seems oblivious to his close companion's emotional distress.

A vengeful Hardy, quietly furious at being so visibly upbraided by Amanda, hatches a plan to win her back while also arranging for Keith to be attacked in retaliation for his interest in her. Knowing when Amanda and Keith's date is set to take place, Hardy invites them to a house party that he has arranged so that he can carry out his underhand strategy. Keith soon discovers the details of Hardy's scheme, but is so determined to make a success of his date with Amanda that he resolves to go ahead with his original plans, irrespective of the consequences. Amanda, meanwhile, finds herself frozen out of her privileged group of friends when it becomes apparent that she has no intention of backing out of the date.

As the big date draws near, Cliff is incensed when he discovers that Keith has withdrawn his savings – intended to pay his way through his first year of college – in order to buy Amanda an expensive pair of diamond earrings. But Keith has no intention of changing his plan now, and explains to his father that the outcome of the date is so significant to him that it has to take precedence over what he might (or, indeed, might not) decide to do in the future. Unrelenting, he arranges to hire a flashy car for the evening, which Watts agrees to chauffer even in spite of being obviously distraught by her unrequited attraction to Keith – and, just as importantly, his apparent ignorance of it.

Thanks to some considerable forward planning by Keith, and the unexpected assistance of some of the delinquent acquaintances that he has gained while in detention, the date with Amanda is indeed an event worth waiting for. In a painstakingly organised schedule, Amanda is whisked from an upmarket restaurant to an art gallery before visiting an open-air performance arena, where they finally have a frank discussion about the way in which – unwittingly or otherwise – they have used each other for their own respective benefit. Keith then confounds Amanda by proposing that they attend Hardy's party after all. Knowing what lies in store for them there, Amanda is less than enthusiastic about the idea, but Keith is insistent. But is the strength of Keith's attraction for Amanda really compelling enough to thwart Hardy's malevolent scheming? And will Watts ever be able to penetrate Keith's lack of responsiveness to the feelings that she holds for him?

On the release of *Some Kind of Wonderful*, many commentators were to make the observation that the film could, in many ways, be considered a gender-reversed reinterpretation of the narrative of *Pretty in Pink*, exchanging Keith for Andie Walsh, Watts for Duckie, and Amanda for Blane McDonnagh.[1] Indeed, although the love triangle aspect is mutual to both films, they share a number of other commonalities including the theme of the distribution of wealth determining social strata within the complex echelons of high school life,[2] and of course the psychological anguish of unrequited love (although Watts's emotional journey does admittedly reach a markedly different conclusion to that of the hapless Duckie). Like *Pretty in Pink*, *Some Kind of Wonderful* benefits from a skilfully understated sense of humour, which manages to maintain the film's pleasantly offbeat tone without ever disrupting the overriding sincerity of the treatment of its prevailing themes.

Yet if the film is predominantly concerned with issues of the class divide, both in high school and the world at large, Hughes also revisits the issue of parental expectation in his examination of Keith's determination to protect his own control over his individual goals for the future – even if he is unsure of their exact nature. By making Cliff Nelson a decent and encouraging parent, albeit one with high expectations for his son, Hughes completely avoids any clichéd treatment of this theme; Cliff does not seek to live his life vicariously through Keith, nor is he entirely unsympathetic to his son's artistic ambitions, but by that same token he is determined to ensure that valuable opportunities do not pass Keith by. Cliff's resolve in offering Keith the best possible start to his adult life is neatly contrasted by Watts's surreptitious yearning for a stable family unit of her own, and the even more subtle fact that in spite of her musical talents, no lofty prospects have been placed upon her by anyone. Here Hughes foregrounds something of the intensity of the evolution of the pair's friendship into a far deeper and more substantial bond, for both characters are shown to take considerable pleasure from living in the moment, enjoying the small details of life as it passes by their youthful eyes. Yet for Amanda, who is – at least initially – completely in thrall to the expectations of her richer and more influential peers, popularity and success is entirely predicated upon saying the right things and behaving in a certain approved manner. Thus when she does eventually make the break from this elitist clique, she finds that in order to stand alone she must develop from scratch the same kind of casual detachment that has come as second nature to perpetual outsiders like Keith and Watts. It is an observation that Hughes makes in a characteristically subtle and controlled way.

Eric Stoltz makes for an appealing lead player as Keith, and his contemplative, slightly ethereal central performance is a crucial factor in setting the film's generally thoughtful ambience. Stoltz, who had featured in many well-received films of the eighties including *Fast Times at Ridgemont High* (Amy Heckerling, 1982), *The Wild Life* (Art Linson, 1984) and *Running Hot* (Mark Griffiths, 1984), was later the recipient of a Golden Globe nomination for Best Performance by an Actor in a Supporting Role as Rocky Dennis in the emotional drama *Mask* (Peter Bogdanovich, 1985). His performance in *Some Kind of Wonderful* is no less accomplished, and Stoltz excels in expressing Keith's emotional turbulence with regard to the romantic allure of Amanda and the changing nature of his friendship with Watts. He is particularly astute in his judgement of the character's subtle but dogged approach to psychological manipulation, an attribute which is laid bare when he and Amanda finally speak candidly about the complexity of their intentions toward each other.

Lea Thompson is equally impressive in her rendering of the strikingly attractive but troubled Amanda Jones. From the character's growing anger and contempt towards Hardy's deceptiveness to her emotional turmoil when her one-time friends snootily close ranks on her, Thompson shows a considerable acting range that built upon previous solid performances in films such as *All the Right Moves* (Michael Chapman, 1983), *Jaws 3-D* (Joe Alves, 1983) and *Red Dawn* (John Milius, 1984). By the time of *Some Kind of Wonderful* she had become particularly well-known to audiences as a result of her appealing appearance as Lorraine Baines McFly in the enormously successful smash hit *Back to the Future* (Robert Zemeckis, 1985). The grace and self-assurance that she brings to her portrayal of Amanda contrasts very effectively with the deeply pragmatic and down-to-earth qualities embodied in Watts, as so skilfully rendered by Mary Stuart Masterson. Masterson manages to walk a very fine line in developing Watts's minimalist, boyish self-image and irresolute disdain of social expectation, while still emphasising the character's inner and outer beauty as well as her desperate desire to be accepted by Keith as far more than just a close friend. Active in film since *The Stepford Wives* (Bryan Forbes, 1975), Masterson had also appeared in critically successful eighties features including *Heaven Help Us* (Michael Dinner, 1985) and *At Close Range* (James Foley, 1986), and the well-judged qualities of her touching performance complete an impeccably cast group of central players which make

Hughes's unconventional love triangle a truly memorable one.

Just as the main cast members had each delivered accomplished portrayals of their respective characters, the performances provided by the film's broad range of supporting players were no less capable. Craig Sheffer is excellent as the conceited, derisive Hardy Jenns, full of sneering malice and condescension. Sheffer's performance is every inch the equal of James Spader's rendering of the snobbish manipulator Steff McKee, and he demonstrates considerable skill in presenting the character's bilious pomposity which – by the film's conclusion – eventually becomes so deflated that Hardy's underlying cowardice is laid bare for all to see. Mention is also due to John Ashton and Jane Eliot as Keith's beleaguered but caring parents, and also Maddie Corman and Candace Cameron as his two squabbling but entertainingly sardonic younger sisters. Much of the film's comic relief is provided by Elias Koteas as Duncan, the leather-jacketed oddball with whom Keith strikes up an unlikely acquaintance while languishing in detention. Koteas is in absolutely top form throughout *Some Kind of Wonderful*, adding surprising dimensional layers to an unusual character who ultimately becomes strangely charismatic and amiable as the film progresses. Whether discovering new (and somewhat unorthodox) artistic talents or devising new ways to act contrary to the expectations of the school authorities, Duncan acts almost as a faintly anti-heroic shadow of Keith, and Hughes makes good use of the character to help lighten the otherwise reflective and thoughtful disposition of the narrative.

As was the case with *Pretty in Pink*, Howard Deutch's direction is never less than efficient and skilfully employs some attractive location shooting, most especially in the arena auditorium scenes near the conclusion. The film's pace is also very well judged, allowing the optimum opportunity for character development without ever allowing the overall sense of momentum to slacken. *Some Kind of Wonderful*'s original score, by Stephen Hague and John Musser, is proficient and spirited, and is amply augmented throughout by a range of tracks from famous artists ranging from Billy Idol to the Rolling Stones.

Some Kind of Wonderful met with general critical approval at the time of its release, with commentators praising the film for Hughes's keen eye for class-related issues,[3] well-implemented range of characters,[4] and its appealing central cast.[5] If anything, more recent analyses of the film have been even more appreciative of its merits. Some modern reviewers have considered it to be the most underrated teen movie in Hughes's canon,[6] while others deem it to be an ideal nostalgic experience for eighties cinemagoers,[7] and a note-perfect rendering of high school life in the United States of the time.[8]

Lea Thompson was to win the Best Young Actress in a Motion Picture at the Young Artist Awards in 1988 for her part in *Some Kind of Wonderful,* and the achievement of her performance was evocative of the film's wider success with audiences in America and across the world. Although it was to be Hughes's final teen movie of the eighties, *Some Kind of Wonderful* typified much of what had come to epitomise his approach to the genre. With its quirky characters, star-crossed young lovers and low-key celebration of suburban family life, the film encapsulated much of what made Hughes's output so accomplished; as always, he had managed to capture not only the ambience of a specific place and time, but he had also perfectly captured the mood and sentiment of what it means to be young and in love, with all of the complications and intricacies that come with this most unique and ephemeral of sensations.

Some Kind of Wonderful was released in American cinemas on 27 February 1987. The same day saw the first national screenings of Robert Altman's comedic stage-to-screen adaptation of *Beyond Therapy*, which starred Julie Hagerty, Jeff Goldblum and Glenda Jackson. Also being released in the United States for the first time that day were Chuck Russell's horror sequel *A Nightmare on Elm Street 3: Dream Warriors*, Lizzie Borden's bleak prostitution-based drama *Working Girls*, and Danièle Huillet and Jean-Marie Straub's adaptation of Franz Kafka's *Klassenverhältnisse* (*Class Relations*), which had first been screened at the Berlin International Film Festival in 1984. At the top of the Billboard Charts at the time was Bon Jovi's 'Livin' on a Prayer'. Appearing in current affairs at the time, the Tower Commission reported its findings on the Iran-Contra affair, Donald Regan resigned as the White House Chief of Staff, and albums by The Beatles were released on compact disc for the first time.

'It's easy to empathize with Hughes' nobler adolescent themes, like finding your own path when the group is against you (kinda like screenwriters), but it is hard to sympathize with kids who feel left out because they don't have their own diamond earrings.'
Rita Kempley, *The Washington Post*, 27 February 1987.

'*Some Kind of Wonderful* is yet another film in which Hughes and his team show a special ability to make an entertaining movie about teenagers, which is also about life, about insecurity, about rejection, about learning to grow. I sometimes have the peculiar feeling that the kids in Hughes's movies are more grown up than the adults in most of the other ones.'
Roger Ebert, *The Chicago Sun-Times*, 27 February 1987.

'Smart and caring teenagers searching for identities is the trademark that made the rich characters of John Hughes survive all these decades. Even though they are hopelessly dated by fashion and music, time has been kind to titles like *Some Kind of Wonderful.*'
Brett Cullum, *DVD Verdict*, 29 August 2006.

12

PLANES, TRAINS AND AUTOMOBILES (1987)

Hughes Entertainment/Paramount Pictures

Director: John Hughes
Producer: John Hughes
Screenwriter: John Hughes

MAIN CAST

Steve Martin	-	Neal Page
John Candy	-	Del Griffith
Laila Robins	-	Susan Page
Michael McKean	-	State Trooper
Kevin Bacon	-	Taxi Racer
Dylan Baker	-	Owen
Carol Bruce	-	Joy Page
Olivia Burnette	-	Marti Page

With *Planes, Trains and Automobiles,* John Hughes was entering the third act of his eighties output. Following the ribald zaniness of his screenplays early in the decade, and then later his stylish studies of teenage life distinctive to the commoditised urbanity of the age, as the eighties neared their end Hughes was to move his creative focus from the subject of youth and return his attention to the adult world once again. His wry examination of popular culture and his sharp social commentary, evident throughout all of his teen movies, was once again to come to the fore as he broadened his assessment of American mores to encompass the complexities of adult life and the profound significance of the family unit.

As had been the case with *Ferris Bueller's Day Off,* Hughes was to direct and produce *Planes, Trains and Automobiles* in addition to writing its screenplay. Yet the film had another major benefit in its highly effective casting against type of two of the decade's most successful comedy actors, Steve Martin and John Candy. The result was an eruditely humorous film which perfectly captured the spirit of the season in which it is set.

Advertising executive Neal Page (Steve Martin) is really looking forward to the Thanksgiving season. Although held up in a board meeting in New York City, thanks to the staggering indecisiveness of his boss Bryant (William Windom), he has high hopes of catching an early flight home to Chicago so that he can rejoin his family for the holidays.

Unfortunately for Neal, things don't go quite according to plan. After a mad dash for a free taxi, a commodity that is at a premium in New York at the start of Thanksgiving weekend, Neal just manages to find a vacant cab only for it to be unintentionally purloined from under his nose by travelling shower curtain-ring salesman Del Griffith (John Candy). Neal eventually arrives at the airport too late for his flight, and is stunned to find himself seated across from Del in the waiting area. The two recognise each other, and after discovering Del's courteously sociable nature Neal grudgingly appears to bury the hatchet over their earlier misunderstanding. Neal manages to arrange a later flight with the airline, but later discovers that there is no available seating in the first class cabin, and is forced into coach class... where he discovers that the only remaining seat is located next to Del, who promptly drives him up the wall with his incessant banal attempts at conversation.

During their flight, O'Hare Airport in Chicago is hit by a heavy snowfall, causing Neal and Del to be unexpectedly diverted to Wichita in Kansas. There, they discover that the flight has been not delayed but cancelled. With no immediately available alternative flights likely for some time, the local accommodation fills up quickly. Neal is unable to arrange lodgings, but Del fortunately has a contact in the area who is a motel owner. Del had sold shower curtain-rings to the motel in the past and is still on good enough terms with the proprietor to secure a room at short notice. Neal has no appetite whatsoever to spend the night with a stranger in a motel room, much less an exasperatingly irritating one, but knows that his only other choice is an indeterminate amount of time sleeping on the floor of the airport's departure lounge.

Neal somehow manages to survive an evening in Del's company, replete with his slobbish untidiness and incessant chatter, but the pair awake in the morning to discover that all of their cash has been stolen during the night by an opportunistic thief (Gary Riley). They do, however, still have their credit cards to hand, and thus try to hammer out a workable way of getting from rural Kansas to Chicago. As luck would have it, Del has another acquaintance in the area who is connected with the railroad system; after a freezing cold ride in an open truck to the closest railway station, they arrive just in time to book two tickets to Chicago.

Before Del and Neal's journey is anywhere near complete, the train breaks down in the middle of nowhere, somewhere in the depths of Missouri. Leaving on foot, they eventually find their way onto a bus which terminates at St Louis. There, Neal decides that they should go their separate ways, but is soon thwarted when he discovers that the hire-car that he has arranged isn't in its designated space. Del, on the other hand, has succeeded in renting a car, and offers to give Neal a lift to their intended destination.

Hitting the road, a rather extreme mishap at Del's hands soon leads to the car being virtually wrecked. Though it is still technically capable of moving in a straight line (though only in the loosest sense of the term), their flame-grilled car is eventually confiscated by a concerned state trooper (Michael McKean), leaving Neal and Del to try to book themselves into a cheap motel with molten credit cards and no ready cash.

Eventually, and only after a Herculean effort, Neal finds himself on a train to his home in Chicago. But as the last leg of his journey beckons, he begins to question Del's woolly explanation of his own domestic life. Deducing that his unintentional travelling companion may be hiding a tragic truth from him, Neal resolves to ensure that his family's Thanksgiving cheer – that is, what little remains of it – will be shared with his new friend.

Planes, Trains and Automobiles is a film which succeeds on many levels. Its observational comedy is pitched absolutely on-beam, its dialogue is sharp and perceptive, and the film's emotional heart is moving and poignant without ever tipping over into outright sentimentalism. Hughes makes the most of the film's Thanksgiving setting to depict a highly accomplished tapestry of scenes from modern America, from chilly urban cityscapes to frosty rural panoramas. More so even than Hughes's other films of the time, the location shooting is exceptionally well-handled, distinctively showcasing the country's roadsides and landmarks with equal aplomb. Combined with Ira Newborn's atmospheric score, there is a real sense of seasonal ambience throughout, and the optimistic idealism of Neal's beautifully presented home – glimpsed tantalisingly throughout the course of the film – contrasts very effectively with the grimy motel rooms and jury-rigged modes of transportation that he and Del are forced to endure as their journey progresses.

Key to the film's success is the standout performances by its two lead actors. Steve Martin and John Candy had both previously appeared in the Oscar-nominated musical remake of *Little Shop of Horrors* (Frank Oz, 1986), loosely based on Roger Corman's 1960 horror comedy of the same name. But here, sharing the screen for almost the entirety of the film's duration, both performers excel in balancing comedic proficiency with dramatic import. Steve Martin, a talented writer, producer and actor as well as a multiple Emmy and Golden Globe nominee, had previously appeared in many prominent comedies over the past decade, including *The Muppet Movie* (James Frawley, 1979), *The Jerk* (Carl Reiner, 1979), *Dead Men Don't Wear Plaid* (Carl Reiner, 1982), *The Man with Two Brains* (Carl Reiner, 1983), and *Roxanne* (Fred Schepisi, 1987). Often cast at the time as madcap oddballs and wildly eccentric characters, here he succeeds brilliantly in his depiction of a mild-mannered everyman who, through exceptional demands on his not inconsiderable supply of patience, finds himself spiralling into a state of mounting hysteria. Though his irritated outbursts towards Del are matched only by his biting criticism, his frustration is best illustrated by an unforgettable scene at the car rental depot, where he subjects the firm's ineffectual representative to an impressive eruption of profanity as his exasperation finally reaches boiling point.

Although Martin delivers a performance of comic brilliance, he is matched scene for scene by John Candy, who manages to walk an impossibly slender tightrope in his portrayal of a character who is lovable, good-natured and kind-hearted but, through no intended fault of his own, is quite spectacularly annoying. Candy, whose role in the success of *SCTV Network 90* (1981-83) led to multiple nominations and wins at the Emmy Awards, also appeared in a variety of well-known eighties comedy features including *The Blues Brothers* (John Landis, 1980), *Stripes* (Ivan Reitman, 1981), *Splash* (Ron Howard, 1984) and

Brewster's Millions (Walter Hill, 1985). He had also appeared in *National Lampoon's Vacation*, in a cameo performance as a security guard at Walley World. With the incessantly talkative Del Griffith, Candy constructs a character of many touching contradictions. Just as Hughes's script never allows Neal to fall into the trap of becoming simply the foil to his companion's irritating excesses, so too is Del elevated from the role of irksome buffoon into a multi-layered, emotionally-aware individual. Just as his rousing rendition of the theme song to Hanna Barbera's *The Flintstones* (1961-66), leading an impromptu sing-along on the bus travelling through Missouri, perfectly sums up his cheery attitude in the face of adversity, he is also shown to be a resourceful and pragmatic character. This latter aspect is amply showcased by his inventive retailing of his endless supply of shower curtain-rings, as he sells them in a variety of highly unconventional guises (mostly as designer earrings) to the unsuspecting denizens of St Louis.

Although *Planes, Trains and Automobiles* features some solid supporting performances, particularly from Laila Robins as Susan Page, it is the cameo appearances peppered throughout the film which really stand out. The ever-watchable Michael McKean impresses as a poker-faced state trooper, and Bill Erwin also makes an impression as Neal and Del's near-catatonic co-passenger on their flight from New York. Kevin Bacon has an effectively comical character part as the 'Taxi Racer'; he would, of course, later star in Hughes's next feature, *She's Having a Baby*. Sharp-eyed viewers will also spot appearances by a number of *Ferris Bueller's Day Off* alumni, including Lyman Ward as John, one of Neal's fellow advertising executives, Ben Stein as an announcer at Wichita Airport, and perhaps most notably Edie McClurg as the customer services representative at the St Louis car rental agency who finds herself on the receiving end of Neal's memorable profanity-fuelled tirade. And in Owen and his seemingly-nameless wife (Dylan Baker and Lulie Newcomb), Hughes introduces us to a pair of entertainingly-rendered characters who appear to be cut from the same cloth as the *Vacation* series' Cousin Eddie Johnson.

Hughes exercises considerable restraint in articulating the film's themes of familial love and inclusiveness, especially given the generally warm seasonal atmosphere which is evident throughout. We are never less than aware of the message that family can (and should) extend beyond blood relations, as we see demonstrated at the film's conclusion, but Hughes is content not to drive the point home too forcefully. The narrative's many humorous situations always manage to defuse any pervading sense of mawkishness, from the slow-motion dismantling of Neal's sorely tested patience to a hilarious scene in a motel room where Del and Neal, awakening next to each other in a double bed and finding themselves rather too close for comfort, immediately jump into an overtly manly mindset to affirm their respective masculinity. It is much to Hughes's credit, and that of his exceptional cast, that the film manages to maintain its delicate balance of observational comedy and emotional weight throughout its duration.

It is also of note that the film projects a remarkably effective correlation between Neal's love for his spouse and children and Del's yearning for his late wife and the home he no longer has. Both men, though wildly dissimilar in temperament and personality, are both possessed of a strong moral character, and this sound ethical locus – even when they are desperately trying everything and anything they can in order to get to Chicago – is a quality that Hughes takes time to approve and promote. It is also interesting to observe that the young Page family appear much closer to Jack Butler's affectionate brood in *Mr Mom* than the dysfunctional families of *Sixteen Candles* or *Some Kind of Wonderful*, their idealised nature further emphasising their function as the ultimate goal in the most deeply unconventional of quest narratives.

Planes, Trains and Automobiles was warmly received by commentators of the time, who praised the film for its excellent characterisation,[1] entertaining central double-act,[2] and perceptive sense of comic observation.[3] The only dissenting voices were relatively mild in their difference of opinion, considering the film's comedic situations to be only sporadically funny, and perceiving that this led the overall pace of the narrative to lag at times.[4] However, modern reviewers have overwhelmingly continued to voice admiration for the film, making it one of Hughes's most enduring critical successes. A few have noted that screenings of the film have come to form something of a Thanksgiving tradition,[5] while others commend the timelessness of its outstanding lead performances,[6] the inspired way that Steve Martin is cast so effectively against type as an uptight straight man,[7] and the valuable contrast that Hughes's film provides to the iconic teen movies that had immediately preceded it.[8]

With *Planes, Trains and Automobiles*, Hughes had proven that he was more than capable of producing material which was the equal of his teen movies in terms of style, content and popularity. The film's considerable critical acclaim has led to it becoming one of Hughes's most rounded and satisfying comedies, as well as a celebrated contemporary high-point in the careers of Steve Martin and John Candy. Not only had Hughes demonstrated that his comedic and dramatic range was more than broad enough to encompass issues of relevance to an ever more extensive demographic, but his persuasive theme of celebrating and valuing the family unit was a highly compelling one which was also to play a part in his next feature.

Perhaps appropriately, given its Thanksgiving season theme, *Planes, Trains and Automobiles* went on general release in America on 25 November 1987. The only other film making its United States debut that day was Leonard Nimoy's *Three Men and a Baby*, which starred Tom Selleck, Steve Guttenberg and Ted Danson, and which was an enormously popular remake of French comedy *Trois Hommes et un Couffin* (Coline Serreau, 1985). 'Mony Mony' by Billy Idol was number one in the Billboard Charts that week. In current affairs that week, outgoing Premier Zhao Ziyang was succeeded by Li Peng as the People's Republic of China's head of state, 159 people were killed when a South African Airways Boeing 747 crashed into the Indian Ocean, and tragically a further 115 people perished when a Korean Air liner was lost near Burma mere days afterwards.

Representative Critical Opinion

'What John Hughes, who wrote, directed and produced the film, has done here is make a weirdly inventive, off-kilter comedy out of the horrors of modern travel. And in the process, he's also managed to make the funniest road movie since *Lost in America*.'
Hal Hinson, *The Washington Post*, 25 November 1987.

'There wasn't much of an idea here to begin with, and when Mr Hughes works with non-teen-age characters he has smaller reserves of colloquial humor upon which to draw.'
Janet Maslin, *The New York Times*, 25 November 1987.

'What may seem to the outsider as just another 80s comedy has maintained its immense popularity not solely because of its consistency at producing laughs, but because it displays the kind of heart that we can all relate to.'
Gary Panton, *Movie Gazette*, 28 May 2003.

13

SHE'S HAVING A BABY (1988)

Hughes Entertainment/Paramount Pictures

Director: John Hughes
Producer: John Hughes
Screenwriter: John Hughes

MAIN CAST

Kevin Bacon	-	Jefferson Edward Briggs
Elizabeth McGovern	-	Kristen Briggs
Alec Baldwin	-	Davis McDonald
William Windom	-	Russ Bainbridge
Holland Taylor	-	Sarah Briggs
Cathryn Damon	-	Gayle Bainbridge
James Ray	-	Jim Briggs
Isabel Lorca	-	Fantasy Girl

Hughes's next feature, *She's Having a Baby*, marked an interesting development of the themes that he had addressed over the course of his last few films. By combining notions of the responsibilities of adulthood, as had been tackled by *Some Kind of Wonderful*, and the exploration of the significance of the family unit in *Planes, Trains and Automobiles*, he was to employ a textured, multi-layered approach to *She's Having a Baby*'s poignant domestic drama, while still ensuring that the weight of the themes under discussion would not leave the film devoid of the characteristic Hughesian sense of humour.[1]

Once again combining writing, directing and production responsibilities, Hughes was to create a subtly nuanced approach to the emotionally-driven drama of family life with *She's Having a Baby*, as a result engendering one of his most structurally complex films. With a highly experienced cast of performers, and many ingenious narrative quirks planned along the way, the scene was set for one of Hughes's most unusual features of the decade.

It should be the happiest day in the life of Jefferson 'Jake' Briggs (Kevin Bacon). Marrying his childhood sweetheart Kristen Bainbridge (Elizabeth McGovern), even in the face of unrelenting derision from her curmudgeonly father Russ (William Windom), everything should be more or less perfect. So why does he find himself assailed by last-minute doubts at the altar, fuelled by the cynical observations of his narcissistic best friend Davis McDonald (Alec Baldwin)?

Jake and Kristen tie the knot in spite of his eleventh-hour reservations, and move into their first home together soon after. Their lodgings are sparse and their income meagre, due to their shared decision that Jake should return to university as a postgraduate to obtain a Masters degree. However, lethargy quickly sets in as his studies begin, as does the strain of chronic cashflow problems. Jake resolves to drop out of graduate school and, after concocting an outrageously fraudulent CV, manages to talk his way into a job with a Chicago advertising firm. He and his new wife then move into a more comfortably-sized home, with

Kristen taking up a job in the corporate sector.

The newlyweds are barely settled into their new house when Davis arrives unexpectedly from New York, where he has recently settled. His return to Illinois is only short-term, as he is just passing through to attend a funeral in his new girlfriend's family. However, his grandiose tales of the fast-paced city life on the East Coast give Jake pause for thought, and he begins to contemplate whether his new life of domestic contentment really has any long-term hope of containing the full extent of his elaborate ambitions.

Time passes, and Jake and Kristen settle into their new suburban existence, discovering and dealing with all of the responsibilities of adulthood including keeping up with mortgage payments, fitting in with the neighbours, and keeping their warring in-laws at bay. Yet Jake remains determined to continue work on his first novel, which he has been developing ever since leaving college. His colleagues at the advertising agency voice some scorn at this ambition however, claiming to have heard it all before from past employees, but rarely seeing any actual literary success coming to fruition. Although Jake's confidence in the direction of his future is tenuous at best, he finds that his love for his wife is much more resilient than he had ever predicted. When he spots a beautiful woman (Isabel Lorca) at a nightclub and later fantasises about a relationship with her, he ultimately cannot be swayed from his devotion to Kristen – even when he meets the same fantasy woman in a face-to-face encounter some time later.

Kristen, however, has other long-term plans for their marriage. Without discussing the matter with Jake, she decides to stop taking the contraceptive pill, only divulging this fact to him three months afterwards when the revelation is too late to make any difference. As it happens, nature has the last laugh, and Kristen's scheme to conceive is unsuccessful due to Jake's low sperm count. Jake, meanwhile, has been grudgingly starting to warm to the idea of fatherhood, not least in an attempt to silence the incessant cajoling of his mother (Holland Taylor) and Russ.

They seek medical advice, and after some intervention Kristen soon discovers that she has finally fallen pregnant.

As Kristen carries their child to term, Jake continues to find himself faced with big questions about where his life is headed. Another visit from Davis, back in town for the funeral of one of his own parents, ultimately reveals that far from revelling in his status as a high-flying, autonomous free agent, he has come to envy the warmth and stability that exudes from Jake and Kristen's marriage. As the mildly neurotic Jake wrestles with the daunting notions of parental obligations, Kristen takes comfort in her belief in their marriage and the family that is to come. But when Kristen goes into labour, last-minute complications lead to an emergency medical procedure. Jake is forced out of his emotional malaise as the wellbeing of their new baby hangs in the balance. Will Kristen be able to give birth as planned? Can Jake find the inner contentment that he so desperately seeks? And will he ever really manage to finish writing that novel?

She's Having a Baby is one of Hughes's most atypical films of the eighties. With a narrative that spans a timeframe of several years, there is an effectively realised sense of time progressing naturally as the audience witnesses Jake and Kristen's gradual development from fresh-faced young newlyweds and recent college graduates into seasoned professionals confronted with increasingly weighty issues in their lives. From questions of marital fidelity to financial stability, and from compromise over long-term ambition to the dizzying responsibility of parenthood, the film addresses many of the anxieties faced by characters in many of Hughes's teen movies – especially *Ferris Bueller's Day Off* and *Some Kind of Wonderful* – who are faced by the dawning pitfalls and accountabilities that are inevitable in the process of growing into adulthood. Jake's difficulty in coming to terms with these responsibilities is inventively articulated through a variety of vivid fantasy sequences including his convoluted but entirely imagined liaison with Isabel Lorca's idealised woman, and also a memorable sequence where his achingly mundane neighbours suddenly strike up an impromptu song-and-dance routine to celebrate the joys of lawn-mowing and the pleasures of the suburban life. Thus Hughes succeeds in making the film a shrewd satire of the social and cultural expectations of middle-class life in the eighties, while at the same time providing an upfront exploration of the significance of these aforementioned expectations.

At the very core of the film's mechanics is the fact that its two leads are able to effectively convey a convincing portrayal of a well-matched, deeply attuned couple, growing closer rather than apart as time goes by. Kevin Bacon had been active in television and on film since the seventies, having appeared in a wide range of well-received cinematic features including *National Lampoon's Animal House* (John Landis, 1978), *Starting Over* (Alan J. Pakula, 1979), *Friday the 13th* (Sean S. Cunningham, 1980), *Diner* (Barry Levinson, 1982) and *Footloose* (Herbert Ross, 1984). He was later to be nominated for a Golden Globe award for Best Performance by an Actor in a Supporting Role in a Motion Picture for his appearance in *The River Wild* (Curtis Hanson, 1994). Elizabeth McGovern was also a highly experienced performer at the time of *She's Having a Baby*, having been nominated for the Best Actress in a Supporting Role Academy Award in 1982, as well as the New Star of the Year in a Motion Picture award at the Golden Globes in the same year, for her appearance in *Ragtime* (Milos Forman, 1981). She had also appeared in a variety of high-profile releases throughout the decade, including *Ordinary People* (Robert Redford, 1980), *Racing with the Moon* (Richard Benjamin, 1984), *Once Upon a Time in America* (Sergio Leone, 1984) and *The Bedroom Window* (Curtis Hanson, 1987). Together, the pair light up the screen with both humour and poignancy as Kristen and Jake try to make sense of their lives, adapting as their circumstances change around them. Although a clear majority of the film's narrative is related specifically from Jake's point of view, Hughes appears very keen to ensure that Kristen's concerns are expressed as the equal of Jake's own, rather than simply as an adjunct to them.

She's Having a Baby also benefits greatly from a relatively small but highly effective cast of supporting players. Crucially significant among them is Alec Baldwin's role as Davis. Baldwin imbues the character with charisma as well as waywardness, and his performance makes it entirely possible for the audience to see exactly why Jake finds him such an appealing friend just as Kristen, simultaneously, treats him with suspicion and distrust. Baldwin, who at the time was perhaps most immediately recognisable to audiences for his recurring role as Joshua Rush on TV's *Knots Landing* (1979-93) between 1984 and 1985, had been a prolific performer both in film and on television. His cinematic output had been accomplished, including an appearance in *Forever Lulu* (Amos Kollek, 1987), and going on to further success at the time with performances in *Beetle Juice* (Tim Burton, 1988), *Working Girl* (Mike Nichols, 1988) and *Talk Radio* (Oliver Stone,1988). Baldwin has been nominated for Emmy awards seven times between 1996 and 2008, and was also nominated for the Best Actor in a Supporting Role Academy Award in 2004 for his appearance in *The Cooler* (Wayne Kramer, 2003). In addition, he has been nominated six times for Golden Globe awards, winning the Best Performance by an Actor in a Television Series award in 2007 for his appearance in Tina Fey's hugely successful comedy *30 Rock* (2006-).

Among *She's Having a Baby*'s other notable performances are William Windom and Cathryn Damon as Kristen's forthright parents, Russ and Gayle Bainbridge, and also Holland Taylor and James Ray as Sarah and Jim Briggs, Jake's slightly more contemplative (but scarcely less interfering) mother and father. The families' respective expectations on Jake and Kristen's married life provide some knowing humour as they exert restrained but persistent pressure on their offspring's prospects. The film's closing credits sequence – where names are suggested for Jake and Kristen's new son – features cameo appearances from a dizzying array of high-profile stars, some of them veterans of past (and future) Hughes films, including Kirstie Alley, Dan Aykroyd, Matthew Broderick, John Candy, Ted Danson, Woody Harrelson, Robert Hays, Michael Keaton, Elias Koteas, Edie McClurg, Bill Murray, Olivia Newton-John, Roy Orbison, Annie Potts, John Ratzenberger, Ally Sheedy, Lyman Ward and a great many others.

The critical reception of *She's Having a Baby* at the time of its release ranged from ambivalent to hostile, and indeed it was to split opinion in ways unmatched by most of Hughes's other features. A number of commentators disapproved of what they considered to be the film's eclectic but ultimately unpersuasive presentation of adult issues,[2] and were unconvinced by the employment of narrative devices which were, in their opinion, attention-grabbing but superficially trivial.[3] Some reviewers did, however, note that although they found the film's combination of weighty subject matter and light-hearted humour to be somewhat jarring, the film was undeniably one of Hughes's most multiply-layered.[4] Modern assessment of *She's Having a Baby* has been slightly more sympathetic, if equally uneven, with the analysis of recent critics considering the film to be passably engaging rather than memorable,[5] or even suffering from an outright lack of success in the achievement of its dramatic aims.[6] Others, however, have felt that the range and maturity of the themes with which the film engaged meant that *She's Having a Baby* had overall been judged more harshly by past critics than it had deserved.[7]

With *She's Having a Baby*, Hughes took a considerable gamble with critical expectation. Although the film formed a logical continuation of the themes that he had begun to explore in his later teen movies, and also carried on the premise of the significance of family life that had been engaged with by *Planes, Trains and Automobiles*, it also marked a distinct break from all of these earlier films. By introducing a narrative timeframe with a much broader scope than he was normally inclined to employ, and by firmly subordinating comedy to drama (though sometimes exploring dramatic themes in a comedic way), Hughes ensured that the film was to explore the broadest possible range of issues related to adulthood responsibilities, and to the widest achievable extent. By focusing on several years of married life rather than specific incidents from one particular point in time, Hughes brings a contemplative sense of long-term development to *She's Having a Baby*, building up the complex characteristics of Kristen and Jake's partnership over time. Observant viewers would also have noticed another link with *Planes, Trains and Automobiles*: just as Kevin Bacon has a small cameo in the earlier film, it also features a scene where Susan Page (Laila Robins) is watching a programme on her bedroom television set and – although the action is never visible – the audible dialogue is drawn from Kristen and Jake raucously disagreeing about Davis staying at their home in an early scene from *She's Having A Baby*.

In spite of its admirable dramatic aims, *She's Having a Baby* has become one of Hughes's least recognisable films of the eighties, and today has become largely dwarfed by the critical and commercial success of the films which came immediately before it in the Hughes canon. The film did, however, mark a further evolution of Hughes's dramatic themes, examining the dynamics of family life and the duties and expectations of adulthood with great energy and considerable inventiveness. For his next feature, however, he was to return to more traditional comedic ground.

She's Having a Baby made its first appearance on American cinema screens on 5 February 1988. Also making their debut release on that date were Steve De Jarnatt's science fiction action adventure *Cherry 2000*, Wes Craven's horror *The Serpent and the Rainbow*, Peter Del Monte's mystery thriller *Giulia e Giulia* (*Julia and Julia*), and James B. Harris's police drama *Cop*, starring James Woods. One of the most prominent releases that day was Philip Kaufman's high-profile adaptation of Milan Kundera's *The Unbearable Lightness of Being*, starring Daniel Day-Lewis and Juliette Binoche. Peter Richardson's British crime comedy *The Supergrass* was to emerge into American cinemas following an earlier 1985 release date in the UK, and Andrzej Wajda's Polish industrial drama, *Ziemia Obiecana* (*The Promised Land*) was also being screened for the first time in the United States, having originally premiered in Poland in 1975. Topping the Billboard Charts at the time was 'Need You Tonight' by INXS. In that week's news, a sinking barge off the coast of Anacortes in Washington State was to inadvertently spill 70,000 gallons of oil, Panamanian General Manuel Noriega was indicted by a United States grand jury, and the Arizona House of Representatives voted to impeach the State's Republican Governor Evan Mecham.

'There are many comedic setups which, if they were with less archetypically drawn characters, might have delivered the laughs with the refreshingly innocent joy that has been the hallmark of other John Hughes pics.'
Variety Staff, *Variety*, 3 February 1988.

'It is some kind of tribute to the strength of the story, and the warmth of the performances by Kevin Bacon and Elizabeth McGovern, that the movie somehow manages almost to work, in spite of the adornments.'
Roger Ebert, *The Chicago Sun-Times*, 5 February 1988.

'This film doesn't deal in big issues. Only the minutiæ of life is given real time, although you could say some of the small stuff is more important in the lives of most people. [...] Most of Hughes' films offer sharp and funny dialogue, and this is no exception.'
Norman Short, *DVD Verdict*, December 2000.

14

THE GREAT OUTDOORS (1988)

Hughes Entertainment/Universal Pictures

Director: Howard Deutch
Producer: Arne Schmidt
Screenwriter: John Hughes

MAIN CAST

John Candy	-	Chet Ripley
Dan Aykroyd	-	Roman Craig
Stephanie Faracy	-	Connie Ripley
Annette Bening	-	Kate Craig
Chris Young	-	Buck Ripley
Ian Giatti	-	Ben Ripley
Hilary Gordon	-	Cara Craig
Rebecca Gordon	-	Mara Craig

With *The Great Outdoors*, Hughes was to make a conscious move away from the subtle satire and heavy dramatic consequence of *She's Having a Baby*, instead revisiting a broader approach to situational comedy. Returning to themes of travel and holidaying in a domestic setting, as per *National Lampoon's Vacation*, he was also to continue to build upon themes of the importance of familial bonds that had been raised in his more recent features.

The Great Outdoors marked Hughes's third collaboration with director Howard Deutch, and was once again to draw upon the considerable talents of actor John Candy in the role of protagonist. Also featuring an energetic performance from Dan Aykroyd, who at the time was enjoying huge acclaim for his appearances in some of the most successful comedies of the eighties, the stage was set for a return to one of Hughes's most recognisable subjects, an exploration of the great American vacation.

It's the summer, and kind-hearted Chester 'Chet' Ripley (John Candy) has a plan. A hard working family man from Chicago, he is determined to treat his doting wife Connie (Stephanie Faracy) and young sons Buck (Chris Young) and Ben (Ian Giatti) to the best possible vacation at a beautifully scenic lake resort in remote Pechoggin, Wisconsin. Chet had visited the resort with his father many years beforehand, and enjoyed the experience so profoundly that he can't wait to share the same good times with his own young family. Buck and Ben are far from convinced of the merits of Chet's chosen location, but seem resigned to their father's determination that they're going to have a good time at any cost.

However, no sooner have the Ripleys started to unpack at their rented lake house (affectionately named 'The Loon's Nest') when they receive some unexpected visitors – Connie's sister Kate (Annette Bening) and her husband Roman Craig (Dan Aykroyd), along with their vaguely creepy twin daughters Cara and Mara (Hilary Gordon and Rebecca Gordon). Roman explains that he has cancelled his family's intended holiday in Europe in order to spend more time with the Ripleys, whom they rarely see throughout the year. The fact that his surprise arrival was entirely uninvited (and is wholly unwelcome) appears lost on him.

Hailing from the prosperous Chicago community of Oakpark, the Craigs are as snobbish as they are dysfunctional. Mercedes-driving Roman is an upmarket investment broker who seems to believe that he knows everything about everything (and a few other things besides). Kate seems to be on a permanent short fuse, and is deeply sexually frustrated by her husband's apparent lack of interest in her. And, as Chet observes, the peculiar twins look as though they've escaped from *The Exorcist* (William Friedkin, 1973). As soon as they move into the Ripleys' lake house for the week, tensions rapidly begin to mount.

Undaunted by the unanticipated new arrivals, even although his cheerfulness has been somewhat dented, Chet remains resolutely determined that everyone is still going to have a good time. He tries teaching his son Ben how to water-ski, a task which (thanks to Roman) ends with a quite unexpected result. Then a trip to see some bears in the wild takes an alarming turn when the animals develop a sudden fondness for Chet's car. Other incidents include a memorable visit to a local man's 110th birthday party at the resort's nearby Perk's Pine Lodge, where a golden photo opportunity is ruined by a reluctant admission from manager Wally (Robert Prosky) that the elderly gent in question is actually dead, having expired while getting there in the car journey.

In spite of Roman constantly getting on his nerves, Chet discovers that the vacation has a few plus points to offset the negative factors. He manages to terrify everyone rigid (including Roman, much to his satisfaction) with a tall tale of a grizzly bear who he managed to scalp with a shotgun while on his honeymoon. Then later, he succeeds – against all expectation – in eating his way through a staggering 96-ounce prime beef steak at a nearby restaurant, amazing his relatives and securing a free meal for everyone. Even his son Buck has reason to be cheerful when he discovers beautiful local girl Cammy (Lucy Deakins) playing pool at an amusement arcade. Although the two have their fair share of misunderstandings, eventually they become close and spend some time together, which gives Buck ample opportunity to explore the town off the beaten track and discover the real Pechoggin that lies beyond the tourist attractions.

Back at the lake house, tensions are finally reaching fever pitch. Chet's deep reserves of patience are beginning to run dry thanks to Roman's constant sniping and know-it-all pronouncements. He decides to call time on the holiday and intends to pack up and leave, but is eventually talked out of it by the everdiplomatic Connie. However, matters eventually boil over when Chet later blows a fuse and all but challenges Roman and Kate to depart instead. This they do, but not before Roman attempts to shame Chet with an account from the remote past, claiming that Chet had allegedly defamed Roman's character. Having no recollection of this, but being a highly principled individual, Chet is appalled that he would have slighted Roman's name in such a way and seeks to make amends. Roman asks him to invest in a 'rock-solid' $25,000 investment scheme that he is keen to buy into. Humbled by his earlier apparent slander, Chet signs him a cheque for this amount, even although it costs him more than he can afford – almost half his annual salary. But as Roman leaves, he assures Chet that the investment will ultimately pay dividends in the long run.

On the road back to Illinois, however, Roman has an attack of conscience and returns to the lake house. There, he tears up the cheque and confesses to Chet – much to the amazement of Kate and Connie – that he is a fraud. After having made a bad investment two years ago, Roman had effectively bankrupted himself, and he and his family are living on borrowed time. In a desperate attempt to keep himself solvent, he had plotted to invade Chet's holiday with the sole intent of conning him out of $25,000 for an investment opportunity that had never existed. Even his tale of Chet's defamation was entirely fabricated.

In spite of the deviousness of Roman's deceit, Chet decides

that family is more important than the settling of scores. He resolves to help his obnoxious brother-in-law any way he can, even although the two patently can't stand the sight of each other. However, before they can come to any further resolutions a major storm hits Pechoggin, precluding any chance of a departure. When Roman's daughters go missing down an abandoned mine-shaft in the middle of the torrential downpour, it comes down to him and Chet to try to avert a tragic end to the vacation. But things take a turn for the worse when Chet accidentally happens upon an angry-looking bald bear with an apparent taste for revenge...

The Great Outdoors employs a different approach to the traditional holiday-based comedy of the earlier *National Lampoon's Vacation* films. Firstly, it was to take place entirely within a static location, making good use of its abundant natural features to present a wide variety of comic situations rather than adhering to the madcap travelogue aspect of *Vacation* and *European Vacation*. Secondly, the chaotic, larger-than-life eccentricities of the inspired Clark Griswold were supplanted by the shrewdly-rendered warring characters of Chet and Roman. The mild-mannered, compassionately benevolent Chet is very effectively counter-balanced by the vain, arrogant Roman, a man who (in the grand yuppie tradition of the late eighties) knows the price of everything and the value of nothing.

Dan Aykroyd, an experienced writer and producer, had appeared in many high-profile features for several years prior to *The Great Outdoors*, including *1941* (Steven Spielberg, 1979), *The Blues Brothers* (John Landis, 1980) and *Trading Places* (John Landis, 1983), and *Ghostbusters* (Ivan Reitman, 1984). One of the most recognisable names in film comedy throughout the eighties, he was later to be nominated for the Best Actor in a Supporting Role Academy Award in 1990 for his appearance in *Driving Miss Daisy* (Bruce Beresford, 1989). Aykroyd and Candy had appeared together in a number of films throughout the eighties, including *1941*, *The Blues Brothers* and also *It Came from Hollywood* (Malcolm

Leo and Andrew Solt, 1982). Their onscreen collaborations would continue in features such as *Masters of Menace* (Daniel Raskov, 1990), *Canadian Bacon* (Michael Moore, 1995), and of course Aykroyd's own *Nothing But Trouble* (1991). Although Roman Craig was one of his lesser-known comedy portrayals of the decade – hardly a Ray Stantz or Elwood Blues – Aykroyd nonetheless imbues the character with distinctive vigour and dynamism, creating a conceited, pompous and insufferably supercilious individual. Roman symbolises everything about the eighties culture of corporate excess that was antithetical to traditional family values and, by extension, to the co-operation with the long-established social order. When Roman berates Chet for having the antediluvian attitude of wishing to enjoy nature instead of aspiring to harness it for corporate ends, he gives voice to the one great difference which divides the two men so profoundly; whereas Chet is content to live in accord with the world around him, Roman instead seeks to manage and manipulate anything that carries with it the potential for development and exploitation, all in the dubious name of progress.

John Candy delivers another fine performance, effortlessly articulating the pent-up frustration of a benign family man watching his dream holiday turning into a nightmare by degrees. He is well complemented by Stephanie Faracy as his endlessly tolerant and astute onscreen wife, and the pair share a touchingly believable chemistry. Annette Bening also impresses as the irascible Kate in what was her cinematic debut performance. Active on television since the mid-eighties, Bening would go on to considerable success in the coming years with appearances in films which included *Regarding Henry* (Mike Nichols, 1991), *Bugsy* (Barry Levinson, 1991) and *Mars Attacks!* (Tim Burton, 1996). She was also to receive Academy Award nominations for her performances in *The Grifters* (Stephen Frears, 1990), *American Beauty* (Sam Mendes, 1999) and *Being Julia* (István Szabó, 2004). As the frosty Kate, Bening succeeds in providing an effective contrast between the Craigs' marriage and that of the Ripleys. Chet and

Connie are as close as Roman and Kate are distant; whereas the Ripleys are emotionally devoted and enjoy good relations with their children, the Craigs are aloof and detached from each other, coolly reserved in their relations with the twins, and often seem more like strangers than spouses. This juxtaposition is repeatedly used for dramatic as well as comedic effect throughout the course of the film.

Director Howard Deutch makes excellent use of the stunning North American woodland scenery on display, and the many action sequences in the film are handled efficiently – particularly Chet's ill-fated (and unintentional) attempt at high-speed water-skiing. Thomas Newman's soundtrack is also highly competent in its execution. However, much of the charm of *The Great Outdoors* lies in the proficiency of its supporting performances, from Lucy Deakins's brief but touching turn as Cammie the disillusioned waitress to the eccentric husband and wife pairing of Wally and Juanita, played with much panache by Robert Prosky and Zoaunne LeRoy.

Although its comedy was, by and large, more erratic in its application than the generally more consistent *National Lampoon's Vacation* films, *The Great Outdoors* did feature a variety of standout sequences. Hughes employs a wonderfully tongue-in-cheek (and quite literal) use of the Chekhov's Gun principle when Wally, brandishing a shotgun-turned-lampstand that is introduced at the beginning of the first act, uses it to scare off a grizzly bear at the conclusion of the third. The recurring visual gag of garbage-scavenging raccoons, their dialogue provided via subtitles, is also inspired. And Chet and Roman's marvellously over-the-top attempts to trap a bat that has invaded the lake house in the dead of night is played out with impressive dramatic overstatement.

Contemporary criticism of *The Great Outdoors* was, in the main, deeply unreceptive. Reviewers of the time considered the film to be, at best, an average comedy which demonstrated humour that was only sporadically engaging.[1] Others came to denigrate it for performances which were, in their opinion, disappointingly lethargic.[2] The film's harsh criticism at the time of its release may have suffered, to some extent, from its proximity to the similarly-themed *Summer Rental* (Carl Reiner, 1985), a comedy that had also starred John Candy and which had already gone over much of the same vacation-themed ground as *The Great Outdoors*. Modern commentators have been more ambivalent about the film. Some reviewers have condemned *The Great Outdoors* as being one of the least successful films that John Hughes has ever been involved in.[3] At the other end of the spectrum, the film has also been retrospectively praised as a highly enjoyable comedy with an entertaining cast of central players.[4]

The Great Outdoors had seen Hughes return not only to the traditional comedy format, but also to the persistent theme of the importance of family relationships and the emotional support that they can provide – a subject which would continue into the next feature in his filmography. Although largely unsuccessful with the critics of the time, the film has enjoyed something of a revival of fortune in recent years with its DVD release. In spite of the fact that it is generally recognised as one of the less significant films of Hughes's eighties output, there is still much to recommend a viewing of *The Great Outdoors*.

The Great Outdoors was released in America on 17 June 1988, the same day as the first appearance of Penelope Spheeris's musical documentary *The Decline of Western Civilization Part II: The Metal Years*, Anthony Hickox's knowing horror *Waxwork*, Chris Menges's South Africa-based drama *A World Apart*, James Kenelm Clarke's satirical thriller *Yellow Pages*, and Aleksandr Askoldov's Russian Revolution-based drama *Komissar* (*The Commissar*), originally produced in 1967. Also debuting on that date was Walter Hill's crime thriller *Red Heat*, starring Arnold Schwarzenegger and James Belushi. At number one in the Billboard Charts was George Michael with 'One More Try'. In current affairs at the time, the government of Haiti faced a *coup d'etat*, Microsoft released the fourth version of its famous MS-DOS operating system for IBM-compatible PCs, and Greek President Andreas Papandreou met with Turkish Prime Minister Halil Özalin in Athens.

'Though the film never becomes actively unfunny, neither does it do much more than tread water.'

Janet Maslin, *The New York Times*, 17 June 1988.

'[If it] had a few more laughs we might be tempted simply to write it off as mediocre and let it go at that. But this woodland farce is just coarse enough, and unfunny enough, to achieve true awfulness.'

Hal Hinson, *The Washington Post*, 17 June 1988.

'Man, were there ever high hopes when this one opened. Alas, John Hughes was about to enter his second phase of career advancement... the family comedy phase. And those of us who held him as a generational icon would never be the same.'

Chris Parry, *eFilmCritic.com*, 31 July 1999.

15

UNCLE BUCK (1989)

Hughes Entertainment/Universal Pictures

Director: John Hughes
Producers: John Hughes and Tom Jacobson
Screenwriter: John Hughes

MAIN CAST

John Candy	-	Buck Russell
Jean Louisa Kelly	-	Tia Russell
Gaby Hoffman	-	Maizy Russell
Macaulay Culkin	-	Miles Russell
Amy Madigan	-	Chanice Kobolowski
Elaine Bromka	-	Cindy Russell
Garrett M. Brown	-	Bob Russell
Laurie Metcalf	-	Marcie Dahlgren-Frost

Following on from *The Great Outdoors, Uncle Buck* was to see Hughes returning behind the camera to present a new and inventive take on the issue of familial bonds and dysfunction. Once again starring John Candy as the film's protagonist – albeit in a rather different portrayal from those witnessed in his earlier collaborations with Hughes – *Uncle Buck* was to unleash Hughes's sharply observational humour to motivate a poignant and dryly humorous narrative based around an inspired central situation.

In addition to showcasing even more of Candy's range as an actor, the film was also to feature an early role for Macaulay Culkin, who would later go on to huge success the following year as Kevin McCallister in *Home Alone* (Chris Columbus, 1990). Hughes's script for *Home Alone* was among the most commercially successful of all his screenplays, and – in some ways similar to the central scenario of *Uncle Buck* – was to centre on the theme of a child being unexpectedly left to cope without parental supervision, and the ramifications that this entails both for him and his parents. But whereas *Home Alone* was to examine the consequences of a single child being accidentally left alone while the rest of his family unwittingly go on vacation without him, *Uncle Buck* was instead to observe the outcome of an unmarried man, totally inexperienced in the art of child care, who is forced into the role of surrogate parent when a family crisis compels him to take up supervisory responsibilities for his young nieces and nephew. Thus Hughes was to return to some of the most prominent themes that were to recur in his work throughout the late eighties and early nineties, namely those of familial duty and the domestic importance of the family unit.

It's fair to say that life could be going better for Tia (Jean Louisa Kelly), Maizy (Gaby Hoffman) and Miles Russell (Macaulay Culkin). Their parents have recently relocated them all to Illinois from Indianapolis, where the kids had been happy and settled, in order to pursue better career prospects. Now faced with making new friends in the area, the three siblings are downcast at the prospect at starting from scratch. This is especially true of sullen teenager Tia, who is forever needling her parents Cindy and Bob (Elaine Bromka and Garrett M. Brown) for being so preoccupied with their new careers that they have much less direct interaction with their children.

Things take a sudden turn for the worse when Bob receives a phone call in the middle of the night to inform him that Cindy's father has suffered a heart attack. Cindy realises that she and Bob need to get to her father's bedside in Indianapolis as soon as possible, but none of their neighbours are either available or suitable to look after the children during the Russells' absence. Eventually, Bob suggests contacting his brother Buck, who lives locally. Cindy, however, is extremely reluctant to do so, as she considers Buck to be a workshy, irresponsible idler with whom they have had little recent contact. But when it becomes clear that they have no real choice in the matter, Bob calls Buck on the phone and, after explaining the situation, asks him to come over as quickly as possible.

Buck Russell (John Candy) is a bachelor nearing middle-age who revels in enjoying the single life without any concerns of marital accountability. This forms something of a running sore with his girlfriend Chanice Kobolowski (Amy Madigan), who is desperate to marry Buck and start a family with him – much to the horror of this unshakable free-wheeler, who isn't even seeking employment commitments. The news that he will be unable to start work for Chanice at her tyre service firm, in light of having to look after his nieces and nephew, does not go down well (to say the least).

Grabbing a few belongings and heading off in his extremely rickety car, Buck arrives in the suburbs and immediately causes a faux-pas by loudly trying to gain entry to the wrong house. Eventually, however, Bob manages to steer Buck in the right direction, and he and Cindy reluctantly depart, leaving Buck in charge of their children.

The next morning, Tia – who had overheard Buck's arrival the night before – is standoffish and dismissive towards her uncle, who she has not seen in many years. However, although resentful at being left at home while her parents return to Indianapolis without her, even the worst of Tia's glowering moroseness is unable to chip into Buck's seemingly endless reserves of chirpy sociability. He does, however, strike up a much better rapport with Maizy and Miles, not least after patiently answering an incessant round of rapid-fire questions from his inquisitive young nephew.

Buck gets his own back on Tia, to an extent, when he drops her off at high school in his dilapidated car – much to her intense embarrassment. He then tries to rediscover the delights of housework in a less than orthodox way – no small feat given his generally slobbish approach to living. On leafing through his brother's wedding album, however, he is hurt to discover that some of the photos have been framed in a very particular way that suggests that he has been all but airbrushed out of the family's history.

Buck returns to pick up Tia from school, in spite of her earlier protestations that she would find her own way back. In doing so, he inadvertently breaks up a tête-à-tête between Tia and her boyfriend Bug (Jay Underwood), which is not at all well received. Tia is incensed that Buck should object to Bug's public displays of affection, and demands that he keep out of her private life. But Buck, who is rapidly gaining the measure of his feisty niece, grows increasingly resilient in the face of her indignant protestations.

Tia attempts to get revenge later, finding her opportunity when Cindy calls Buck from Indianapolis to check that everyone is well. Intercepting the call, Tia spins Cindy a yarn that Buck is repeatedly leaving Miles and Maizy alone (he had only done so for a short while, to pick Tia up from school), and then wrongly infers that he has been drinking heavily. Unfortunately Buck does little to help his case when he eventually gets to the phone, as he spends much of the time outlining his plan to let the family dog drink out of the toilet, thus saving the need to regularly refill its water bowl.

The next day, Buck has an unexpected encounter with Cindy's neighbour, Marcie Dahlgren-Frost (Laurie Metcalf), who lets herself into the house and sneaks up on Buck in what she believes is a compromising position. Buck, who is actually trying to persuade a washing machine to work, soon overcomes the misunderstanding and introduces himself. Still slightly aloof, Marcie asks him out to lunch, but Buck is politely (yet firmly) resistant to the idea.

At night, Buck takes the kids out for an evening of ten-pin bowling. Tia is resolutely opposed to the idea, but Buck – keen to keep her apart from her predatory boyfriend – manages to persuade her to come along by threatening to shave her hair off during the night. While Maizy and Miles enjoy themselves, Tia sits gloomily on the sidelines. Buck meets an old friend, E. Roger 'Rog' Coswell (Brian Tarantina), who tells him that a mutual acquaintance of theirs – Jimmy Bean – will soon be in town. Bean, who owes money to both of them, is a horse-fixer, and will be involving himself in a forthcoming race which has the potential to net Rog and Buck a serious amount of cash. Buck appears very interested in the scheme.

The next day sees the arrival of Miles's birthday. To celebrate, Buck has baked a collection of pancakes that verge on a gargantuan scale. He oversees a party for Miles and his friends, while Cindy had booked a clown for the event before her unexpected departure. This does not impress the kids, who feel they have outgrown clowns years ago. Buck, however, is even less impressed when Pooter the Clown (Mike Starr) finally turns up at the door, very late and heavily drunk. Although Pooter is surly and aggressive, Buck is so irritated by his bad attitude and the fact that he plans to entertain children while heavily inebriated that he demands that the clown waste no time in leaving the premises. Buck's method of removal, when he is forced to use it, is one that Pooter finds anything but funny.

At night, Tia is enjoying a romantic clinch with Bug at a leafy out-of-town hook-up spot. Bug is pushing her to take things much further than a passionate kiss, but Tia is impervious to his supposed charms. Before Bug can press any more forcefully, however, Buck arrives in his car with Miles and Maizy in the back seat. Although Tia had told him that she would be staying at the home of a cheerleader friend, Buck had seen through her ruse and goes out in search of her. Sure enough, on arrival he discovers that Bug has been drinking, and decides that he will pick Tia up in his own car rather than risk leaving her at the mercy of Bug's intoxicated driving skills. Tia can't see that Buck is trying to help her out, and swears vengeance on him for humiliating her in front of her boyfriend once again.

The next morning, Buck heads for Miles and Maizy's elementary school, where he has a pre-arranged meeting with the fearsome assistant principal Anita Hoargarth (Suzanne Shepherd). Mrs Hoargarth is concerned about Maizy's progress at school, believing her to be an easily distracted daydreamer rather than the ambitious, academically-minded individual that she would prefer. Hoargarth is arrogant and curt towards Buck, especially when he reminds her that Maizy is, in point of fact, only six years old. However, when she continues her venomous diatribe Buck quickly sees red and furiously lambastes her for the close-mindedness and errant disrespect of her acidic invective. By the time he has finished, she seems quite literally lost for words.

Buck leaves a message on Chanice's answering machine, telling her that he misses her company. Chanice rings back later in the evening, but Tia takes the call and lies that Buck has been seeing Marcie from across the street, and has regularly been staying out late at night with her. Chanice seems both saddened and slightly dazed by this news.

Unfortunately for Buck, reality is not so far away from Tia's falsehoods. The next day, the increasingly intense Marcie, who is obviously tired of being single, lets herself back into the Russells' house and makes an unwelcome move on Buck. She persuades him to dance with her, much to Buck's manifest reluctance, but he soon finds that she has an unusually amorous approach to the art (even if the two are almost completely uncoordinated). To complicate matters, Chanice turns up to confront Buck after Tia's revelations the night before. When he is unable to hear the doorbell due to the loud volume of the music, Chanice lets herself in and finds Marcie and Buck dancing together. Immediately believing Tia's tall tale that the two of them are having an affair, Chanice storms off without giving Buck a chance to explain.

Later, Tia tells Buck that she intends to go out the following night, but Buck insists that she stay in until her parents get back and she is no longer his responsibility. Furious, Tia taunts Buck by rubbing his nose in the fact that Bob and Cindy obviously have no desire to be associated with him, and indirectly admits to having set up the confrontation between him and Chanice. Although he remains impassive, the encounter later makes him reflect on the direction of his life and whether he is really following the path that he needs to – especially as he is getting older.

The next day, Tia sneaks away from the house, heading with Bug for a house party that's being held elsewhere. She tells Maizy and Miles not to expect her back for a couple of days. Buck is waiting to pick her up at the school, but quickly realises that she has managed to evade his supervision. He returns to the house dejected to find that Tia has absconded, in spite of earlier having promised him that she'd look after her siblings – being Friday, Buck had intended to lay the bet that he expects to net him a small fortune. However, as his hopes of an entire year's financial resources are pinned on a big win, he has no choice but to take Miles and Maizy with him to the race-track.

However, before Buck can take the car out of the driveway he has an attack of conscience. He realises not only that he can't take the kids with him to a fixed horse race, but also that his top priority has to be retrieving Tia for her own safety. Desperate, he calls Chanice and explains the situation to her. Still fuming at the belief that she has been jilted by him, she is initially reluctant to help out, but on hearing that children are involved she ultimately agrees to look after Miles and Maizy while he goes in search of Tia. He then abandons any plan to attend his meeting at the race-track, and sets out to find his wayward niece. After some location work in his car, Buck eventually pinpoints the street and house in which the party is taking place, and wastes no time in making his way there.

Meanwhile at the house party, Bug is upstairs in a darkened bedroom making some unwelcome advances on his prey. Buck wastes no time in infiltrating the massed revellers and – although he is the living embodiment of a fish out of water – succeeds in tracking Bug down. Drilling open the lock on the bedroom door, he forces his way into the room only to discover that Tia isn't with Bug after all – he appears to have found a new (if similarly reluctant) partner.

A distraught Tia is walking alone along a darkened street. Buck soon finds her and picks her up in his car, and the two quickly arrive at a long-overdue rapprochement. Tia, upset at Bug's unfaithfulness, apologises to Buck for her behaviour during the week. Buck responds that his own directionless life hardly gives him the right to judge anyone else's relationship. However, the melancholic atmosphere is lightened when Buck reveals that he has Bug tied up in the trunk of his car. Buck appears to let him go after the younger man half-heartedly apologises, but when Bug later begins to shout insults at him, Buck decides instead to use the rapidly-fleeing charlatan as the target for some impromptu golfing practice instead.

Back at the house, Tia confesses to Chanice that she had lied earlier about Buck's 'affair' with Marcie. Chanice explains that while she appreciates Tia's honesty, Buck's apparent infidelity was just the tip of the iceberg when it came to the problems that lay between them. She bemoans Buck's lack of commitment, but soon begins to suspect that he has persuaded Tia to emphasise all of his positive aspects to her in an attempt at reaching a new, shared understanding. But with Bob and Cindy due back imminently, how will Buck's surrogate parenting skills ultimately be judged by the Russells? And after an eight year courtship, will Buck and Chanice ever manage to work things out between them?

With *Uncle Buck*, Hughes was to combine a healthy dose of observational comedy with a never less than interesting interpretation of suburban family life. John Candy is on top form as the good-natured Buck Russell, whose free and easy (yet ultimately aimless) life is shaken up by the unexpected responsibilities of proxy parenthood. Candy makes full use of the considerable comic and dramatic potential that the role presents, creating an oddly charming character who manages to be simultaneously humorous and complex in roughly equal measure. He works hard throughout the film to bring a touching believability to this outcast family member, frozen out by his more affluent brother and sister-and-law because of his irresponsible ways, who finds himself slowly becoming integrated with his relations in ways that he had never before considered achievable. From the highly unconventional packed lunch that he puts together for Miles to his idiosyncratic habit of microwaving wet laundry when the washing machine breaks down, Buck reaches the apex of his new-found substitute parental powers at the elementary school, when he triumphantly manages to slap down Mrs Hoargarth's conceited superciliousness. His exultant defence of childhood innocence, challenging Hoargarth's hard-faced determination to pigeonhole and homogenise the life of every youngster in the school, is one of the film's most memorable high-points.

Uncle Buck featured many notable supporting performances from an accomplished group of actors. Elaine Bromka and Garrett M. Brown put in solid if brief appearances as the anxious Russell parents, while Amy Madigan also contributes a well-considered performance as Buck's long-suffering girlfriend Chanice. Laurie Metcalf is also nicely cast as the Russells' impulsive, rather anomalous neighbour Marcie, wringing out every ounce of the character's sexual frustration to good comic effect. Metcalf had appeared in films such as *Stars and Bars* (Pat O'Connor, 1988) and *Candy Mountain* (Robert Frank and Rudy Wurlitzer, 1988), though was perhaps best known at the time for her regular role as Jackie Harris in TV's long-running sitcom *Roseanne* (1988-97).

Yet if the film's adult supporting cast all deliver entirely dependable performances, its younger actors are if anything even more adept. Gaby Hoffman and Macaulay Culkin are both amusingly wry and sardonic in the roles of the two younger Russell kids, Maizy and Miles, and the two enjoy an excellent chemistry with Candy which efficiently articulates the developing family relationship between the three of them. Jean Louisa Kelly engages fully with the role of Tia, exploring every nuance of the morose teen to present an effective appraisal of her emotional upset and gnawing sense of alienation from her parents. *Uncle Buck* was Kelly's cinematic debut; she would later become a prolific performer on television and in film, and was to appear in features including *Mr Holland's Opus* (Stephen Herek, 1995), *Origin of the Species* (Andres Heinz, 1998), *Landfall* (Dan Hamilton, 2001) and *Aspects of Love* (Gale Edwards, 2005). Also worthy of note is Jay Underwood's entertaining depiction of the calculating, predatory Bug. He manages to strike a good balance between the character's posturing wiliness and his wide-eyed disbelief at Buck's matter-of-fact intimidation towards him, an aspect that is never too far away as the older man seeks to protect the safety of his niece. Underwood was best known at the time for performances in films including *Desert Bloom* (Eugene Corr, 1986) and *Promised Land* (Michael Hoffman, 1987), as well as appearing in the lead roles in *The Boy Who Could Fly* (Nick Castle, 1986) and *The Invisible Kid* (Avery Crounse, 1988).

Hughes makes excellent use of the autumnal atmosphere throughout the film, guaranteeing a very distinctive ambience during the location shooting. He also shows considerable skill in juxtaposing Bob and Cindy's beautifully decorated, well-appointed home with the much shadier world that Buck inhabits, which ranges from downmarket bowling alleys to his own slightly seedy apartment. The characteristically Hughesian eye for peculiar comedic detail is also very much in evidence, particularly with Buck's frantic attempts to retrieve a cat late at night only to discover that the family doesn't own it, and also when he is caught short while visiting an elementary school and is forced to make use of a miniature urinal while trying to evade prying eyes. Also worth mentioning is the inspired use of Buck's only-just-roadworthy automobile, so ancient and decrepit that a running joke is made of the gunshot noise the exhaust makes every time the engine is turned off.

Uncle Buck generally fared well with critics at the time of its release, with commentators approving of the film's well-observed characterisation,[1] John Candy's bravura central performance,[2] and the effective fusion of a typically Hughesian teen movie and a broader comedy of family tensions.[3] Not all criticism was as affirmative however, as some reviewers considered *Uncle Buck* to be ultimately a waste of Candy's considerable comic potential[4], accused the film of culminating in an emotional mawkishness that is at odds with its general air of unruffled pragmatism,[5] and humour that occasionally felt flat and uninspired.[6] Modern reviews have generally been more positive about the film's merits than negative. Commentators have considered *Uncle Buck* to be possessed of an amiable charm and pleasantly consistent sense of humour,[7] and demonstrating a family-friendly appeal,[8] with only a few considering the film's comedy to be lifeless or predictable in hindsight.[9]

Buck Russell's colourful story was later revived as a short-lived television series, *Uncle Buck* (1990-91), which was to star Kevin Meaney in the title role. The series' premise was somewhat altered from that of the film in that parents Bob and Cindy are killed in a car accident, leaving Buck with much longer-term responsibility for his young nieces and nephew. However, despite exploring a number of different comedy situations throughout its short run of episodes the series was not successful with either audiences or the critics, and was cancelled relatively quickly.

Uncle Buck marked another interesting development for Hughes, blending the subtle character observations of his teen movies with the wide-ranging socio-cultural comedy of his more recent features. Connecting these two elements was Hughes's long-running theme of familial cohesion, and the redemptive qualities that it can potentially bring. Just as Tia's emotional journey ultimately draws her closer to her family, we see in Buck a dawning realisation that the single life – once exhilarating in youth – is now isolating him in middle-age. There is even an indication at the end of the film that Buck plans to put his transient approach to a career behind him, as Chanice strongly hints that he will soon finally be working for her after all. Hughes again stresses the importance of the family unit in affirming the emotional wellbeing and overall stability of the individual, and this was a topic that he would explore once again in his final contribution to film in the eighties.

Uncle Buck first appeared on general release in America on 16 August 1989. It was to have a relatively clear run at the box office on that date, as the only other film debuting at the time was David Greenwalt and Aaron Russo's hippie-themed comedy *Rude Awakening*, starring Cheech Marin, Eric Roberts and Robert Carradine. At the top of the Billboard Charts was 'Right Here Waiting' by Richard Marx. Appearing in the news that week, Archbishop of Cape Town Desmond Tutu led a huge anti-apartheid protest march in South Africa, 171 people lost their lives when a French DC-10 plane crashed near Niger, F.W. De Klerk was sworn in as President of South Africa, and 85 people were killed in South Carolinian city of Charleston as a result of Hurricane Hugo.

'Hughes succeeds more than he has any right to in *Uncle Buck* because he's able to override sitcom cliché with generosity. It's a smart idea to let Candy play feelings instead of just fatness and bluster. For a movie that isn't really that good, *Uncle Buck* is surprisingly likable.'

Jay Carr, *The Boston Globe*, 16 August 1989.

'Though acceptable family fodder for moviegoing parents who prefer not to blush in front of their kids, Hughes' continued foray into so-called adult cinema continues to be less than promising. If *Uncle Buck* is an adult comedy, The Hucklebuck is one of this century's enduring pop-tune standards.'

Mike Clark, *USA Today*, 16 August 1989.

'*Uncle Buck* is better than it has any right to be. It's basically one plot contrivance after another, all designed to put the inexperienced Buck in charge of kids he has no idea how to take care of, and who don't really want him there in the first place. [...] *Uncle Buck* hits every story beat you'd expect, and yet it works not only as a comedy, but as a movie with believable relationships.'

Erich Asperschlager, *DVD Verdict*, 20 August 2011.

16

NATIONAL LAMPOON'S CHRISTMAS VACATION (1989)

Hughes Entertainment/Warner Brothers

Director: Jeremiah Chechik
Producers: John Hughes and Tom Jacobson
Screenwriter: John Hughes

MAIN CAST

Chevy Chase	-	Clark Griswold
Beverly D'Angelo	-	Ellen Griswold
Juliette Lewis	-	Audrey Griswold
Johnny Galecki	-	Russell 'Rusty' Griswold
Randy Quaid	-	Cousin Eddie Johnson
Miriam Flynn	-	Cousin Catherine Johnson
William Hickey	-	Uncle Lewis
Mae Questel	-	Aunt Bethany

For his last contribution to the cinema of the 1980s, Hughes was to return to the erratic world of Clark Griswold and his luckless family. This time, however, the Griswolds would not be terrorising the United States or continental Europe while on vacation, but would instead be bringing the holiday season into their home as they enjoyed Christmas celebrations with their many eccentric relations. While the film marked a more family-oriented turn for the *National Lampoon's Vacation* series in comparison to the first two ribald entries in the cycle, Hughes takes care to ensure that the festive theme and staunch emphasis on domestic merriment would not compromise laughs for the sake of emotional sentiment.

National Lampoon's Christmas Vacation was the first cinematic outing for director Jeremiah Chechik, who would later go on to direct films including *Benny and Joon* (1993), *Tall Tale* (1995) and *Diabolique* (1996) as well as a number of features for television. The film was also to see the return of original cast members Chevy Chase and Beverly D'Angelo as Clark and Ellen Griswold, along with Randy Quaid and Miriam Flynn reprising their roles as the ever-entertaining Johnson cousins from the original *Vacation* movie. They were joined by actors Juliette Lewis and Johnny Galecki as the latest incarnations of the two hapless Griswold kids, Audrey and Rusty.

It's December in Chicago, and Clark W. Griswold (Chevy Chase) has taken his resigned but endlessly-patient wife Ellen (Beverly D'Angelo) and kids Audrey (Juliette Lewis) and Rusty (Johnny Galecki) on a long drive out of the suburbs to find their family Christmas tree in order to mark the start of the year's festivities. Clark is absolutely determined to make the most of Christmas, whereas his long-suffering family seem reconciled to the notion of simply trying to survive it.

After a few close shaves with other drivers on the way into the wilderness, Clark eventually discovers the one flawless tree that he knows will look perfect in the family's living room. There's only one problem: it's absolutely gargantuan. Having forgotten to take his saw with him on the journey, Clark and company are forced to dig out the huge tree (roots and all) and bring it home atop their car. The outsized tree's massive scale leads to smug derision from Clark's stuck-up yuppie neighbours, Todd and Margo Chester (Nicholas Guest and Julia Louis-Dreyfus), though he wastes no time in giving as good as he gets in response. Ultimately, however, Todd and Margo's reservations may not have been entirely misplaced, as Clark discovers to his detriment when he unties the tree only to watch its unfettered branches shoot out and shatter his living room windows.

In bed at night, Ellen voices her concern about Clark's determination to host a large family gathering over the Christmas period, which will include her parents as well as his own. She points out that they all inevitably end up bickering over the most meaningless of small details whenever they meet, which will put a strain on the festivities. Clark nevertheless assures her that everything will be fine, due to the unique ability of Christmas to reconcile misunderstandings. Ellen is far from convinced by his optimistic take on the situation.

At his office in the city, Clark is looking forward to the lucrative Christmas bonus that he is due to receive from his work in food additive design. He reveals to one of his colleagues, Bill (Sam McMurray), that he has put down a hefty deposit on a new pool that he intends to have installed in his back yard. Even the cantankerousness of his irritable boss Frank Shirley (Brian Doyle Murray) does nothing to dampen his festive spirit. After work, he goes shopping for some lingerie for Ellen at a large department store, though he quickly becomes tongue-tied when he finds himself being served by a staggeringly beautiful sales assistant (Nicolette Scorsese).

Later, the family are each making their own individual preparations for Christmas when an ominous doorbell sounds, signalling that their relatives have arrived: Clark's parents Nora and Clark Senior (Diane Ladd and John Randolph) and Ellen's father and mother, Arthur and Frances Smith (E.G. Marshall and

Doris Roberts). Even before the front door has been opened, they have already started arguing in earnest. Audrey, on the other hand, is more concerned by the prospect of them sleeping in her room during their stay.

Clark commandeers Rusty into helping him festoon the house with external Christmas lights. As ever, he goes completely overboard and enshrines every inch of the house's exterior with cabling and bulbs, though he suffers a number of minor injuries as he does so. At one point, Clark misses his footing on the ladder and clings to the house's guttering for dear life. As he does so, a sharp-edged length of ice is fired from a now-detached segment of gutter and smashes through the Chesters' bedroom window, destroying their expensive-looking stereo system. However, as the 'evidence' quickly melts, they have no clue on their return as to what can have caused the damage (though of course, their suspicions quickly fall in the general direction of their neighbour).

His work now complete, Clark insists on his relatives joining him outside in the freezing cold – in their pyjamas and dressing gowns – as he attempts to build their collective anticipation for the activation of the lights. However, much to Clark's dismay the big switch-on proves to be a damp squib when he throws the switch... and nothing happens. His relatives are far from impressed by this non-event, leaving Clark frustrated. He resolves to keep checking every single light in the system until he can uncover the source of the hitch.

Having worked late into the night to find the fault in the lighting (though ultimately to no effect), Clark is late getting up the next morning. Still in his pyjamas, he sneaks up into the loft to hide away some Christmas presents. Frances, unaware of Clark's whereabouts, sees the open loft hatch and closes it to keep out the cold air. This leaves Clark trapped in the loft while all of his relatives go out shopping. He wastes no time in finding some warm clothing in a dusty trunk, and in the process uncovers a bundle of home movies from the fifties and sixties on old film reels. He then whiles away the rest of the day watching scenes of his childhood Christmases on a projector, though the warmth of his nostalgia is rapidly dissipated when Ellen – unaware of his position – pulls open the loft hatch and sends both Clark and the projector clattering down onto the upstairs landing.

At night, Clark is still fastidiously checking every bulb on the exterior of the house – though still to no avail. As his aggravation mounts, Ellen eventually realises that he hasn't properly connected the power extension, and soon remedies the situation. Clark is stunned by the spectacle before him, which draws so much electricity that the nearby power station has to switch over to auxiliary nuclear reserves just to keep the rest of the city's lights on. The family are belatedly amazed by Clark's triumph, though it goes down less well with the Chesters who find themselves momentarily blinded by the intensity of the lights (especially as they were enjoying a romantic night in at the time of the switch-on).

The exhilaration of Clark's accomplishment is short-lived, however, as he unexpectedly finds himself face-to-face with the dreaded Cousin Eddie (Randy Quaid), who has driven up from Kansas in his ancient RV to spend the festive season with him. Eddie has brought along his wife Catherine (Miriam Flynn) and a few of his extensive family, Ruby Sue (Ellen Hamilton Latzen) and Rocky (Cody Burger), along with his rather-too-friendly dog Snots. Clark is both startled and dismayed to see Eddie and his brood, not least as no-one had invited them. However, Eddie soon makes it clear that he's planning to stick around for a while, much to Clark's consternation.

Resigned to the fact that Eddie and his family are there to stay for the holidays, Clark takes them along with his own kids to a night of sledging. Clark intends to make use of a secret weapon – a prototype kitchen lubricant that his company has been developing. He treats the base of his sledge with it in the hope of reducing its friction against the ground. However, it works rather too well, and he ends up careening through the air at a worryingly fast rate. Tearing into a forest and then along a busy road at a rate of knots, Clark is fortunate to get through the encounter in one piece.

At work, just before he and his colleagues leave for the Christmas season, Clark is worrying about the fact that he still hasn't received his bonus. Bill assures him that he has just heard that an envelope has been delivered to his home by courier, and that surely Clark's own notification letter can't be far behind it. Back home, Clark stares out of the kitchen window and daydreams about his family enjoying themselves in the still-to-be-installed pool. He then lets his imagination run riot, picturing the beautiful lingerie saleswoman frolicking on the springboard, before he is interrupted by Ruby Sue. His little niece is concerned that she and her brother won't be receiving any Christmas gifts – the previous year, even although they had both been on their best behaviour, no presents had been forthcoming on Christmas Day. Clark feels humbled by Ruby Sue's obvious gratitude at being allowed to stay at his family's house, and makes her a promise that he'll prove to her not only that Santa Claus is real, but also that he'll bring presents for her and Rocky.

The next morning, after Clark and Ellen watch dumbfounded as Eddie empties the contents of his RV's chemical toilet into the street's sewerage drain, they agree to lend Eddie and Catherine some financial aid in order to give their children some Christmas presents. When Clark later broaches the subject with Eddie, however, he is surprised to find not only that he readily accepts the idea, but that he already has a list made out – including gifts for Catherine – which he promptly hands over to the flabbergasted Clark.

Christmas Eve arrives, and with it comes the elderly Uncle Lewis and Aunt Bethany (William Hickey and Mae Questel). Lewis is tetchy and argumentative, while Bethany is cheerful but slightly bewildered. Clark and Ellen are taken aback to discover that Lewis and Bethany have (accidentally or otherwise) wrapped up their cat as a Christmas gift, and discreetly let it loose.

Christmas dinner then follows, though it quickly transpires

that the turkey has been grossly overcooked and is now little more than a desiccated husk. However, as Catherine was responsible for cooking it, the family chew their way through the remnants in order to spare her feelings. In the meantime, Lewis and Bethany's cat is gnawing on the power cord of the Christmas tree's lights and inadvertently electrocutes itself underneath one of the living room chairs. Clark and Eddie circumspectly remove the evidence from the house, during which Clark notices a worrying gaseous vapour starting to emanate from the sewer where Eddie had emptied his chemical toilet earlier.

Clark has barely rejoined the dinner table when he notices an unusual flash from the living room – Lewis has accidentally burnt down the Christmas tree with his omnipresent cigar. Just as Rusty begins to worry that Clark is heading for one of his legendary meltdowns, a knock at the door signals the late arrival of the envelope containing Clark's bonus. However, upon opening it – amongst much fevered expectation from the rest of the family – he is astonished to discover that rather than a cash windfall, the envelope actually contains an annual membership to the Jelly of the Month Club. This proves to be the final straw, and Clark flies into a hysterical rage, angrily proclaiming that all he wants for Christmas is his boss, Frank Shirley, brought from his affluent home to account for his miserliness in depriving all of his employees of their expected cash bonus. Eddie begins to look thoughtful, and slips away soon afterwards.

Still slightly unhinged, Clark promptly goes into the garden and cuts down a conveniently-placed tree with a chainsaw, in order to provide a replacement for the char-grilled original. In the process, he manages to smash the Chesters' dining room window, though he shows little sign of remorse at this (or even awareness). As Clark embellishes the tree with hastily-sourced replacement decorations, he quickly discovers a manic squirrel hiding amongst the branches. A panicked frenzy ensues as the family try to evade the squirrel, which culminates when the front door is thrown open and the interloping rodent jumps onto Margo, who has arrived to confront Clark about her broken window. The squirrel is soon followed by the frantic Snots, who dives onto Margo in order to attack it. Now bruised and tattered, the livid Margo eventually withdraws.

With the ground floor of the house now virtually in ruins thanks to the squirrel debacle, Clark and Ellen's parents decide that they want to leave. But Clark, now nearing a full-fledged state of mania, is having none of it. For a quiet life, everyone settles down in front of the fire while Clark recites *The Night Before Christmas* for the benefit of the younger members of the family. But before he can complete the story, Eddie returns with a surprise guest – Frank Shirley, in his pyjamas, gagged and tied up with ribbon. Shirley is initially incensed, threatening to fire Clark and have Eddie jailed. However, when Clark elaborates on how cheated he feels at having been unexpectedly deprived of his bonus – which he has relied upon for years – Shirley relents and decides to reinstate it... with a generous additional increase of 20%. Clark is stunned at this unexpected turnaround in fortune. However, his elation is merely transitory, for immediately afterwards a police SWAT team arrives – having been called by Shirley's concerned wife Helen (Natalia Nogulich) – and hold Clark and his family at gunpoint. In spite of all the odds that are stacked against him, can Clark still somehow manage to pull the perfect Christmas out of his Santa hat before it's too late?

With its all-encompassing festive spirit and pervasive sense of geniality, *National Lampoon's Christmas Vacation* was an effective deviation from the earlier entries in the series, relying on the comic strengths of Clark's infectious enthusiasm to provide the perfect holiday season while also providing plenty of keen observational insight into the delights (and potential pitfalls) of Christmas. Hughes's well-judged visual device of a traditional Advent calendar counting down towards Christmas Eve is highly effective in leading the audience towards the apex of the festivities – and the height of Clark's ever-building hysteria. Yet in spite of the film's sense of warmth and good nature, Hughes provides more than enough touches of the requisite *Vacation* anarchy to save the film from ever risking a headlong dive into sentimentality. Just as Clark and Eddie drink egg-nog from a pair of matching Marty Moose mugs (Marty having been the mascot of Walley World in the original *Vacation* film), the audience is provided with plenty of evidence – from Clark's manic sleigh-ride to the later slapstick of the squirrel infiltrator – that this is undisputedly Christmas the way that only a *National Lampoon* film could depict it.

Chevy Chase once again slips effortlessly back into the role of the good-hearted but mania-tinged Clark Griswold. Having appeared in a number of high-profile films since the time of *European Vacation*, including *Spies Like Us* (John Landis, 1985), *Funny Farm* (George Roy Hill, 1988) and *Fletch Lives* (Michael Ritchie, 1989), Chase once more delivers a pitch-perfect performance as the perpetually unlucky father who just wants to deliver a wonderful holiday season (no matter how ill-fated his attempts may be). From the running gag with the tree sap – Clark's hands end up sticking to everyone and everything after he arranges his new Christmas tree – to his exquisitely ham-fisted delivery as he falteringly tries to buy lingerie for Ellen from a strikingly beautiful department store attendant, Chase's portrayal of the character constantly impresses with a continuously witty, astute delivery and in his endless capacity for physical comedy.

There is no weak link in the supporting cast either, starting with Beverly D'Angelo as the ever-accommodating Ellen. Having appeared in prominent roles in *Big Trouble* (John Cassavetes, 1986), *In the Mood* (Phil Alden Robinson, 1987) and *High Spirits* (Neil Jordan, 1988) since the time of *European Vacation*, D'Angelo again makes the most of Ellen's drollness and silent despair at Clark's well-intentioned exploits, though it could be argued that she has less to do in this film when compared to other entries in the series. Johnny Galecki and Juliette Lewis are both effective as the new iteration of the Griswold kids, articulating well the frustration of warring siblings faced with the unwelcome intrusion of older relatives. Lewis, who would later be nominated for an Academy Award, Emmy and Golden Globe, was at the time best known for appearances in films such as *My Stepmother is an Alien* (Richard Benjamin, 1988) and *The Runnin' Kind* (Max Tash, 1989). William Hickey and Mae Questel are both memorable as the crotchety, cigar-chomping uncle and affably ditzy aunt respectively, and Brian Doyle-Murray (who had appeared in a cameo in the original *Vacation*, though in a completely different role) impresses as Clark's hard-faced boss Frank Shirley. The film's standout performance, however, is from Randy Quaid, who comes close to stealing the show as Cousin Eddie. If anything even more unhygienically repellent than on his first appearance in *Vacation*, Quaid makes full use of his character's greatly-expanded screen time, brilliantly articulating both Eddie's sponging guile and his ingenuous charm.

Although the film takes place almost exclusively in one snowy suburban locale, Jeremiah Chechik is skilled in making full use of every situation for well-timed comedy effect. This is true from Clark's high-wire stunts as he staples Christmas lights to his roof all the way through to the slow-motion demolition of the Chesters' upmarket but pretentiously-decorated home. Hughes's script makes good use of the intermittent interludes away from the house, be they at Clark's inner-city office or the area's pleasant woodland regions, and employs them efficiently in a way that enhances the film's festive flavour instead of diminishing it. Angelo Badalamenti provides a dynamic score which nicely accompanies *Christmas Vacation*'s sense of manic action, as well as providing the obligatory holiday atmosphere whenever required. (Badalamenti was later to achieve huge success with his haunting theme music for David Lynch's *Twin Peaks* television series, 1990-91.) Given the static nature of the family Christmas celebrations, Lindsay Buckingham's 'Holiday Road' – so prominent in early Griswold outings – is nowhere to be heard this time around. In its place, however, is the film's lively title song, 'Christmas Vacation', which is performed by

Mavis Staples.

Although *National Lampoon's Christmas Vacation* exudes seasonal charm, not all contemporary critics were convinced of the film's merits. At the time of its release, some reviewers believed that the film was not fully the sum of its parts[1], suffering from uneven humour and a few flaccid performances.[2] Yet others were to praise the film's entertaining evocation of the potential drawbacks of the holiday season,[3] and were warmly approving of its likeable ensemble cast.[4] Modern commentators have generally tended towards favourable criticism of *Christmas Vacation*. While a few have claimed that the film is unable to endure close scrutiny outside of its festive context,[5] others have admired the nostalgia value of its distinctively eighties take on the traditional Christmas movie.[6] Some have singled out Hughes's witty dialogue and the emotional warmth of the script for particular approval,[7] while others believed it to be one of the best films in the *Vacation* series, presaging much of the slapstick physical comedy that would appear in many of Hughes's later scripts, such as *Home Alone* and its sequel, throughout the course of the nineties.[8]

The fourth and final film in the series, *Vegas Vacation* (Stephen Kessler, 1997), was an entertaining but critically under-rated return to the traditional holiday format of the original film. It was, however, crucially devoid of *Vacation*'s amusing sense of the offbeat travelogue, focusing on one singular location rather than a cross-country trek. Although the film was not to carry the *National Lampoon* brand name, it did retain key cast members of the *Vacation* series including Chevy Chase, Beverly D'Angelo, Randy Quaid and Miriam Flynn. However, for the first time the screenplay was not to be written by John Hughes, but instead by Elisa Bell (from a story by Bell and Bob Ducsay). *Christmas Vacation* was also followed by a belated made-for-television sequel, *National Lampoon's Christmas Vacation 2: Cousin Eddie's Island Adventure* (Nick Marck, 2003), written by Matty Simmons. Although Chase and D'Angelo did not feature this time around, the TV movie did star Randy Quaid and Miriam Flynn, once again reprising their roles as Eddie and Catherine Johnson, as well as Dana Barron as Audrey Griswold.

Hughes's wryly-observed take on the traditional family Christmas, with all of its irritations as well as its many pleasures, was an inspired one which has proved to stand the test of time. This has meant that *National Lampoon's Christmas Vacation* has quite comfortably taken a place among the wider pantheon of classic eighties festive films, including *Gremlins* (Joe Dante, 1984), *Santa Claus: The Movie* (Jeannot Szwarc, 1985) and *Scrooged* (Richard Donner, 1988). With its entertaining medley of eccentric relatives, teenagers both surly and engaging, chaotic comedy situations and a continual emphasis on the importance of the family, the film marked an appropriately fitting end-point for John Hughes's substantial contribution to the cinema of the eighties.

National Lampoon's Christmas Vacation made its first appearance in American cinemas on 1 December 1989. Also appearing on that date was Ted Mather's drama *Dance to Win,* and Andrei Konchalovsky's crime comedy *Homer and Eddie,* starring Whoopi Goldberg and James Belushi. Another significant feature making its debut was Deborah Shaffer's musical documentary *Dance of Hope,* which would later be nominated for the Grand Jury Prize at the Sundance Film Festival. Milli Vanilli were at number one in the Billboard Charts that week with 'Blame It on the Rain'. In the news at the time, Soviet President Mikhail Gorbachev met with Pope John Paul II at the Vatican, Vishwanath Pratap Singh was sworn in as India's new President following the resignation of Rajiv Gandhi, and Luis Alberto Lacelle was elected as the President of Uruguay.

'Whether it's *Uncle Buck* or *Mr Mom* or the booby-footed Clark, Hughes has found an irresistible formula in fatherly ineptitude. [...] *Christmas Vacation* may not be a fancy package, but it is a diverting stocking stuffer.'

Rita Kempley, *The Washington Post*, 1 December 1989.

'With the Griswold saga [Hughes] seems to set up sequences that Chechik isn't able to make pay off. You have the odd sensation, watching the movie, that it's straining to get off the ground but simply doesn't have the juice.'

Roger Ebert, *The Chicago Sun-Times*, 1 December 1989.

'Full of funny moments and one-liners, and sporting good performances from the main roles, *National Lampoon's Christmas Vacation* should warm the coldest heart, and is the perfect film to watch during the holiday period.'

Daniel Stephens, *DVD Times*, 17 November 2003.

Conclusion

Teenage Hopes and American Dreams

It is difficult to imagine the world of American film in the eighties without the movies of John Hughes springing instantly to mind. His output has become so synonymous with the decade that it is a challenging task indeed to track down an historical account of commercial film-making in the 1980s that does not make mention of films such as *The Breakfast Club, Pretty in Pink* or *Ferris Bueller's Day Off*. Yet although his pioneering and highly influential work in the teen movie genre has tended to overshadow his copious achievements in other areas of comedy writing, perhaps his greatest accomplishment throughout the eighties was his characteristic skill in emphasising the importance of social cohesion and family values in a starkly acquisitive age of high capitalism.

It is particularly interesting to note the way in which Hughes's films – which generally tended to focus squarely on characters who were almost always white, usually male and often upper-middle class – were nevertheless inclined towards an overarching willingness to address themes of unfaltering universality in American life of the time. And yet while this wide-ranging remit is discernible in many Hughes movies, his protagonists do generally have a propensity to be anything but run-of-the-mill everymen and everywomen, ranging from amiable psychological manipulators like Ferris Bueller to nerdish outsiders such as *Weird Science's* Wyatt and Gary, to say nothing of many memorable eccentrics who include Clark Griswold, Duckie Dale, 'Cousin Eddie' Johnson and Del Griffith among their number. But far from alienating his audiences, Hughes's choice of unconventional, nonconformist characters became a key attribute of many of his films, utilising an outlandish lens through which to connect the audience to a distinctively idiosyncratic and never less than uniquely rendered view of the world.

In using the unorthodox to illuminate aspects of conventional expectations in society, and thus to explore the boundaries of conformity and traditionalism in the American culture of the eighties, Hughes was to succeed in presenting the viewer with a complex melange of comic anarchy and perceptive social commentary throughout the decade. This was especially relevant from the monumental success of his teen movies – still regularly reissued on DVD and Blu-Ray even today – which focused on issues of perennial social anxiety in ways so profound that they established resonance not only with their intended teenage demographic, but also with many older audiences into the bargain.[1] Teen film enthusiasts who had enjoyed features such as *American Graffiti* (George Lucas, 1973) during the previous decade were now witnessing a discernible shift in tone with early eighties entries in the genre, such as *The Outsiders* (Francis Ford Coppola, 1983) and *Class* (Lewis John Carlino, 1983). These sophisticated audiences found themselves able to engage with Hughes's output as an erudite, socially-aware evolutionary development within the teen movie genre, which built upon previous critical expectations while also subverting and revising them to meet the complex and distinctive tastes of a new generation.

In this regard, one of Hughes's most lasting achievements may well be his skill in the cross-pollenisation of recognised generic features. Following Hughes's contribution to eighties cinema, teen films would no longer automatically face lazy categorisation as unsophisticated campus comedies or heavily issue-based melodramas; his ground-breaking entries in the genre were stylish, polished and mature, combining waspish dialogue with sensitively-rendered characterisation in order to create a vibrant new approach to the genus which was to redefine convention.

So what were the defining characteristics of Hughes's films that ensured not only critical and commercial success at the time of their release, but also their enduring popularity amongst new audiences even today? Certainly his engagement with class-related issues – which pulled few punches – was skilfully and sensitively handled, chiming in with much contemporary cultural debate. Especially in his teen movies, social statements were made with quiet power and admirable restraint even when issues of class difference formed the main thrust of the narrative (especially in films such as *Pretty in Pink* and *Some Kind of Wonderful*). With the use of this method, Hughes demonstrated a highly proficient ability to connect with prevalent social criticisms which manifested themselves throughout the decade, particularly with regard to a class divide which was perceived to be constantly widening, without ever diluting the comedic content of his films.[2] Yet his observations about the hierarchical social structure which operates in high schools (a construct which is predicated upon popularity rather than family income, although we soon discover that the two are often closely interconnected) are perhaps even more adroitly employed, and form far more than a straightforward satire on broader class anxieties. With films such as *Sixteen Candles*, *The Breakfast Club* and (to a lesser extent) *Weird Science*, Hughes explores with great passion the rigid strictures which separate peer groups, dexterously emphasising the point that pressure from the unwritten rules of these social interactions are equalled only by the profuse apprehension that surrounds the need to meet parental expectation.

Hughes's depiction of the adult world is also an interesting one, for it too transcends issues deriving from the time of the films' respective production to address concerns of a more universal nature. Parents in Hughes's films certainly never fit into any one easily definable bracket, ranging from the caring, dysfunctional Jim and Brenda Baker (*Sixteen Candles*) to Cameron Frye's dictatorial father Morris (*Ferris Bueller's Day Off*) by way of the loving but despondent Jack Walsh (*Pretty in Pink*). Hughes offers the audience a pragmatic view of parenthood, where mothers and fathers are flawed individuals who are depicted in a purposefully lifelike way; some are well-intentioned and strive to relate, others are autocratic and out of touch, but all are portrayed in a credible and ultimately convincing manner. It is thus interesting to compare these various parents to other adult characters in the teen films, such as Ben Stein's beautifully-played economics teacher in *Ferris Bueller's Day Off*, a monotonically droning symbol of the establishment whose intellectually repressive status divides him from his hopelessly bored class even when he fruitlessly attempts to engage them in debate. Such characters, strongly emblematic of social institutionalism and almost always deriving from the education system, contrast effectively with more sympathetic characters such as John Kapelos's Carl the Janitor in *The Breakfast Club* and *Pretty in Pink*'s shop-owner Iona, who successfully engage with the protagonists by means of mutual respect rather than falling back upon a strained or condescending means of interaction. Thus adult characters who are willing to connect (or at least attempt to connect) with their more youthful counterparts are inevitably treated more sympathetically than the distant and disinterested representatives of established authority. This harmonises with observations made in *The Breakfast Club* that the aging process inevitably changes individual personalities, ineradicably separating adults from the heightened emotions and ambitions of their youth. Hughes perfectly symbolises this argument in the form of tyrannical authoritarians Richard Vernon (*The Breakfast Club*) and Edward Rooney (*Ferris Bueller's Day Off*), both of whom seem vaguely dissatisfied with their lot in life and who are largely content to vent their pent-up frustration on their teenaged charges as a kind of proxy for a meaningful existence.

In an era where teen movies often took the form of unsubtle sex comedies or laboured social commentaries, Hughes's acute attention to characterisation and dialogue seemed like a breath of fresh air. He takes great care never to patronise his audience, and in doing so made his young characters multifaceted and possessed of considerable depth and dimension of personality.[3] Hughes captured perfectly the cadence and tone of authentic teen conversation while never falling into the trap of relying upon fashionable buzz-words and colloquial idiolect solely for the sake of it, preferring instead to employ sharp and incisive wit. This may also be a reason for the enduring success of his films; his refreshing lack of faddish, anachronistic dialogue allows modern audiences a more direct connection to the ebb and flow of his respective narratives, making them perennially accessible while the distinctive fashions and music of the eighties create a world of social and cultural authenticity, thus preserving the films' potent sense of nostalgia.[4]

Hughes's writing throughout the eighties does raise some very interesting ideological issues. Although he expresses disdain at the inequitable and unavoidably isolating effects of class division, his approach to capitalism is much less clearly demarcated. Acquisitive yuppies such as Roman Craig of *The Great Outdoors* and the pretentious Todd and Margo Chester, Clark Griswold's upmarket neighbours in *National Lampoon's Christmas Vacation*, become subjects of ridicule and derision. Yet the materialism of characters such as Ferris Bueller, for instance, is much more obscurely delineated. Ferris, for whom money holds the key to resolving many of life's complications, seems nevertheless to be under no illusion about the fact that existence is nothing without certain aspects that will always remain beyond the reach of purchase, such as hope and companionship. His anxieties about the fragility of friendship and romance, as well as his perceptive observations about the small, beautiful aspects of perceiving the world around him as it passes by, indicates much more depth to his character than the gloss of his affluent upper-middle class exterior may initially suggest.[5] Yet there is little doubt that for all this, money is still a considerable motivating factor in Ferris's world: consider his insistence in dining at the most expensive of restaurants, or his cutting edge electronic equipment. This is also the case in the lush suburbs of *Weird Science*, where the plot is motivated by the kind of ground-breaking fantasy technology – in the hands of teenage protagonists – that even modern research scientists could only dream of. Yet the enervating effects of surplus wealth in the teen movies are counterbalanced by other depictions, such as the self-important arrogance of *Pretty in Pink*'s Steff McKee, the manipulative Hardy Jenns in *Some Kind of Wonderful*, and especially the acquisitive obsessions of the unseen Mr Frye in *Ferris Bueller's Day Off*, whose avaricious materialism has all but completely divided him from the emotional needs of his family. Thus Hughes is highly proficient in his adaptive exploration of the complex economics of the eighties, in all of their capitalistic glory, to illustrate both the liberation and potential corrosiveness of wealth.

While it is true that Hughes's teen films have become his best-remembered of the eighties, being both commercially successful and vastly influential,[6] his other output throughout the decade is also worthy of note. Films such as *Mr Mom* delineated his concerns about the influence of economic forces on lives of working- and lower middle-class families, and his observations would prefigure later discussion of the issue in *Pretty in Pink*. Others, such as *She's Having a Baby*, *The Great Outdoors* and *Uncle Buck* put greater emphasis on the importance of familial bonds – irrespective of how dysfunctional the families in question may be. They also underscored the fact that the maintenance of harmony in domestic situations, though often challenging and emotionally intricate, is of at least as much importance to the individual as personal or material ambition. This is very much the case in the *National Lampoon's Vacation* series, where the coherence of the family unit always manages to transcend the situational chaos and slapstick carnage of the films' narrative. Clark Griswold, for all his accident-prone haplessness and occasional lapses into mania, always remains a steadfast family man, devoted and supportive even when held in the apparent grip of single-minded obsession. Yet Hughes also takes care to stipulate that although the family unit is vitally important, it need not necessarily be based upon the traditional model of the nuclear family; this can be seen, for instance, in the resilient relationship between Andie and her single father Jack in *Pretty in Pink*, and in the fiercely independent Watts of *Some Kind of Wonderful* who – through her emotional allegiance to Keith – has in effect made him into her own honorary family.

Given that he was writing and directing at a time when materialism and Cold War fatalism had propagated a significant amount of cultural and political cynicism, Hughes's unwavering espousal of the importance of interpersonal relationships in the modern world seemed stimulating and buoyant, particularly given his emphasis that the extension of such attachments could and should extend beyond the ties that bind blood relations. We witness this in the unlikely central friendship of *Planes, Trains and Automobiles* as well as in Hughes's most uncharacteristic work of the eighties, *Nate and Hayes*, and indeed it is a motif that he was to carry on into his work during the following decade.

Although the commercial and cultural success of Hughes's output throughout the decade has meant that his legacy to modern film-making tends to focus on his filmography throughout the 1980s, this impression may also be owed in part to the fact that almost all of his directorial work took place during this period. Beyond the confines of the eighties, Hughes was only to direct one further film – the family comedy *Curly Sue* (1991) – although his screenwriting and production talents would continue to generate significant commercial success throughout the course of the 1990s and beyond.[7] In spite of the fact that his contribution to cinema remained prolific in the following decade, and his name certainly continued to be a box-office draw, the films that he would produce beyond his eighties heyday would prove to have a very mixed response from the critical community in comparison to that of his earlier triumphs.

Hughes's first feature as screenwriter and producer in the nineties, *Home Alone* (Chris Columbus, 1990), has become one of his most recognisable, in no small part due to the film's meteoric commercial success. Relating the tale of a young boy named Kevin McAllister (Macaulay Culkin) who is accidentally left alone in the family home while his parents and siblings head off on an overseas vacation, the film became one of the decade's biggest box-office smashes, eventually being charted in the Guinness Book of Records as the most commercially successful live-action comedy film of all time. Its Christmas setting has lent *Home Alone* additional longevity thanks to repeat screenings over the festive period, and its most memorable sequence – where the protagonist uses ingenious improvised traps to fight off a duo of dim-witted burglars (an excellent, cast-against-type Joe Pesci and Daniel Stern) – has been endlessly parodied in subsequent years.

Hughes next acted in a production and screenwriting capacity on *Career Opportunities* (Bryan Gordon, 1991), a film which – of all his nineties output – arguably shared the most commonality with his earlier creative work. A romantic comedy starring Frank Whaley and Jennifer Connelly, the plot centred on a nightshift cleaner and a shoplifter who find themselves locked in a department store after closing time only to wind up being harassed by two bungling intruders (Dermot and Kieran Mulroney). In spite of the superficial similarities with the storyline of *Home Alone* that is suggested with the above break-in plotline, the film marked Hughes's brief return to some of his signature eighties themes. The male lead character is an imaginative slacker struggling to find a place for himself in a world where he finds himself to be an awkward fit, while his unexpected companion for the evening attempts to maintain the facade of a social high-flyer but simultaneously fights to conceal the fact that she is on the run from an abusive parent. Both discover new aspects to their worldview as the story progresses. Although Hughes handles the film's dramatic issues with his customary finesse and moderation, *Career Opportunities* met with a lukewarm response at the box-office and is largely forgotten today.

His subsequent film, *Only the Lonely* (Chris Columbus, 1991), marked an unusual anomaly for Hughes's career in that he was to act as its producer but not its screenwriter (scripting duties being assumed instead by the director, Chris Columbus), though the movie did involve the return of two well-remembered Hughes alumni from the eighties in the form of leads John Candy and Ally Sheedy (with Macaulay Culkin also making an appearance in an extended cameo). A romantic comedy, the story involves a police officer who must balance his affections for a quirky funeral parlour worker with his familial obligations to his obstinate elderly mother (Maureen O'Hara). Although the film contains many touching moments, and treats sympathetically the difficult emotional issues of caring for an ageing parent, *Only the Lonely* ultimately found itself faced with a largely indifferent critical response.

Hughes followed this with a screenplay for the Robert Weissman-produced comedy drama *Dutch* (Peter Faiman, 1991), helmed by the director of the previous decade's massively successful *Crocodile Dundee* (1986). Starring Ed O'Neill and Ethan Randall (an actor later to be better known as Ethan Embry), the film focuses on the tersely spiky interplay between a cheerful but calamity-prone free spirit and his new girlfriend's snooty estranged son when the pair are forced to endure an eventful journey home prior to the Thanksgiving period. Although this summary may suggest more than a passing resemblance to *Planes, Trains and Automobiles*, *Dutch* greatly suffers by comparison to the earlier film. The antics of the eponymous hero and his obnoxious ward seemed overly familiar to audiences of the time, and the film performed poorly with many critics.

Curly Sue (1991) was to be Hughes's final film as director; he also served as the film's producer and screenwriter. It has also, regrettably, come to be seen as the least successful of all his directorial efforts in the eyes of many commentators. The film starred James Belushi and Alisan Porter as a pair of homeless drifters who are forced to enact desperate scams in order to eke out their continued existence. When attempting to hoodwink a glamorous Chicago lawyer (Kelly Lynch), they inadvertently set in motion a series of events which will call into question the sustainability of their nomadic lifestyle. Although *Curly Sue* called once more upon Hughes's perennial theme of valuing familial bonds and never neglecting the family unit even when it confounds traditional expectation, the film's handling of these topics often seems rather unsubtle and emotionally manipulative in ways that had been hitherto uncommon in Hughes's *oeuvre*, and it has since become arguably the most obscure of all his features.

Hughes assumed a rare co-writing role on the next film he was to engage with, *Beethoven* (Brian Levant, 1992), a collaboration – using his Edmond Dantès pen-name – with screenwriter Amy Holden Jones. Relating the misadventures of the Newton family (led by Charles Grodin and Bonnie Hunt) as they unexpectedly adopt a St Bernard puppy who comes to be known by the name of Beethoven, the film's whimsical line in family entertainment played well with many critics, and the film benefits from entertaining performances by Oliver Platt and Stanley Tucci as two 'dog-nappers', as well as a brief appearance by a pre-*The X-Files* David Duchovny. In spite of some critical scepticism *Beethoven* performed very strongly in commercial terms, and spawned no less than six sequels along with an animated television series.

Commercial success also followed *Home Alone 2: Lost in New York* (Chris Columbus, 1992), a seemingly-inevitable sequel to the colossally successful original. Hughes once again assumed production and screenwriting duties, and the film saw the return of the majority of the main cast (including Macaulay Culkin, John Heard and Catherine O'Hara) as well as Joe Pesci and Daniel Stern as the hapless antagonists. The film transplants the action from Chicago to New York, where Kevin McAllister (the still-youthful protagonist) discovers that his flight has diverged from his parents', who have unwittingly landed in Florida instead. Kevin then finds that he must call on all his reserves of cunning in order to charm his way into a high-class New York hotel while also thwarting his old adversaries from the previous film in their attempt to burgle a nearby toy store. Although the film exhibits many parallels with the original (a fact noted by many critics), it seldom seems overly repetitive, and in spite of the fact that it could not hope to match the overwhelming success of *Home Alone* at the box-office it still performed very strongly, ultimately becoming the second-highest-grossing film of the year in the United States.

The family-oriented theme continued in *Dennis the Menace* (Nick Castle, 1993), a film based upon the popular Hank Ketcham cartoon strip which was scripted by Hughes and produced by himself and Richard Vane. Featuring an all-star cast which included veteran actors Walter Matthau and Joan Plowright, the movie also reunited two stars from *Back to the Future* (Robert Zemeckis, 1985) in the form of Christopher Lloyd and Lea Thompson. Following the character interactions and comedic situations of the comic strip fairly faithfully, the film met with a mixed critical reception but nonetheless performed convincingly in cinemas both domestically and abroad.

Next came *Baby's Day Out* (Patrick Read Johnson, 1994), where Hughes once again shared production duties with Richard Vane while penning the screenplay himself. Starring Joe Mantegna, Joe Pantoliano and Lara Flynn Boyle, the film boasted an impressive cast but was widely criticised by reviewers for its hackneyed comedy set-pieces (a trio of woefully inept kidnappers abducts a baby from a wealthy family, only for the infant to run rings around them in increasingly implausible ways). While the film has many inventively-shot sequences, *Baby's Day Out* did badly at the box-office and has since sunk from public view largely without a trace.

More successful was *Miracle on 34th Street* (Les Mayfield, 1994), an energetic remake of George Seaton's festive classic from 1947 which starred Dylan McDermott, Elizabeth Perkins and Mara Wilson, along with a suitably jovial turn from Richard Attenborough as Kris Kringle, the role previously made famous by Edmund Gwenn. Scripted by Hughes, updating Seaton's original screenplay from the forties, the film was produced by Hughes, William Ryan and William S. Beasley. Transporting the action from the Macy's Department Store of the original to the fictitious New York 'Cole's' store, the story remained largely true to the original but for a few refashioned amendments employed to bring the story more in line with modern sensibilities. The film featured some sumptuous set design as well as a rousing Bruce Broughton score. As might be expected from any remake of a classic film from the age of the silver screen, critics were divided as to the virtues of this updated *Miracle on 34th Street*, but the film went on to modest commercial success and has remained a popular Christmas staple on television, DVD and Blu-Ray ever since.

Following this were two Disney remakes, *101 Dalmatians* (Stephen Herek, 1996) and *Flubber* (Les Mayfield, 1997). The former was a live-action updating of the original animated classic (Wolfgang Reitherman, Hamilton S. Luske and Clyde Geronimi, 1961), while the latter was a radical modernisation of old family favourite *The Absent-Minded Professor* (Robert Stevenson, 1961) with Robin Williams assuming the Fred MacMurray role. Both films were scripted and produced by Hughes (though Flubber was produced in collaboration with Ricardo Mestres), and they shared a strong box-office performance as well as a decidedly tepid critical reception.

Hughes then returned for a third and final time to the *Home Alone* universe with *Home Alone 3* (Raja Gosnell, 1997). The film was written by Hughes and produced in collaboration with Hilton A. Green and himself, though it shared neither the cast nor characters of the first two films in the series. Chris Columbus, who had directed both earlier films, was succeeded by Raja Gosnell who had served as the film editor on *Home Alone* and *Home Alone 2*. Replacing Macaulay Culkin was Alex D. Linz in the role of Alex Pruitt, an eight-year-old boy who soon discovers that he must defend his home against an international criminal syndicate who are in search of a prototype computer chip hidden in his remote-controlled toy car. The film's far-fetched premise (even in comparison to the series' first two entries) led to a reasonably cool reception from many critics, but it nevertheless performed solidly at the box-office, even if the record-breaking commercial returns of its predecessors were now little more than a distant dream. A fourth entry in the series, *Home Alone 4: Taking Back the House* (Rod Daniel, 2002), was broadcast as a TV movie by ABC some years later, but its production was to feature no involvement from

Hughes.

The following year was to see Hughes produce and direct *Reach the Rock* (William Ryan, 1998), a contemplative drama starring William Sadler and Alessandro Nivola. The story was to centre on a senior police officer who enters into a psychological battle with an incarcerated small-time criminal, raising questions along the way about individual choice and the nature of freedom in modern society. After a long run of successful family features, Hughes's sudden change in tone seemed as jarring as it was welcome, and though the film has become largely overlooked on account of its modest profile, it remains a genuinely fascinating curio in Hughes's eclectic filmography which is well worth seeking out.

The turn of the century was to see Hughes's involvement with *Just Visiting* (Jean-Marie Poiré, 2001), produced by Patrice Ledoux and Ricardo Mestres and also known as *Les Visiteurs en Amérique* on the international market. Hughes was to collaborate on the screenplay for the film with Jean-Marie Poiré and Christian Clavier, and the storyline – a time-travelling romance set between mediæval Europe and twenty-first century Chicago – was populated by many recognisable stars including Jean Reno, Christina Applegate and Malcolm McDowell. The film was not well-regarded by critics, and performed badly at the domestic box-office.

Next was *New Port South* (Kyle Cooper, 2001), a film which was produced by Hughes but (as had been the case with *Only the Lonely*) a rare occasion in his career where he had served as producer but not screenwriter. Scripting duties were instead assumed by Hughes's son, James Hughes. Set near Chicago in the fictional Illinois town of New Port, the film explored familiar themes of authority and intellectual freedom in high school which had informed and typified many of the senior Hughes's output throughout the mid-eighties, but it ultimately demonstrated a much darker philosophical edge (and considerably less subtle ideological overtones) than that which had been on display in films such as *The Breakfast Club* and *Ferris Bueller's Day Off*. Like *Reach the Rock*, the film is challenging and ultimately rewarding, though it polarised reviewers at the time of its release and has since struggled to achieve much of a profile beyond the interest of Hughes aficionados.

John Hughes's final contributions to the world of cinema came in the form of providing the stories for romantic comedy *Maid in Manhattan* (Wayne Wang, 2002), scripted by Kevin Wade, and madcap comedy *Drillbit Taylor* (Steven Brill, 2008), featuring a screenplay by Kristofor Brown and Seth Rogen. Both storylines were credited to Hughes's writing pseudonym Edmond Dantès, and although little of his distinctive artistic imprimatur survives beyond the inventive premise of either film, the movies none-theless went on to success at the box office – dramatically more so in the case of *Maid in Manhattan* than was the case with *Drillbit Taylor*, however. The latter was to mark the thirty-fourth and last time that Hughes was to be credited with a contribution to a film before his untimely passing a year later in 2009.

The inspirational qualities of Hughes's work cannot be overstated, and its influence can be witnessed in the films of later directors as diverse as Cameron Crowe and Whit Stillman. He brought sensitively-rendered characterisation, bitingly intelligent wit and expertly executed dialogue to popular genres in ways that still cause critics and fans alike to consider his eighties films with enthusiasm and admiration more than two decades after their first cinematic release.[8] It may seem difficult to believe that films produced in the time of leg-warmers and Rubik's Cubes could have anything remotely in common with our ever more complex and technologically sophisticated modern world, replete with iPhones and Facebook. Yet somehow Hughes's cinematic output manages to rise above the trends of its originating era in order to address concerns of a more wide-reaching nature. Indeed, Hughes's films have become a rare phenomenon indeed; although fully in tune with the social issues of the time, the universality of their depictions of suburban life and the teenage experience has meant that his distinctive and sympathetically depicted character portraits – articulated by some of the best-known and most fondly remembered performers of the 1980s – have stood the test of time in ways that so many other films of the decade could never hope to match. Whether we perceive his thematic concerns in the hopes and fears of teenagers approaching the uncertainties of adulthood, coming to terms with their own deeply distinctive sense of individual identity, or in adults yearning for the lost opportunities of their youth, Hughes's films offered audiences a relatable and convincing account of ordinary American lives. A snapshot of everyday existence in a decade of political upheaval and material indulgence, Hughes's take on the world of the eighties always managed to appear level-headed and coherent even when presenting the most chaotic, larger-than-life experiences. From the subtle postmodernism of *Ferris Bueller's Day Off* and technological surrealism of *Weird Science* to the ribald physical comedy of *The Great Outdoors* and the *National Lampoon's Vacation* films, there is little doubt that as long as audiences remember the eighties, they will also remember the work of John Hughes.

Prior to his tragic death in 2009, there remained long-running speculation in the film world about whether Hughes would ever have decided to make a return to the director's chair – a question which will now sadly remain forever unanswered. But one fact does remain certain: John Hughes was responsible for helping to define the cinema of the 1980s and, when he became the eloquently expressive voice of Generation X between 1984 and 1987, his penetrating judgements on life and society were to echo down the years, their influence still plainly discernible in popular culture today. Whether you had a well-meaning but embarrassing father like Clark Griswold, a crush on a beautiful girl like Claire Standish or Amanda Jones, a zany best friend like Watts or Duckie Dale, an overbearing teacher like Richard Vernon, a bullying sibling like Chet Donnelly, or even if you simply aspired to be like the wily urbanite Ferris Bueller or the caring, sensitive Andie Walsh, there was almost always someone in a Hughes film that we could find a way of relating to, and perhaps that was what made the Hughesian take on life more insightful and socially aware than was the case with so many other cinematic releases of the time.

Today, John Hughes's work is celebrated by film historians and fans alike, and many of the films that he directed and screenplays that he wrote throughout the eighties have come to be seen as a high water-mark in the cinema of the decade. In spite of his many later commercial successes, it seems almost certain that he will always be best known for his filmic output throughout the course of the 1980s, and indeed features like *The Breakfast Club* and *Ferris Bueller's Day Off* have become as closely wedded to the cinema of the time as Reaganomics and the collapse of the Berlin Wall came to characterise the geopolitics of the era. While other cultural vestiges of the eighties have faded and diminished with the passing years, Hughes's refreshingly upbeat and honest appraisals of American life have always managed to transcend the age of their production, his optimistic evaluation of the human condition ensuring that his films are still being discovered and enjoyed by new audiences even today.

ILLUSTRATIONS

Illustrations are from the following movies:

National Lampoon's Class Reunion (1982)
National Lampoon's Vacation (1983)
Nate and Hayes (1983)
Sixteen Candles (1984)
The Breakfast Club (1985)
National Lampoon's European Vacation (1985)
Weird Science (1985)
Pretty in Pink (1986)
Ferris Bueller's Day Off (1986)
Some Kind of Wonderful (1987)
Planes, Trains and Automobiles (1987)
She's Having a Baby (1988)
Uncle Buck (1989)
National Lampoon's Christmas Vacation (1989)

They were five teenage students with nothing in common.

But to each other... They would always be.. THE BREAKFAST CLUB!

B|C

The Criminal

The Jock

The Kook

The Brain

The Princess

Far over two thousand years, Europe has survived many great disasters. Now for the real test...the Griswolds are coming from America!

NATIONAL LAMPOON's
EUROPEAN VACATION

A MATTY SIMMONS PRODUCTION
AN AMY HECKERLING FILM CHEVY CHASE
"NATIONAL LAMPOON'S EUROPEAN VACATION"
BEVERLY D'ANGELO · DANA HILL
JASON LIVELY · VICTOR LANOUX as The Thief
and ERIC IDLE as The Bike Rider
Music by CHARLES FOX
Co-Produced by STUART CORNFIELD
Story by JOHN HUGHES
Screenplay by JOHN HUGHES
and ROBERT KLANE
Produced by MATTY SIMMONS
Directed by AMY HECKERLING

COMEDY
DOUBLE FEATURE

CHEVY CHASE
NATIONAL LAMPOON'S
VACATION

CHEVY CHASE
NATIONAL LAMPOON'S
EUROPEAN VACATION

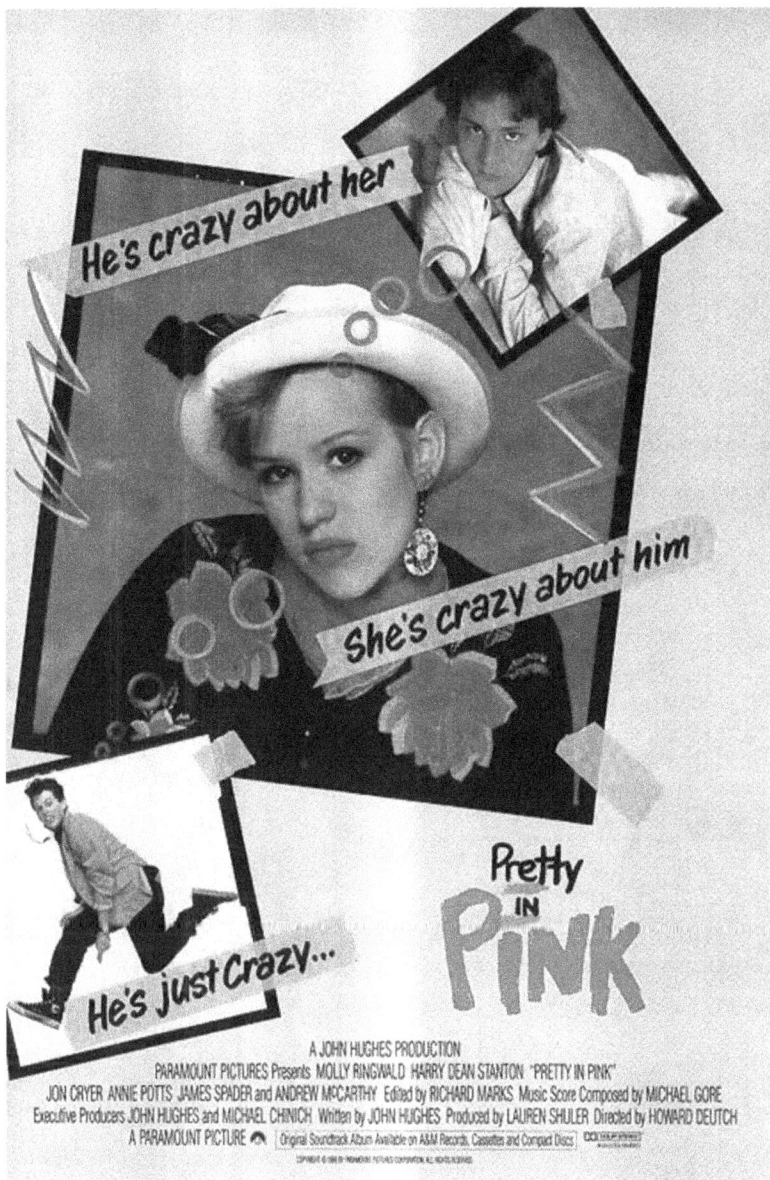

He's crazy about her

She's crazy about him

He's just crazy...

Pretty IN PINK

A JOHN HUGHES PRODUCTION
PARAMOUNT PICTURES Presents MOLLY RINGWALD HARRY DEAN STANTON "PRETTY IN PINK"
JON CRYER ANNIE POTTS JAMES SPADER and ANDREW McCARTHY Edited by RICHARD MARKS Music Score Composed by MICHAEL GORE
Executive Producers JOHN HUGHES and MICHAEL CHINICH Written by JOHN HUGHES Produced by LAUREN SHULER Directed by HOWARD DEUTCH
A PARAMOUNT PICTURE   Original Soundtrack Album Available on A&M Records, Cassettes and Compact Discs

pretty in pink

(Image © Paramount Pictures)

A JOHN HUGHES PRODUCTION

SOME KIND OF WONDERFUL

MUSIC FROM THE MOTION PICTURE SOUNDTRACK

MCAD-6200

PLANES, TRAINS AND AUTOMOB

STEVE MARTIN

What he really wanted was to spend Thanksgiving with his family.

What he got was three days with the turkey.

JOHN CANDY

PARAMOUNT PICTURES PRESENTS
A JOHN HUGHES FILM

PLANES, TRAINS AND AUTOMOBILES
Music Score by IRA NEWBORN Edited by PAUL HIRSCH Director of Photography DON PETERMAN, A.S.C.
Executive Producers MICHAEL CHINICH and NEIL MACHLIS
Writen, Produced and Directed by JOHN HUGHES A PARAMOUNT PICTURE

Soundtrzk Album Available on
Hughes Music/MCA Records, Cassettes and Compact Discs.

TM & Copyright ©1987 by Paramount P
All Rights Reserved.

SPECIAL FEATURES

- WIDESCREEN VERSION ENHANCED FOR 16:9 TVs
- DOLBY DIGITAL
- ENGLISH 5.1 SURROUND
- ENGLISH SUBTITLES (For the deaf and hard of hearing)
- INTERACTIVE MENUS
- SCENE SELECTION

SPECIAL FEATURES NOT RATED

Neal Page is an advertising executive who just wants to fly home to Chicago to spend Thanksgiving with his family. But all Neal Page gets is misery. Misery named Del Griffith — a loud mouthed, but nevertheless lovable, salesman who leads Neal on a cross-country, wild goose chase that keeps Neal from tasting his turkey.

Steve Martin (Neal) and John Candy (Del) are absolutely wonderful as two guys with a knack for making the worst of a bad situation.

If it's painful, funny, or just plain crazy, it happens to Neal and Del in "Planes, Trains and Automobiles." Every traveler's nightmare in a comedy-come-true!

PARAMOUNT PICTURES PRESENTS A JOHN HUGHES FILM
STEVE MARTIN · JOHN CANDY
PLANES, TRAINS AND AUTOMOBILES Music Score by IRA NEWBORN Edited by PAUL HIRSCH
Director of Photography DON PETERMAN, A.S.C. Executive Producers MICHAEL CHINICH and NEIL MACHLIS
Written, Produced and Directed by JOHN HUGHES A PARAMOUNT PICTURE
Soundtrack Album Available on Hughes Music/MCA Records, Cassettes and Compact Discs.
TM & Copyright © 1987 by Paramount Pictures. All Rights Reserved.

This film is presented in "widescreen" format. The black bars on the top and bottom of the screen are normal.

1987/COLOR/92 MIN./U.S. R/CAN. PG
www.paramount.com/homevideo

This is a Region 1 disc, designed to be compatible with NTSC Region 1 DVD Players

5555 Melrose Avenue, Hollywood, California 90038
Licensed for Sale Only in U.S. and Canada.
TM, ® & Copyright © 2000 Paramount Pictures. All Rights Reserved.

STEVE MARTIN   JOHN C

A JOHN HUGHES FILM

PLANES, TRAINS AND AUTOMO

PLANES, TRAINS AND AUTOMOBILES

WIDESCREEN   DVD   COLLECTI

A JOHN HUGHES FILM

Man.
Woman.
Life.
Death.
Infinity.
Tuna casserole.

One movie dares to tell it all.

KEVIN BACON · ELIZABETH McGOVERN

SHE'S HAVING A BABY

A New Comedy About the Labor Of Life

FERRIS BUELLER'S DAY OFF

SCENE BY SCENE

When **Ferris Bueller's Day Off** *first went on general release in America during the summer of 1986, audiences were presented with one of the most multifaceted and structurally refined of all John Hughes's films. In this section, I will take a detailed look at the way in which Hughes carefully constructs this well-loved movie, examining the skilful manner that he employs irony, wit and inspired characterisation in order to densely permeate his narrative with many distinctive contrasts and rewarding connections.*

Hughes chooses to begin *Ferris Bueller's Day Off*, inventively enough, not with an image but a line of dialogue from a breakfast radio broadcast. Against a dark background, we are told not only that the weather is favourable, but also where the action is going to be situated – the Chicago area. This is followed soon after by the voice of Ferris Bueller's mother Katie repeatedly trying to wake her son and, when he doesn't respond, calling out for her husband Tom. As she does so, the opening credits (still being shot on a dark background) suddenly give way to a wide-angle shot of the Bueller family home – a location which is pivotal throughout the course of the film.

As we hear Tom running upstairs to his son's room, we see Ferris for the first time. He is lying in bed, open-eyed but apparently comatose. A concerned Katie explains that although Ferris claims not to have a fever, he is feeling unwell. Ferris then claims to have difficulty recognising Tom, further fuelling his parents' concerns. Katie notes that Ferris's hands are cold and clammy – a notion which Tom puts to the test. But after he does so, Ferris makes an apparently laboured attempt to get out of his bed. Tom and Katie are alarmed, given the symptoms he has outlined to them, but Ferris is insistent, claiming to have a test at school that he doesn't want to miss.

Here we see Ferris's reverse psychology at work for the first time – by trying to convince his parents of his profound sense of responsibility, even in the face of illness, he hopes to persuade them of the seriousness of his condition. Even as he emphasises his concern that he doesn't want to put his chances of attending a decent college at risk, Tom and Katie are determined that he not leave his 'sick bed'.

We then meet his sister Jeanie, introduced by close-up shots of her impatiently tapping feet in trainers, and her hands resting on her hips in an assertive fashion. The cynicism of Jeanie's tone of voice clashes with the earnestness of her parents' obvious concern. She is unimpressed by Ferris's performance, and totally unconvinced of his malaise – even when he tries an even more ostentatious demonstration of his lack of depth of vision after she enters the room. He does, however, risk a cheeky wink to her – unseen by his parents – which inflames her temper even further. Jeanie rails at the injustice of Ferris's attempt to evade his classes, claiming that even if she were at death's door her parents would insist on her attendance at school. Ferris weakly chides her, telling her to be grateful that she is still in good physical condition. But this time he pushes the envelope still further, giving her a signal of mock-secrecy by theatrically putting his finger to his lips. Obviously as intended, Jeanie is outraged, though she barely manages to contain her indignation. With one final barb at her parents, she storms out.

With the introduction of Jeanie, Hughes presents the lesser of the film's two ostensible antagonists, and also sets up the sibling rivalry which exists between this unconventional brother and sister act. Jeanie's hot temper is made evident, as is Ferris's innate sense of playful deceit. He also lays out the beginning of their shared antipathy which plays out during the day ahead – Jeanie's grievance at the injustice of Ferris's seemingly-effortless duping of their parents, and the danger of Ferris's scheming being exposed by Jeanie.

With Jeanie's departure, Ferris continues to ramp up the intensity of his bedridden performance to his parents. Katie, and then Tom, both assure Ferris that they'll keep in regular touch with him even while they're at work during the day. Ferris pours on the sentiment, thanking them for being such kind and considerate parents. They accept his dying swan routine without question, so convincing do they find his alleged ailments, and they even seem reluctant to depart from his side. The minute that Tom and Katie leave the room, however, Ferris sits bolt upright in bed and – addressing the camera directly – revels in the fact that he's managed to fool them so successfully.

There follows a montage from MTV, shown on Ferris's television set, before the camera returns to Ferris himself once again. Still talking directly to camera, he voices incredulity that his parents were so easily fooled when he considered his presentation to be – compared to earlier performances – relatively poor. Triumphantly, he throws back the curtains to his bedroom, and asks why anyone should want to be in high school on such a day. To prove his point, we are then presented by a beautiful blue sky soaring above leafy green trees. Lively music begins to strike up in the background. Returning to Ferris, we can plainly see a look of unadulterated exultation spreading over his face.

As he adjusts the equaliser of his impressive-looking hi-fi system, Ferris explains to the audience that this has been the ninth day of absence that he has managed to engineer during the current semester, and laments the difficulty of having to present new and diverse forms of illness. As he points out, he'd have to go all-out for a tenth day, and is thus determined to make the most of this day away from school.

We move next to a wide-angle shot of Ferris's bedroom, which provides a good panorama of his plentiful (and eclectic) collection of belongings. Taking a relaxed seated position, Ferris gives the audience a primer on how to fool their parents into giving them the day off. His points are represented onscreen with superimposed captions. First, he recommends clammy hands – an unfocused kind of symptom that is difficult to diagnose. However, he advises against a bogus fever, warning that it can lead to parents seeking a medical opinion – never a good thing. As he talks, Ferris is tying a sports trophy to a length of string, but offers no explanation for his action. (This will become relevant later.)

Next, he provides his sick-day masterplan: simulate a stomach cramp, lean over holding your abdomen while giving vocal expression to your pain, and then give your palms a lick. As he points out, even although it may appear a puerile scheme, it is no more infantile than the school you're trying to avoid. Then, as he leaves his room to walk down the hall to the bathroom, he delivers one of the film's most iconic lines, informing the audience that life is so fast-paced that – every once and again – they should make sure that they stop to appreciate it before it's gone forever.

Already, less than five minutes into the film, we have been introduced to a great deal of what makes Ferris such an appealing character. Although wilfully cunning and devious, he is also charming and charismatic. His attitudes are both life-affirming and vaguely philosophical, albeit in a playful way. We know that not only is he a past-master at getting his own way, not least with regard to his attendance at school, but also that he is both meticulous in his planning and contemplative in his approach to life. We will see ample evidence of these two traits later.

Ferris gets out of his bathrobe and, in a tastefully framed shot, has a shower. Having sculpted his hair into a Mohican style with shampoo, he assures the audience that he wasn't lying about having a test at school – he really did have one scheduled – but as the topic was European socialism, he saw little point in participating. As he points out, seeing that he has no interest in ever becoming European, the inhabitants of that continent can follow whatever political model that pleases them – it isn't a big issue to him, unlike the fact that he doesn't have his own car. (Ferris's lack of a car of his own is quite possibly the most major irritant in his life, and here Hughes provides the first indication of it.) He then switches from a fixed shower-head to a mobile one, bursting into song as he rinses himself off (and playfully covering his face to mock-protect his identity).

Back in the upstairs hallway, his hair and lower body shrouded by towels, Ferris adds a small caveat to his earlier pronouncement about European politics. He says that he doesn't feel that allowances should be made for extreme political systems, regardless of nationality, but instead believes that people should believe in themselves rather than in ideologies. But at any rate, as he points out, none of this changes the fact that he still needs to sponge a ride in other people's cars because he has no transport of his own.

We then suddenly switch to Ferris's alma mater, Ocean Park High School, where his economics teacher is droningly going through the class register. Various students respond to their names – vocally or by gesture – as he tediously goes through the roll-call. When he reaches Bueller on the register, there is no response – yet even although Ferris's desk is clearly empty, the teacher continues to repeat his name in the same monotonous tone of voice. One of Ferris's classmates points out that she has heard on the grapevine that Ferris is ill, having passed out at a café the night beforehand. The teacher thanks her, but is so monumentally dull and expressionless that it is not entirely clear whether he believes this account or not. Next on the register is Frye – a name which the teacher again reads out repeatedly, but to no response.

Hughes uses a very effective switch in tone here, moving from Ferris's upbeat, confident assertions of the importance of liberty to the school's comparatively oppressive environment, as suggested by his economics teacher's repetitive droning. The muted colours of the school are in stark contrast to the vibrancy and eclecticism of Ferris's home, and the audience is left in absolutely no doubt that Ferris – even before his day has really started – is indisputably enjoying himself more than his semi-catatonic fellow students. It is a skilful comparative distinction that is used several times throughout the film.

The next shot is of an upmarket residence surrounded by tall green trees. Upon moving inside the house, the first image that greets the viewer is of an expensive-looking multi-function telephone surrounded by various small bottles of medicine. A hand is feebly lowered from the side of a bed to engage the speakerphone. An equally weak voice asks who is calling: the person on the other end of the line is indistinguishably Ferris. Ferris's voice reveals who we are being introduced to: his closest friend, Cameron Frye. We then move back to see Cameron's room in its entirety; it almost looks like a kind of high-tech mortuary, with closed curtains framing his bed in the foreground, a couple of small mirror-balls suspended from the ceiling, and a plasma globe mounted on a pedestal nearby. Ferris enquires after his friend's health. Cameron responds that he is feeling very unwell, and when asked about the whereabouts of his mother replies that she is currently away from home. As their conversation continues, a number of additional shots provide further glimpses of medicine bottles lying around, and various other malady-related paraphernalia including what appears to be a mixed cold cure in a glass (not yet drunk) and a box of paper tissues on Cameron's beside cabinet.

In a complete change of ambience, we then suddenly switch to a relaxed Ferris – still holding the conversation with Cameron, a cordless phone in his hand – as he suns himself on a garden lounger. He is now wearing Hawaiian-style beach shorts and sipping a cocktail from an ostentatious-looking receptacle. Ferris tries to cajole his friend into coming over, explaining that he's taking the day off. However, Cameron – who genuinely does seem to be unwell – refuses. But Ferris won't take no for an answer, apparently not because he wants Cameron's company so much as for the reason that his friend has his own car. Hughes continues to repeatedly move between Ferris's carnivalesque corner of his back yard and the sombre appearance of Cameron's sickbed. Ferris rings off, frustrated, but then calls back again immediately afterwards to convince Cameron that he isn't really unwell, just unimaginative – there is so much more to do than lying around in bed.

In a sense, Hughes is using this scene to foreground the major issues which will later confront Cameron; the character is hidebound by neuroses which Ferris compels him to deal with as the day continues. As Ferris explains to camera, he is keen to assist Cameron in becoming less repressed and self-conscious before he leaves high school, so that he will better be able to appreciate college. This is juxtaposed with an image of Cameron, still in bed, wallowing in self-pity.

The audience next find themselves in a leafy commercial area. Moving closer, we see that our location is a realtor agency, Koenig and Strey. Inside, Katie is at her desk in a plush communal office area. She is answering her phone, on the other end of which is Edward R. Rooney, the dean of students at Ferris's high school. Katie's soft but professional phone manner is immediately contrasted with Rooney's officiously pompous tone. Katie is apologetic, as she had intended to call the school to inform them of Ferris's absence. There is then an establishing shot of the school exterior, with a running student (presumably late for class) in the background and a couple of parked bicycles in the foreground. As Rooney presses the issue, asking Katie if she is aware that Ferris is not present at school, we move inside the school to see a variety of students departing at high speed to their respective classes, save for one hapless character who has dropped a loose-leaf folder and is now surrounded by piles of random sheets of paper. As Katie again apologises for not having been in touch, we are introduced to Rooney's eccentric secretary Grace, who is deep in thought at her desk. Without warning, she produces a pencil out of her hair. She then stops, confused, and pulls out another pencil. And another. Rooney, meanwhile, is emphasising his disdain for Ferris's record of attendance at school. He stresses to Katie his concern that Ferris has not been paying adequate attention to his studies. We then move to Rooney's desk, upon which lies a highly-polished nameplate. Any immediate effect of impress-iveness that this is meant to convey is slyly undermined by Hughes with the placement of a half-eaten packet of indigestion tablets next to the nameplate. (Hughes may be underscoring Rooney's uptight nature here even before we see the character himself – could it be that Rooney's constant irritation has already led him to develop a peptic ulcer?)

As Rooney flicks a tiny speck of dirt from the edge of his desk, the audience gets their first look at the film's main antagonist. Still on the phone, he explains to Katie that Ferris has now been absent from school on nine occasions during the current semester. Rooney takes great pleasure in telling Katie that, if he is not fully satisfied by Ferris's academic performance, he will not hesitate in forcing her son to repeat his current year of high school. Katie is surprised at this news, but Rooney is insistent – he has checked the school's computer database, which holds the school's attendance details. As Katie continues to voice her disbelief, punctuated by Rooney needling her with his scepticism over Ferris's honesty (or perceived lack of it), he continues to search for further miniscule fragments of grit or dust scattered around his desk. A shot at another angle shows his office to be fastidiously tidy, perfectly reflecting his anally-retentive obsession with methodical order. Rooney, now becoming indignant, stresses the fact that no matter how Katie may refuse to accept the fact, Ferris really has been absent on nine separate occasions. However, as he makes this declaration, he watches in shock as the number on the monitor screen before him is reduced in front of his eyes from nine down to two days of absence.

Switching back to Ferris's bedroom, we can see the same record being displayed on Ferris's home computer (an IBM PCjr). As Ferris points out, he may not have a car, but a computer – while not as useful on a day to day basis – does have some uses. His skill at network hacking marks a neat tip of the hat to Matthew Broderick's well-received performance in *WarGames* (John Badham, 1983), where he played a teenage computer expert who breaks into the U.S. government's defence network and very nearly manages to trigger World War III by accident.

Back at the school, Rooney is apoplectic. He repeatedly calls for his secretary Grace with mounting vehemence, but cutting back to her desk we can see that she is currently occupying herself by sniffing a bottle of correction fluid. While Rooney continues to furiously call out to Grace, his hand momentarily covering the receiver's mouthpiece, Katie calmly explains to him that while some students may well feel inclined to bunk off school at certain times of the year, she is absolutely convinced of Ferris's ill-health, so much so that she even debated taking the day off herself to look after him. As she says this, we cut back to Ferris – still in his bedroom – as he blows tunelessly on a clarinet. He claims never to have taken any lessons; from his musical performance, it's unlikely that anyone would disbelieve this fact.

This is the first example of Ferris managing to outsmart Rooney, and with considerable aplomb. Although Rooney, with all his overbearing self-importance, believes himself to be in a position of absolute primacy at the school, Ferris will continue to undermine his self-satisfied sense of authority as the film progresses.

In the economics class, the teacher is giving a mind-bogglingly dull appraisal of the 1930 Hawley-Smoot Tariff Act. Although he makes some token attempts to engage class participation, all of the students appear on the verge of falling into a coma by his colossally boring style of delivery. Shots of the teacher hovering in front of his blackboard are intercut with brief portraits of the staggeringly uninterested students, one of whom has fallen asleep in a puddle of his own saliva. We then suddenly cut to Ferris at home who, in sharp contrast, is blithely dancing around in a Hawaiian shirt, striped trousers and Converse trainers. Once again, the distinction could not be more apparent.

Jeanie is walking down a bustling high school corridor, bag over arm, when a friend catches up with her and expresses her regret over Ferris's condition. When Jeanie – irritated – asks why she thinks that he's ill at all, the friend explains that it's an issue that is being widely talked about. Apparently one of the fellow students in her biology class has become convinced that Ferris, should his condition worsen and eventually kill him, wants to donate his eyes to Stevie Wonder. Jeanie is quietly incensed by Ferris's popularity among the student body at large, and his seemingly-effortless ability to con virtually everyone that he meets. Another friend then approaches Jeanie, but – now more sullen than ever – she brushes her off and wanders out of shot. As Jeanie does so, she reveals a group of younger male students using a payphone in the background.

It transpires that the students are calling Ferris to ask about his condition. Ferris explains that he is still in a poor way – a fact which he 'proves' with the inventive use of an electronic synthesiser (an E-MU Emulator II) which has been loaded with various samples of coughing, sneezing and other sounds of general malaise. The students are relieved to know that Ferris is still alive, not least as he has promised one of them that he'll help them to trick their way out of summer school. They then pass the phone on to a passing female student, who also asks after Ferris's health. Ferris responds with an ever-more ostentatious collection of ailing body sounds, claiming that he may need a kidney transplant to ensure his recovery. The female student seems saddened by this, but brightens up when Ferris tells her that he'll probably still be alive at the weekend – she hopes to catch up with him then. Ferris thus perpetuates the now near-mythic reputation of the gravely poor condition of his health amongst the student body at large. Returning to Ferris's bedroom, we find him performing a rather unorthodox rendering of Johann Strauss's 'Blue Danube' waltz on his synthesizer keyboard, replete with a variety of snorts and sniffles.

In the dean's office, Rooney is going through a huge pile of paper printouts – presumably hard-copies of attendance records. He tells Grace of his manifest distrust of Ferris, voicing his concern that the miraculous Bueller ability to pull the wool over the eyes of authority will have a corrosive effect on the rest of the school. Rooney is disturbed by the thought of having to deal with a legion of students duplicating Ferris's schemes, as it will hamper his ability to run the school efficiently. And, as Grace helpfully pipes up, it will inevitably make him look even more stupid than Ferris has already done. In spite of Rooney's protestations, Grace continues by saying that the key to Ferris's success is his popularity – he is respected by all of the school's diverse cliques, regardless of age, gender or social background. That, asserts Rooney, is why he absolutely needs to prove without any possibility of doubt that Ferris has been lying to the school and to his parents, thus putting a stop to his free-wheeling disrespect for authority. Grace then unwittingly plays into Rooney's considerable vanity, comparing the intensity of his anti-

Ferris diatribe to that of Clint Eastwood's eponymous hero in *Dirty Harry* (Don Siegel, 1971). Rooney responds to this with a magnificently ham-fisted attempt at an Eastwood-esque snarling expression, though his demonstration appears totally lost on Grace.

Back in his bedroom, Ferris is on the phone to Cameron trying to cajole him to get out of bed and drive over. As Ferris speaks, we can see that he is using a mouse to sketch a picture of a naked woman with a graphic design package on his computer. Switching over to Cameron, who is now sitting up in bed, there seems to be little difference from his earlier appearance. He insists that his blood pressure reading is unfavourable and that he has no intention of leaving his bed. But Ferris becomes ever more adamant. Pointing out that he'll be lucky to graduate from high school if he's caught truanting, and is unlikely to have the same golden opportunity presented to him again, he is determined to make this day off count. He is interrupted by another call, which turns out to be from his father Tom. Instantly affecting an ailing tone of voice, Ferris answers the call. We then move to an establishing shot of a busy commercial sector of Chicago, followed by the interior of Tom's upmarket office. His desk appears splendidly lavish. Tom is still concerned for Ferris's wellbeing, particularly as he sounds no better than when he left home in the morning. Quickly switching back to his conversation with Cameron, Ferris warns his friend to get over with his car as soon as possible. Then returning to his father's call, he claims that the conversation is making him dizzy and that he should be returning to bed. Tom recommends that he take a hot bath, swathe his head with a hot towel, and then make some soup before getting some sleep. Ferris tells his dad that he loves him before hanging up and returning to converse with the camera. He laments the fact that Cameron seems to have let him down, and speculates that by now he will probably be sitting in his car agonising over whether he should stay at home or acquiesce to his friend's wishes.

True enough, we then move to a medium close-up of Cameron in the driver's seat of his car. And equally true is the fact that he is torturing himself over what course of action to take. Talking to himself, he comes to the conclusion that disagreeing with Ferris will only delay the inevitable, as his friend is unrelenting in the pursuit of his aims and never loses an argument. Though he is monumentally frustrated at being so obviously manipulated, punching the front passenger seat in irritation, he revs the engine and prepares to depart. And then changes his mind. Moving to a camera position some distance further away, a shot which takes in both his car and the exterior of his residence, Cameron removes his seatbelt and gets out of the car. Then, returning to the medium close-up of the driver's seat view, we watch as he casts around in rage, his movements just visible from the car's rear window.

Here Hughes reveals more of Cameron's character, juxtaposing his sense of inner repression with his loyalty to Ferris – and, of course, his unconscious longing for the kind of liberation that Ferris's artful scheming represents. Ultimately, the audience already knows – as Cameron probably does – that he will eventually go along with his friend's machinations, irrespective of his misgivings.

We move next to an English literature class, where another deathly dull teacher – who has a stilted, almost staccato means of delivery – is lecturing his class. A wide shot of his class reveals, on the extreme right of the frame, Ferris's girlfriend Sloane Peterson. Like the rest of her classmates, she appears bored rigid. There is then a cut to a pair of legs adorned with neatly creased white trousers and neat white shoes, striding purposefully down a school corridor. Panning up, we are introduced to a school nurse, wringing her hands as though anxious about something. Cutting back to Sloane, who is now yawning with boredom, the English teacher is continuing to drone on with his lecture. He is interrupted when the nurse arrives via the classroom's main doorway. Before the nurse has even had a chance to explain her purpose there, Sloane is already in the process of putting on her jacket. The nurse calls out for her, and Sloane affects an exaggerated look of total surprise. Moving back out of the classroom, Sloane and the nurse head down the corridor together. The nurse delicately explains to Sloane that her father has called the school to explain that her grandmother has unexpectedly passed away. Sloane appears distraught (almost comically so, under the circumstances), and the nurse does her best to comfort her.

Although at this point we are unaware of Sloane's identity, or indeed her relevance to the film, her humorously calculating actions presage her relationship with Ferris and her complicity with his elaborate schemes. (Also germane is the fact that we later learn that the nurse is called Florence Sparrow, a play on the name of the eminent historical nurse of the Crimean campaign, Florence Nightingale.)

In Ed Rooney's office, Grace is explaining that she'd taken the aforementioned phone call from Sloane's father, and has asked the nurse to inform Sloane of the death in the family. Rooney immediately smells a rat, and asks Grace who Sloane is currently dating. When Grace replies that she often sees Sloane and Ferris together, Rooney becomes certain of foul play. He asks Grace to find Sloane's father's phone number, but before she has the opportunity to do so she takes an incoming call... which turns out to be from none other than George Peterson himself. Rooney, however, is convinced that rather than Sloane's father, Ferris is on the other end of the line impersonating him. Taking the call, Rooney feigns sympathy when 'George' asks for Sloane to be excused from class, but then demands to have sight of the grandmother's dead body before he'll release Sloane from school. Grace is stunned by Rooney's callousness and enquires about his uncaring approach to the conversation, but Rooney assures her that he's merely setting a snare to trap Ferris into revealing his attempt at deception. However, a second incoming line then rings on Grace's desk; Ferris is calling in to speak to Rooney. Alarmed,

Grace runs back into Rooney's office and gesticulates wildly. Annoyed, Rooney asks what the matter is, only to be told that he's not in fact speaking to Ferris at all. A hilariously dramatic jarring chord, coupled with a tight focus on Rooney's alarmed expression, underscores the monumental depth of his gaffe.

Switching to the second line, Rooney listens as Ferris crisply explains that as he is currently absent from school, he wonders if Jeanie might possibly pick up any class-related work for him so that he can catch up on any assignments before his return. Rooney is too shocked to answer, his expression growing ever more distressed. After Ferris hangs up, Rooney switches back to 'George'. Immediately apologetic, he meekly expresses regret for his earlier insensitivity. But 'George' is furious at Rooney's lack of consideration. We then cut back to Ferris's house, where 'George' is actually revealed to be Cameron (wearing, appropriately enough, a T-shirt bearing a medical caduceus). As Cameron cranks up the irritation that Sloane's father would likely be feeling at the earlier slight, Rooney becomes tongue-tied with apprehension. He frantically signals Grace to find out what class Sloane is in so that she can be released from school for the day. However, while Grace and Rooney have difficulty in finding the information they need, Cameron begins to overplay his hand. Ferris, now sharply dressed, assures Cameron that his perform-ance is impeccable, even though his friend is starting to lose his nerve. On the other end of the line, Grace impersonates Rooney while the dean agitatedly rifles through notes in an attempt to pin down Sloane. As Rooney returns to the phone receiver, Cameron demands that Sloane be sent out to the front of the school so that he can pick her up. Ferris is concerned that this will look suspicious, so Cameron improvises and tells Rooney to accompany Sloane to the car. Ferris is now getting worried, and slaps Cameron to quickly persuade him to change the plan. Ad-libbing frenetically now, Cameron ends the call by telling Rooney that he's changed his mind – he doesn't have time to talk, but will get back in contact later so that the two of them can have lunch together.

These scenes underscore not only Ferris's continuing and innate ability to run rings around Rooney (and, by extension, the school system), but also Rooney's inflated perception of his own ability to smoke out Ferris's conniving plans. His dawning horror at his supposed error of mistaken identity, coupled with his Keystone Kops-style slapstick antics as he tries in vain to pin down the paperwork he needs to locate Slone, articulate much about the way that his character thinks and operates.

Back in Ferris's painstakingly ordered kitchen, Cameron is annoyed at Ferris for having slapped him. Now calm, Ferris explains that they will have difficulty extracting Sloane from the school if Rooney is watching them too intently. But Cameron is irritated with Ferris for not only manoeuvring him into leaving his home and driving over to the Buellers' house, but also for having asked him to make a fake call to Rooney's office (not least considering the potentially disastrous consequences if things had gone wrong). Infuriated at Ferris's lack of respect for his feelings, Cameron grabs his jacket and moves to walk out of the house. Ferris, however, turns on the charm and manages to talk Cameron out of a hasty departure.

At the school, Rooney is racing down one of the corridors, comically slowing down as he passes every doorway so as to conceal his urgency from any student who might happen to see him. Cutting back to the Buellers' kitchen, Ferris and Cameron have now made amends. However, Ferris explains that because picking up Sloane has now been made a much more potentially hazardous undertaking, he will require Cameron to supply a little something extra in order to make his plan work.

Moving then to Cameron's father's garage, we watch as the camera pans up from Ferris and Cameron's feet to their heads as they gaze in awe at the sight that awaits them. That sight is then revealed to be an extremely rare 1961 Ferrari 250GT California – Mr Frye's pride and joy, which he has spent years restoring to a state of perfection. On our first view of the car, the distinctive sound of Yello's song 'Oh Yeah' (1985) strikes up. As Cameron underscores his father's absolute devotion to this vehicle, the audience is treated to several lingering close-ups of various parts of the car's bodywork, including shots of the distinctive Ferrari emblem. Although there are other vintage cars in the attractive glass-panelled garage, the Ferrari is clearly in pride of place. Ferris moves over to assume a posing position near the Ferrari as he explains to Cameron that he intends to take the car out of the garage to pick up Sloane. Cameron is horrified at the prospect, and frantically tries to talk Ferris out of the scheme while his friend – in love with the very sight of the car – wanders around it to take in the full extent of its splendour. In spite of Cameron's grave misgivings, not least at the almost certain ire of his tyrannical father, Ferris is insistent. He explains that Rooney will never accept that George Peterson would drive a banged-up old car like Cameron's, and that only arriving in the Ferrari will convince him that the situation is a believable one. Cameron is resolutely opposed to the idea, but by now Ferris is in the driver's seat and raring to go. Cameron pleads with him, saying that his father will notice that the odometer will have increased with every mile that they've travelled, but Ferris brushes off his concern, explaining that they'll leave the car in reverse gear later so as to reduce the figures on the odometer. But while Cameron crosses himself and makes one last desperate attempt to talk Ferris out of his plan, offering to rent a Cadillac or hire a limousine instead, Ferris is already driving out of the garage, stopping just long enough to let Cameron into the car.

Mr Frye's Ferrari, perhaps the single most prominent visual symbol in the film, represents not only his avaricious acquisitiveness, but also the disciplinary powers that he ruthlessly wields over his son Cameron. Although Hughes has already established Cameron's hypochondria and slightly neurotic nature, we are somehow left in no doubt from his reactions in this scene that his father's fury will potentially be severe indeed. Nor indeed do we have any hesitation in believing Cameron's account that the ownership and condition of the car really does mean more to him than his son.

Eagle-eyed members of the audience will note that the Ferrari's numberplate reads 'NRVOUS', appropriate given Cameron's state of mind throughout most of the film. The other main characters' cars also bear numberplates that are made up of abbreviated titles from earlier Hughes films. Ed Rooney's car is designated '4FBDO' ('For *Ferris Bueller's Day Off*), while Jeanie's is 'TBC', after *The Breakfast Club*. Even Ferris's parents get in on the act; Tom's car bears a 'MMOM' (*Mr Mom*) numberplate, while Katie's reads 'VCTN' (*National Lampoon's Vacation*).

Rooney is accompanying Sloane out of the school's main doorway as they await the imminent arrival of her 'father'. From inside the school, Jeanie is watching the situation unfold at a distance. Rooney is now exaggeratedly apologetic after his earlier faux-pas, and quotes from the Old Testament (Job 14:1-2) in a rather surreal attempt to comfort her. However, as Sloane does not respond to his attempts at conversation, the exchange becomes increasingly strained and awkward. A school bus passes by, suddenly revealing Mr Frye's Ferrari behind it. Standing in front of the car is a heavily-disguised Ferris (complete with dark glasses, long overcoat and hat). He calls out for Sloane, thus avoiding having to get near enough to Rooney to face close scrutiny, and fortunately Rooney seems not to notice that the voice of 'George' sounds nothing like it had done during their earlier phone conversation. Sloane pauses only to thank Rooney for his empathy and consideration, inflating his already considerable sense of self-importance, before she heads for the car.

Jeanie is watching all of this from the main school doors, situated just behind Rooney. The droning voice of the economics teacher is just audible in the background. From her expression, we can tell that she is quietly exasperated by the fact that Ferris has managed to pull the wool over the school's eyes yet again.

At the side of the Ferrari, Sloane greets Ferris with a long, lingering kiss on the lips. As their embrace becomes ever more intimate, Rooney looks on with increasing discomfort. He purses his lips in distaste at what appears to be an incestuous clinch between the two. Ferris and Sloane get into the car, and Sloane inconspicuously greets Cameron, who is concealed in the back. When she asks Ferris what his plans are, he reveals that he has ambitious aspirations for the day ahead – much to Cameron's alarm, as he is still massively apprehensive about the use of his father's car. Ferris revs the engine and speeds off into the distance, with Sloane cheering for joy. Still standing at the school doorway, Rooney is beginning to look suspicious.

Here we see that Sloane, now united with Ferris, is of the same mind with regard to the blundering school authorities, effortlessly buttering up Rooney while maintaining (at least initially) the ostensible appearance of a grieving teenager. Rooney's hilariously clumsy attempts to be both apologetic and comforting, on the other hand, are skilfully contrasted with his dawning mistrust of the situation as it unfolds.

Now free from the watchful eye of Rooney, Ferris continues to accelerate as they head down the road from school. Cameron, deciding that he can risk exposing his presence, unearths himself from the back of the car. Ferris triumphantly tosses his hat into the air as Cameron – almost drowned out by the sound of the engine – begs him to slow down.

We are next greeted with a panoramic establishment shot of the Windy City of Chicago. Soaring skyscrapers and busy traffic are evident everywhere. Hughes then shifts to a variety of more detailed shots, some showing well-known Chicago buildings and landmarks. Highly distinctive architecture can be seen in this variety of stunning aerial shots. Eventually, we move back to the Ferrari as it speeds along a road heading into the city. Ferris is still riding the car hard. We switch next to a viewpoint directly in front of the car, as though staring through the windscreen. Without audible dialogue, Cameron is chiding Ferris for not decelerating, and Ferris responds by repeatedly taking his hands off the wheel, predictably causing Cameron to freak out.

Back in high school, a student is collecting donations in an empty cola can as he walks along a corridor. Many passing teenagers rattle coins into the can as they go by. That is, until he meets Jeanie. When she asks what he is collecting for, the student explains that he is helping to raise money in order to purchase Ferris a new kidney. Enraged, Jeanie knocks the can flying out of his hand and storms off. Mystified by her seemingly-heartless actions, the student asks her what she'll do if she ever needs help from Ferris Bueller in the future. Jeanie predictably offers no response.

Grace is dialling the Peterson's home telephone number at Rooney's request. Rooney, meanwhile, is now back at his desk and looking increasingly distrustful. As he lifts the receiver to connect to his extension line, we cut to Sloane's answering machine at her home. Her recorded message plays a tearful message explaining the details of their family bereavement, and also outlines a separate contact number. Rooney explains to Grace that he is now sure that there is a ruse at work, that Ferris is behind it, and that Sloane is implicated. (And, as Grace asks to Rooney's disdain, can we be sure that Sloane's grandmother isn't also mixed up in it somehow?) When the further contact number is dialled, it connects to Cameron's answering machine, which plays a message purporting to be from a mortician. Rooney, now convinced of foul play, tells Grace that he is absolutely determined to uncover Ferris's deception and make him face the consequences of his actions.

Rooney's attitude in this scene is interesting, as he makes a conscious shift from simply seeking to bring Ferris to book, penalising him for not respecting school rules, and instead he begins to develop a personal obsession with pursuing his dispute with Ferris. No longer hoping simply to catch him out, Rooney is now upping the ante considerably, unwavering in his resolve to damage Ferris's future by curtailing his perceived subversive ambitions.

Ferris has now slowed down somewhat as the car has reached

inner-city Chicago. He turns into a multi-storey car park, where he intends to leave the Ferrari for the day. Cameron is alarmed by this, knowing that if the car is even slightly damaged he could face major ramifications at home. But Ferris is persistent, stressing that he'll tip the valet to ensure that no harm comes to Mr Frye's pride and joy. The valet soon arrives, clocking in, and Ferris approaches him with a rather indiscreet enquiry about his language skills. The man responds in heavily-accented English that yes, he does indeed speak the same language. (With an ironic glance to camera, we can see that Ferris is not entirely convinced of this.) Ferris hands over his tip, asking the valet to take particular care of the Ferrari. Cameron is extremely reluctant to leave the vehicle, but is eventually persuaded out by Ferris and Sloane. The valet assures him that he has no cause for concern, before carefully driving the car further into the building. Yet just as Cameron is coaxed out onto the city street by his friends, the Ferrari can be seen – entirely unobserved by Ferris and associates – screeching out of the car park, with the valet in the driving seat and one of his colleagues along for the ride. They are then witnessed racing off into the city at high speed.

These scenes set up the source of a major predicament later in the film – any change in the Ferrari's status, now out of Ferris's control, is bound to have major negative consequences for Cameron. Yet in a more understated way, it also delineates a certain subtle degree of xenophobia on Ferris's part. His rather insensitive questioning of the valet, fundamentally about his nationality, calls to mind his earlier comments about having no interest in the affairs of other countries, their politics or their respective mindsets.

Back at the Buellers' house, Katie is returning to check on Ferris. Parking in the driveway, she quietly enters the house and – as suspenseful music plays – gently creeps upstairs as not to disturb her son. Slowly opening the door to Ferris's room, she looks in to see a gently turning figure in bed. The light sound of contented snoring can also be heard. Satisfied, she closes the door, but reminded of Rooney's earlier warning about excessive absences she feel compelled to have another quick glance. As she does so – though unseen by Katie – the apparatus of Ferris's deception is laid bare. The sporting trophy, which he was seen tying up earlier in the film, is suspended behind the door to act as a counterweight. Through a complex system of strings and pulleys, when the door opens the trophy's suspension is slackened, causing a mannequin (concealed under a quilt) to turn in Ferris's bed. Meanwhile, a looped track of snoring samples is being played on his hi-fi. Still apparently satisfied by her son's apparent infirmity, Katie closes the door behind her for a second time and heads downstairs.

In Chicago, Ferris, Sloane and Cameron are on the observation level of the Sears Tower. Ferris is revelling in being at the top of the highest building on the planet; Cameron, still worried about the Ferrari, is feeling distinctly vertiginous. Taking pleasure in the moment, Ferris invites his friends to stand higher on the observation rail and rest their heads against the glass of the windows. This gives each of them an even more arresting view of the city below. Sloane is amazed at how tranquil Chicago looks from her current height. Cameron, on the other hand, is convinced that he can see his father.

Here Hughes again emphasises the psychological differences between Ferris and Sloane, both obviously deriving gratification in their distant observation of the world below, and Cameron, whose paranoia over his father's inescapable disparagement is inhibiting his ability to let himself unwind even remotely.

The action then briskly moves to the floor of the Chicago Board of Trade, where a horde of traders can be seen frenetically dealing in commodities. This frantic scene is intercut with a view of Cameron apparently giving some broker-esque hand-signals. Eventually it becomes apparent that he, Sloane and Ferris are all sitting within a sealed-off observation area, with the traders some distance away behind a wall of glass. Ferris half-jokingly asks Sloane if she'll consider marrying him during the course of the day. Sloane laughs his offer off, asking him to think about the profound ramifications of what he's asking. Cameron, making annoying noises with his cheeks, glumly cuts across the conversation to interject that his own parents are a perfect demonstration as to why the institution of marriage is futile. As he points out, his mother and father may be married, but they also hate each other. In Cameron's opinion, his father loves his Ferrari, but detests his own wife. Yet Ferris and Sloane do not appear to let their friend's sense of resentment towards his parents dampen their own romantic sanguinity.

Cameron here demonstrates once again the clear difference between his own bleak outlook on the future, and the much more upbeat prospects that Sloane and Ferris have in mind. The scene also serves to further elaborate upon Cameron's miserable home life, underscoring the fact that his mother is at least as much at variance with Mr Frye as Cameron himself is.

Next we see an exterior shot of Chez Quiz, an upmarket restaurant in the city. Moving inside, Ferris and friends are waiting in a high-class reception area, grossly underdressed amongst the other sharply-attired guests. Ferris surreptitiously checks the reservations list before the arrival of a snooty maitre d', who is instantly suspicious of the three teenagers. The maitre d' asks if Ferris has made an advance booking, to which Ferris responds that he has made a reservation for a party of three under the name of Abe Froman – having seen the name on the maitre d's own list. However, the maitre d' is unimpressed. In his opinion, Abe Froman – 'The Sausage King of Chicago' – would clearly look nothing like a casually-dressed teenager. Ferris, however, is indignant at the maitre d's superciliousness, and refuses to leave when asked. His attempt at leaving a tip is also unsuccessful. The maitre d' then threatens to call the police, to which Ferris replies not to bother; he will be phoning them himself. Clandestinely, however, he calls an internal line within the restaurant instead. The maitre d', thinking that an incoming call is pending, tries to take the receiver from Ferris, but is angrily brushed off. Annoyed, he then heads for another phone further into the building instead. Cameron pleads with Ferris to leave before things become any more complicated, but Ferris is determined to get his own way – as he explains to camera, if he's going to be brought down, it certainly won't be by an arrogant snob like the maitre d'. Sloane takes the receiver from Ferris, and when the maitre d' answers she asks to speak to Abe Froman. The maitre d' asks for Froman's general appearance, so Sloane precisely describes Ferris's current outfit. Smelling a rat, the maitre d' then switches to the other active line, only to hear Cameron impersonating a police sergeant.

We then immediately cut to Ferris, Cameron and Sloane, all comfortably seated at one of the tables in the restaurant as they consult their respective menus. The maitre d' is repentant over the earlier 'misunderstanding', and not even Ferris's barbed comments can pierce the older man's studied contrition. As he leaves, Ferris gently chides Cameron for not having enough faith in his legendary powers of persuasion.

Again we see Ferris managing to get one over on an authority figure with considerable panache. Even when his friends are of the opinion that Ferris is about to run out of luck, he manages to pull an ace from out of his sleeve. It seems, as in the case with his running antipathy with Rooney, that the more despotic and draconian his opponent, the more determined Ferris is to get the upper hand.

Jeanie is standing at the end of a high school corridor, deep in thought. We hear her internal monologue as the camera slowly approaches her. She momentarily considers whether Ferris really is as annoying and exasperating as she has always judged him to be. After all, her parents bought her a car, while he had to put up with a computer instead. Eventually, however, her antipathy wins through as she is needled once again by the agonising realisation that Ferris always manages to get what he aims for without ever getting caught out, while she inevitably comes off second-best.

In the gents' toilet of the restaurant, Ferris is washing his hands as he addresses the camera (via his reflection in the mirror). He discusses the fact that, while his own family is undeniably dysfunctional, the peculiarities of the Buellers are as nothing when compared to those of the Fryes. Intercutting with occasional shots of Cameron looking twitchy and socially ill-at-ease in the restaurant, Ferris laments the unhappy environment that makes up his friend's home, which he blames for Cameron's perpetual belief that he is ill. As Ferris continues to preen himself and comb his hair, he expresses concern for his friend, obviously feeling that Cameron deserves better out of life. Tipping the attendant and stopping to take a complimentary mint on the way out, Ferris has only just left the room when his father emerges from one of the toilet cubicles.

Back in Rooney's office, Jeanie arrives looking to meet with the dean. Grace, still at her desk, explains that Rooney has left the building on personal business, but won't elaborate on when he's due back. Jeanie then refuses to discuss her own business with Grace, and leaves in an even worse mood than when she first turned up. Grace asks her if she shouldn't be in her consumer education class, to which Jeanie responds to the effect that she couldn't care less.

This scene signals for the first time that Jeanie's irritation has reached a level such that she may be considering informing on Ferris's waywardness – a course of action that she has so far considered out of bounds. However, her lack of response to Grace also suggests that she may still be taking into account the full range of her options.

At the main doorway of Chez Quiz, Ferris is alarmed to discover his father at the bottom of the restaurant's steps, deep in conversation with some business associates. Ferris bemoans the odds of such an unfortunate coincidence, although as yet Tom has not noticed their presence. Cameron immediately suggests that they confess their truancy to Tom, but Ferris is absolutely opposed to it, believing that the game is never up. All three don dark glasses and stealthily manage to steal Tom's cab, which is waiting beside him on the street. Before Tom can even notice that the taxi has departed, however, another one has already taken its place.

In a much quieter area, Rooney is parking up, obviously on the lookout for Ferris. Ostentatious music strikes up, reminiscent of an old TV detective show. Getting out of his car, he puts on a pair of dark glasses to disguise his appearance; they are of the flip-up variety, but look comical due to the fact that he isn't wearing any conventional spectacles beneath them. He walks into a busy pizza parlour, bustling with activity, as he casts his eye over the multitude within. Eventually he spots a figure at an arcade machine who is wearing a jacket identical to Ferris's, and heads over for a confrontation. (From the design of the arcade cabinet, the game that is being played is Data East's *Karate Champ*, 1984, but the sound effects that are heard throughout the exchange actually sound more like samples from Namco's famous *Pac-Man*, 1980.) However, Rooney's threatening tone doesn't go down at all well when the mysterious figure turns around to reveal the face of a young woman, her hairstyle fashionably cropped. Before he has a chance to withdraw his badly-chosen words, the woman spits a mouthful of cola over him with a straw.

Rooney heads over to the eatery's checkout area so that he can dry himself off with a couple of napkins. A baseball game is being played on a television mounted on a nearby wall. As Rooney is temporarily unable to see while he wipes the cola out of his eyes, he completely misses televised footage of Ferris and Cameron celebrating among the spectators at Chicago's Wrigley Field, which shows Ferris catching a wayward baseball that has been hit into the crowd. By the time Rooney's vision is unimpaired, the television camera has moved on to another shot. A nearby cook is rather nonplussed when Rooney, having been told that the game is currently drawn, asks who is winning.

These scenes mark the beginning of Rooney's catastrophic (and, it transpires, hopelessly doomed) quest to bring Ferris down. Hughes brilliantly juxtaposes the image of Ferris and friends donning stylish shades in their previous scene with Rooney wearing his bizarre-looking flip-top sunglasses. But just as Rooney's dignity is punctured by his unexpected case of mistaken identity – and, more to the point, the drenching that follows it – the worst is most certainly still to come.

Out at the baseball park at Wrigley Field, Ferris is still enjoying himself to the full. Even Cameron is finally starting to let his hair down. Momentarily cutting to an exterior shot of the park, a 'Save Ferris' notice is being clearly displayed on a large digital display. (This marks the beginning of a series of running visual gags throughout the film, each contributing high-profile publicity around the Chicago area of Ferris's plight.) Back among the spectators, Sloane looks bored rigid as more of the baseball game is played out, while Ferris jokingly reminds Cameron that if they weren't bunking off, they'd currently be enduring a gym class.

Moving seamlessly to the school's playing fields, a coach is currently driving around on a small motorised vehicle shouting encouragement to a class of breathless students as they jog around a circuit on the grassy sports ground. In the foreground, Jeanie drives up in her car and momentarily comes to a halt. Glancing at Ferris's panting classmates, she mirrors Ferris's own realisation of where he should be if he hadn't managed to pull off his absence, which makes her resent him all the more.

Rooney is pulling up in his car on the street outside the Buellers' house. Striding up to the front door, he rings the doorbell, which we see – thanks to a very quick shot from the house's interior – has set in motion some elaborate electric circuitry. Seconds later, Ferris's voice is piped through an intercom system. He explains that he is unable to come to the door due to his current state of infirmity, but that his parents are both contactable on their business phone numbers. However, Rooney is having none of it. He repeatedly insists that Ferris should come to the door and discuss the nature of his absence with him in greater detail. However, a more detailed shot of Ferris's jury-rigged doorbell system reveals that all of his responses have been recorded onto a cassette tape, and thus Rooney obviously has no chance of a genuine response. Angered at Ferris's apparent refusal to take the matter seriously, Rooney rings the doorbell again, but when he is faced with an exact repeat of the same message he catches on to the fact that he is listening to a recording.

Moving away from the door, Rooney begins to sneak around the house's perimeter, trying to take a look through some of the ground floor windows. The earth nearby is muddy, however, and he has trouble keeping his balance. When attempting to look over some high window shutters, he loses a shoe in a mucky quagmire, and then ends up soaking the legs of his trousers when he accidentally starts water running through a garden hose. Retrieving his shoe, he desperately tries to rinse the mud from it, but only succeeds in drenching himself further in the process.

Rooney's descent into professional (and possibly psychological) oblivion is being firmly established here, for his increasingly desperate attempts to gain evidence of Ferris's truancy from within his family residence is the ultimate source of his downfall. With the seeds of his determination now fully sown, his growing obsession is demanding to be fed.

Back on the outskirts of Chicago, the car park valet and his colleague are racing Mr Frye's Ferrari along an open stretch of road. A quick shot shows that the odometer has already increased, and the speedometer isn't exactly flat-lining either. As John Williams's opening theme from *Star Wars* (George Lucas, 1977) plays in the background, the valet and his friend seem ecstatic at the exhilarating experience of speed that the Ferrari is affording them.

On the Buellers' back doorstep, a still-soggy Rooney is tying his shoelaces. He turns, spots what appears to be a large cat-flap in the back door, and decides that he's going to try to force entry to the house. Rooney quickly discovers that he has no chance of gaining access through the flap, which is too small to accommodate his frame, but before he can withdraw he is faced by a ferocious, slobbering guard-dog. The dog has been resting in the kitchen, previously unaware of Rooney's presence. Rooney's bungling attempts to sweet-talk it into submission are entirely in vain, however, and the dog chases him back out into the garden. Switching to a view from one of the houses' windows, we can see Rooney racing back and forward as the snapping dog follows in close pursuit. The sound of tearing linen can be heard.

Ferris, Cameron and Sloane are heading for the Art Institute of Chicago, established in an impressive exterior shot. Moving inside, they can be seen joining in with a tour of elementary schoolkids, before the camera moves on to several close-up shots of various different works of art. The characters also strike a variety of poses in front of numerous pieces, many of their stances being ironic, and Ferris and Sloane take a few moments apart to share a kiss. Cameron, meanwhile, becomes fixated on the image of a happy child standing next to its mother in a painting, Georges Seurat's *Sunday Afternoon on La Grande Jatte*. This again reinforces the notion of the pain he suffered during the course of his own melancholic infancy. But the more that Cameron tries to focus on the child, the less detail he is able to discern.

Next we move to a variety of exterior shots showing a vibrant and well-attended street pageant – the Von Steuben Day Parade. The inner-city traffic is shown as being at a near-standstill due to the passing procession. Cameron thoughtfully tries not to look as Ferris and Sloane kiss, but eventually reminds them both that they will all need to leave soon in order to get the car back safely. Ferris disputes the matter, claiming that they still have a few hours to kill, but Cameron is still anxious, claiming that it will be his neck on the line – not Ferris's – if Mr Frye discovers that the car isn't back in the garage by the time of his return from work. Ferris reproaches his friend, reminding him of all the incredible sights they've witnessed in the city so far, but he soon discovers that his protestations are falling on deaf ears – Cameron has become even more anxious than usual. Looking around for the cause of the disquiet, Ferris discovers to his horror that Tom is sitting in a cab directly adjacent to their own. Before Ferris's father can recognise them, however, Cameron and Ferris duck below window-level, leaving only Sloane visible (and disguised with sunglasses). On the floor of the cab, Ferris and Cameron take turns at feverishly rubbing a lucky rabbit's paw. Looking across from his cab, Tom obviously finds Sloane – who he does not recognise – visually alluring, but does his best to stop staring at her indulgently. Instead, he buries his head in his issue of *The Chicago Sun-Times*. The front cover bears a story about a neighbourhood uniting in support of a certain ailing teenager.

Rooney is watching very cautiously through a hole in the Buellers' garden gate as their dog tears into one of his shoes. He tries – incredibly gingerly – to peer over the top of the gate to get a better view, but the dog immediately races for him, almost managing to jump high enough to bite him. Alarmed, Rooney leaps back to consider his next move.

The parade is still continuing as Cameron and Sloane weave their way through the assembled crowd. They have temporarily lost Ferris, much to Cameron's manifest fretfulness. However, before he can rattle through a full list of potential places he may have gone (most of them solely with the intentional purpose of making Cameron panic), a familiar voice booms out of a nearby speaker, dedicating a song to an individual named Cameron Frye. The pair look up in horror to see Ferris, in his element on the crest of a passing float, flanked by dancers in traditional German dress as he mimes along stylishly to Wayne Newton's 'Danke Schoen' (1963). (A directional sign shown behind the float's accompanying accordionist stipulates that the parade is taking place on Dearborn Street.) This time even Sloane is convinced that Ferris has gone too far. However, before she can protest any further, she and Cameron are rounded up and pushed back into the crowd by a couple of passing policemen. Still at the top of his game, Ferris continues with the song as the parade's apparently-impressed panel of judges look on.

As Cameron and Sloane walk away from the parade area,

Cameron bemoans the fact that Ferris always manages to succeed at everything that he sets his mind on, while he finds difficulty in everything, from his miserable home life to facing his fears for the future. His tone is a mixture of admiration and envy. When he mourns the fact that he has no real idea of where he is headed in life, Sloane mentions that he does at least have the certainty of college still to come. But, as Cameron asks, what purpose will be served by his attendance there when nothing really interests him? Sloane replies that nothing much interests her either, and so they do at least have some common ground where that is concerned. Sloane wonders aloud what Ferris will end up doing with his life, to which Cameron speculates wryly that he might become a fry cook.

In this short but pivotal scene, Cameron manages to delineate the core difference between himself and Ferris, even if he can't fully comprehend why this disparity has come to be established. Ferris's success largely comes from his absolute sense of self-belief. Cameron, on the other hand, has virtually no self-esteem whatsoever, which constantly impacts on his worldview and his conception of what he can (and can't) achieve in life. While Ferris appears to be fully cognisant of this distinction, it still seems to be lost on Cameron.

There then follows a short but very entertaining musical interlude, where Ferris – still ensconced atop the parade float – bursts energetically into a mimed rendition of the Beatles's cover of 'Twist and Shout' (1964). He has ample support from a brass band, and his performance is intercut with shots of other Chicago denizens enjoying the music, ranging from a nearby construction worker (complete with hard-hat) to a group of synchronised dancers. Even the judging panel get in on the act. Slightly more surprising is that Tom's office is in one of the buildings overlooking the parade, and we join him as he looks out of the window and can't resist a little boogie in time with the music. Every time Hughes cuts back to Ferris in the float, however, the scene appears a little more lively, and the crowd slightly more densely packed. The assembled multitude burst into rapturous applause as Ferris reaches his triumphant conclusion. He is handed a baton as he waves to the immense audience around him.

Back at the Buellers' house, a delivery man is returning to his van, having dropped something off at the family's front door. We move closer to discover that Rooney has taken possession of the delivery, which is a large potted flower arrangement. He is less than impressed to learn from the attached greetings card that the gift has been sent from the staff and faculty of the school's English department. As the delivery man blows his horn to signal his departure, a livid Rooney gestures obscenely back at him. From the way that Rooney is carrying the arrangement, it is clear that it is actually quite hefty. We then promptly move back to a wide shot of the house's exterior as Rooney advances from the doorway, heading for the gate to the backyard. He whistles and calls for the guard-dog, making clear his intended use for Ferris's floral gift.

Jeanie is parking her car nearby. She gets out to discover – much to her abhorrence and disbelief – a huge balloon flying high over the rooftops in the vicinity which clearly bears the 'Save Ferris' slogan. Her disgusted expression speaks volumes.

Rooney is peeking victoriously over the Buellers' garden gate, his voice dripping derision as he wishes the guard dog pleasant dreams. We then see a medium close-up of the dog lying unconscious on the paving of the yard, the shattered remnants of the floral arrangement scattered around it. However, from its gentle snoring sounds, we are aware that Rooney has stunned the animal rather than killed it outright.

Here we see Rooney's irrationalism continuing to mount. By effectively staking out Ferris's house, he crosses a line from professional rectitude into the territory of a personal vendetta. But now he has gone one step further, stealing private property and then destroying it in an act of unabashed animal cruelty. Whether – as we are led to suspect – this is an act of revenge for the dog's earlier attack on him, or merely another step along the road to gaining entry to Ferris's house, Rooney is continuing to hurtle down the road to catastrophe.

Jeanie's car is now arriving on the Buellers' driveway. She wastes no time in getting out and heading into the house. Rooney, still unseen at the side of the building, hears her arrival. Inside, Jeanie races upstairs and throws open the door to Ferris's room. The force of the door swinging open is too much for Ferris's jury-rigged mechanism to bear, and the mannequin in his bed sits bolt upright. Her suspicions of Ferris's deception now confirmed beyond doubt, Jeanie is enraged.

Rooney, meanwhile, has crept back to the front door. On discovering that the door is now unlocked, he hesitates momentarily, then decides to quietly gain entry. Upstairs, Jeanie is on the phone to her mother's business line. However, from the tone of her conversation it is clear that her mother is out on business and the intended time of her return is not known. Jeanie, if possible, is growing ever more incensed. Back downstairs, Rooney is starting to creep stealthily through the house. Jeanie hears him gently closing the front door, and – confused – gently sneaks down the stairs to investigate. Her trainers make no noise on the stair carpet. Rooney makes his way into the kitchen, still looking for evidence of Ferris's truancy. This is intercut with a shot of Jeanie's legs and feet, still silent, pacing along the parquet flooring of the hall. Jeanie is convinced that it is Ferris who she hears sneaking back into the house. Rooney, on the other hand, believes Jeanie to be Ferris. Jeanie jumps out of the doorway into the kitchen, expecting to ambush Ferris and catch him in the act. Rooney, on the other hand, is near-simultaneously pouncing out of the kitchen in expectation of apprehending Ferris. Shocked, Jeanie now believes that the house has been invaded by an intruder (which, in effect, is has), but is too scared to recognise Rooney. She attacks him with a number of rapid high-kicks to the head, knocking him out cold. He falls hard onto the kitchen floor as Jeanie, screaming, races back upstairs to the relative safety of her room. Unknown to Rooney as he lies unconscious on the ground, his car (which is parked next to a fire hydrant) is currently being ticketed by a traffic warden on the street outside.

Ferris, Cameron and Sloane are laughing and joking back at the car park. Cameron is still expressing his disbelief at Ferris's audacity in taking such a prominent part in the parade, to which Ferris replies that anyone who really wanted to catch him out would never be attending such a stirring event in the first place. As they talk, the valet arrives with the apparently-undamaged Ferrari. Ferris rebukes Cameron for his earlier lack of faith, though Cameron is still not entirely convinced of the valet's honesty. As the friends get back in the car, Ferris tips the valet again – much to the man's silent amusement. When the Ferrari speeds away into Chicago, the valet and his associate celebrate the fact that they've managed to pull off their impromptu joyride without any adverse consequences.

Cutting back to the street outside the Buellers' house, Rooney's car is now heavily ticketed – there are at least four more official documents tucked under the windscreen wipers alongside the original one. Meanwhile, a frantic Jeanie is in her room and on the phone to the police. It soon becomes apparent from the one side of the conversation we hear that the operator is sceptical of her account – though to her considerable disdain, they do take the time to wish Ferris a speedy recovery. Fuming, Jeanie slams down the receiver.

Back outside, Rooney's car is now being prepared for towing by the authorities. In the Buellers' kitchen, Rooney has regained consciousness and is nursing his wounds with some running water from the sink. Jeanie's voice comes over the house's intercom system and informs the 'intruder' that she has telephoned for police assistance. Rooney turns around in alarm, a ragged piece of paper handkerchief poking comically from one of his bloodied nostrils. Jeanie further elaborates on her earlier statement by adding the fact that she is in possession of her father's gun, and – just to ward off any ideas of intimate attack – is suffering from an appallingly intense infection of herpes. Rooney, growing ever more anxious by the minute, wastes no time in departing. As he does so, a close-up of the kitchen floor reveals that he has accidentally dropped his wallet.

Rooney arrives outside just to see his car being towed away. He shouts out to the driver of the tow-truck, but is ignored. He then races to unlock the driver's side door of his elevated car, but the truck is moving too quickly. Rooney, however, is not quick enough to retrieve his keys in time, and so they are lost along with the car. Now in the throes of mounting hysteria, he screams profanely and gestures frenetically at the driver of the truck, but to no avail. Left with no other obvious choice, he tears after the rapidly-accelerating truck – a task made rather more difficult by the fact that he is still missing one of his shoes, reducing him to an amusing waddle as he tries to run.

Here we see Rooney finally starting to tip over the edge from a state of irrationality into out-and-out mental instability. His comical attempts to rail at the authorities, albeit fruitlessly, are all the more ironic given his own draconian adherence to following the official rules above all else. Yet even now we have not quite seen him reach his lowest ebb.

As the Ferrari cruises through downtown Chicago, Cameron – knowing that they are on the homeward stretch – finally seems to be mildly relaxed. Ferris, however, is anything but – he has just noticed that the odometer is registering almost two hundred more miles than it had when they left Mr Frye's garage. When Cameron notices this, the effect is immediate – an extreme close-up of his mouth, slowly drawing back as we follow his scream outward. This in turn reveals an expression of total panic, articulating his frame of mind quite efficiently. A rapid montage of shots then follows, depicting a number of different areas of the city as Cameron's anguished shriek continues unabated. Ferris continues to drive while Cameron appears to be hyperventilating, or possibly on the brink of entering some kind of coma. Sloane is becoming increasingly concerned about their friend's wellbeing.

A close-up shot reveals an unfamiliar-looking finger pressing the doorbell at the Buellers' front door. This, in turn, triggers Ferris's recorded message. Upstairs, Jeanie risks a peek from her hiding place under her duvet. Hugely relieved, believing that the police have come to her aid, she races out of her room and down the stairs. However, on hurriedly answering the door, she is rather crestfallen to find herself face-to-face with what appears to be a strip-o-gram dressed as a nurse, complete with a rather creepy-looking entourage. Obviously having been booked with Ferris in mind, the new arrival isn't given a chance to get through her well-rehearsed introductory spiel before Jeanie slams the door in her face.

At a picturesque waterside sight-seeing spot, Cameron is lying out cold on a low wall while Sloane tries to coax some kind of reaction out of him. To camera, Ferris is expressing trepidation about his friend's mental wellbeing. Knowing how uptight Cameron is at the best of times, Ferris is concerned that the prospect of Mr Frye's ire has finally pushed him to snapping point. Ferris also appears worried that his own freewheeling attitude in inviting Cameron to join his day off may have been – at least partly – to blame for the current predicament. As they only have a few months of high school together, following which they will both take summer jobs and then enrol at college (probably in different places), Ferris knows that their friendship – which has lasted since childhood – will probably only survive a little longer before they both go their separate ways in life. This is part of the reason for his absolute determination that they have a good time on his prized day of absence from school. He goes on to consider his relationship with Sloane; as she is a year younger than him, she still has to go through her senior year in high school, and Ferris is unsure how they will be able to keep their romance alive when he is in college.

Cameron still shows no sign of responding to Sloane's repeated attempts to communicate with him. Ferris bemoans the fact that Cameron has never been in love – or, leastways, has never had his love reciprocated. Thus in Ferris's opinion, when

Cameron does finally end up striking it lucky with a potential partner, his growing desperation for companionship and affection will almost certainly lead him into a unbalanced relationship with a woman who has no respect for him. Knowing that their time is growing short, Sloane worries that their current approach to coaxing Cameron out of his catatonic state is not working, and suggests that they try something else.

The above scene is interesting, for it is one of the very few in the film where Ferris acknowledges that there are certain forces in life that he can neither outsmart nor manipulate. He knows that he and Cameron are almost certain to drift apart, as may also be the case with Sloane. And yet, rather than grieve over the inevitable, he makes a conscious, life-affirming choice instead to revel in the short time that they have left together, and to make the most of their shared company while he still can.

Ferris and Sloane are luxuriating in a large swimming pool located in Sloane's back garden. Cameron is seated on a plastic folding chair at the end of a diving board, still completely spaced out. Sloane continues with her attempts to talk him out of his strange waking unconsciousness, but is still meeting with no success. Ferris opines that perhaps Cameron really has been pushed into a kind of mental flux by the distressing way that events have transpired. Then, without warning, Cameron falls off his chair and pitches over into the pool. As he remains totally unresponsive in the water, Ferris is alarmed that he may drown, and dives in after him. At the bottom of the pool, however, Cameron is showing an awareness of his surroundings. Ferris grabs his friend and manages to drag him out of danger, with help from Sloane on the surface. He tries desperately to revive Cameron, who remains impassive. Then, suddenly, Cameron smiles and starts joking, proving that he has finally emerged from his catatonic state. Realising that the apparent drowning was a hoax, Ferris is initially angered at having been hoodwinked, but soon sees the funny side and is relieved to have his friend back with him. He pulls Sloane down into the pool with them, and the three start to clown around together.

Jeanie is seated in the waiting area of Shermer Police Station. Officers and staff go quietly about their business around her. A delinquent in a leather jacket is seated next to her, cracking his knuckles. His red-rimmed eyes suggest that he has not had any sleep for some time. He tries to strike up a conversation with Jeanie, though she is reluctant to interact with him. Undeterred, he lets her know that he has been taken in for questioning on drug-related charges, and in turn asks what she's doing there. Jeanie responds that she is not entirely sure of the answer to this question. His further attempts at discussion are initially brushed off, particularly when he (rather surreally) criticises her eye make-up. However, his persistence eventually pays off, and Jeanie explains about her grievance with her brother and the fact that he continually manages to evade suspicion or apprehension despite the outlandish audacity of his schemes. She also clarifies how she got to her current location; after calling the police, officers arrived to discover that there was no intruder in the house (Rooney having left the premises), and as such she was taken back to the station on suspicion of making a hoax call. The delinquent listens carefully to her story, then tells her that in his opinion, her problem does not lie with her brother, but rather with herself. He suggests that she should concentrate on the potential that her own life has, rather than resenting her brother for the success of his conniving plans. Jeanie seems to contemplate this, though she continues to remain otherwise disdainful of the delinquent. He does little to help his case when he suggests that she should talk to a very helpful individual that he knows named Ferris Bueller, who might hold the answer to her problems.

Hughes exercises considerable lightness of touch in the juxtaposition of this scene and the one which follows it. Here, we see Jeanie starting for the first time to question whether her animosity towards Ferris is actually a substitute for dissatisfaction with her own life, thus setting in motion a pronounced change in her character. This is contrasted in the next scene with an even more overwhelming transformation of Cameron's character.

In Mr Frye's garage, the stationary Ferrari is mounted on a couple of metal stands. A small concrete block has been wedged against one of its pedals in order to force it into reverse. This, as Ferris indicated earlier, is a desperate attempt to turn back the figures on the now-greatly-increased odometer. The friends are sitting on a couple of benches outside the garage. Cameron is explaining what went through his mind while he was still in a state of catatonia. He describes a process whereby he started to really observe his behaviour for once, and came to the conclusion that his endless worry and self-loathing over the years had all been pointless and in vain. He makes a conscious choice to change his ways and become a more autonomous individual, better equipped to shape his own destiny. Cameron also says for the first time how much he will miss Ferris and Sloane in the coming year, when they will all be studying in different places. Out of the blue, Sloane asks Cameron if he was watching her getting changed into her swimwear while he was supposedly in the throes of his pseudo-coma. Cameron evades answering this question directly, tactfully deciding to return to the garage to check on the car.

Moments later, Ferris hears an alarmed cry coming from near the Ferrari – Cameron has discovered that their plan isn't working, and the odometer won't go into reverse. Ferris suggests breaking open the odometer and moving the figures backwards by hand, but Cameron decides against it. Instead, Cameron tearfully reaches breaking point and rages against the injustices that have been perpetuated on his life by his father. Furious at years of being bullied and told what he should and shouldn't do, he finally comes to the conclusion that the problem never lay with his dictatorial father, but rather with his own inability to stand up for himself. Pledging that from now on he will take control of his own affairs and determine the future of his life, Cameron channels all of his animosity towards his father into an attack on the car. Fuming, he repeatedly kicks the Ferrari, breaking a headlight and denting the hood and bumper. Sloane moves to stop him in case he regrets it later, but Ferris – sensing the landmark alteration in his friend's psychology – holds her back.

The concerted violence towards the Ferrari appears to have the required cathartic effect on Cameron, who seems incredibly relieved that he has finally made a stand against his father's tyranny. Ferris and Sloane look on, slightly dazed at the pending consequences of what is going on in front of them. Cameron explains that when his father returns from work, he will finally be forced to deal directly with him. Cameron will no longer have to continually live in terror of Mr Frye's potential loss of temper, as he is choosing to face it candidly. Only then will he receive the closure that he so desperately desires.

Resting his foot triumphantly on the dented hood of the Ferrari, Cameron looks on in shocked amazement as the car – still running in reverse – is knocked off of its metal support struts, and then careens at speed out of one of the garage's large rear windows. (A very skilful reverse angle shot is taken from the Ferrari's point of view, clearly showing the look of awestruck horror on Cameron's face.) The car lands some distance below, lurching through the tightly-packed green trees behind the house. Stunned, Ferris and Sloane rush to the broken window to survey the extent of the damage. Sloane offers a momentary enigmatic smile, living in the moment and demonstrating an appreciation for the unexpected. Cameron, who still can't quite believe what has happened, desperately questions what he has done. Ferris responds to his question by answering that the Ferrari has met its demise. Dreading every step, Cameron moves to join his friends at the window, peering down to be met with the sight of the car's wreckage smouldering on the ground. It is partially covered by branches, and almost certainly damaged beyond repair. A close-up shot reveals that the car has only been stopped by the presence of a wire-mesh fence at the boundary of the garden.

Cameron is momentarily too shaken to talk. He absently kicks a small piece of broken glass from the frame of the window over into the garden below, still coming to terms with what has happened. None of the three can quite believe what they've just seen. Moving back into the main body of the garage, Cameron is still obviously disturbed. Ferris offers to take the blame for what has happened, based on the fact that Mr Frye already holds him in contempt. He also tells Cameron that he considers himself responsible for the way things transpired, given that it was he who insisted on taking the Ferrari out of the garage that morning. But Cameron has made up his mind. Telling Ferris that he wouldn't have let him drive the Ferrari that day unless he was willing to face the potential consequences, he will face up to his father on his return and have a long-overdue conversation with him. As the scene ends, a lingering close-up of Cameron's face shows the determination and new-found resolve in his expression.

Cameron's emotional journey is at the very core of the narrative of *Ferris Bueller's Day Off*, and these scenes form its triumphant climax. With his new sense of purpose, Cameron has at last put himself in command of his own free will, and we know without doubt that by crossing a crucially important line – the destruction of his father's one true pride and joy – he will force the very confrontation that he has spent his life dreading and trying to avoid. He has now come full-circle from the fearful neurotic of the film's first act, and is ready to face not only his belligerent father Morris, but also his future.

Back at the police station, Katie is speaking to a detective in his office about the situation that has unfolded during the day with Jeanie. Katie expresses incredulity that Jeanie would be out of school without authorisation, much less that she would make a hoax call to the police. The detective responds that for whatever reason Jeanie made the call, she was obviously genuinely frightened. Katie assures him that she and Tom will later be discussing the matter with her in detail. As she heads out of his office, the detective asks Katie to pass on the best wishes of everyone at the station to Ferris, who he hopes will soon make a full recovery. Katie seems mildly nonplussed by this.

In the waiting area, Jeanie is enjoying a passionate (and surprising) clinch with the delinquent. An annoyed Katie clears her throat to break up their embrace, then tells Jeanie that she wants her out of the police station as quickly as possible. As Katie heads off, Jeanie – her general disposition now much more light-hearted than before – says her goodbyes to the delinquent (who asks her name, but when she replies never offers his own). As Jeanie leaves, she finds herself almost dizzy with elation, though Katie – shouting from the ground floor – is less than impressed by what has transpired.

Outside Sloane's house, she and Ferris are making their own goodbyes for the day. Sloane tells him how much she has enjoyed herself, and asks if he's sure that Cameron will be alright given the tumultuous events that took place earlier. Ferris replies that he feels certain that Cameron will be absolutely fine, and quite possibly for the first time ever. Sloane and Ferris look at each other longingly. Smiling, Sloane then asks Ferris if he knew precisely what he was planning from the minute the day started. Ferris won't elaborate though, and kisses her instead. They are reluctant to part their embrace, but Ferris discovers that the time is five minutes to six – his family will be due back at the house at any time. Pausing only to give her a peck on the cheek – and the assurance that he'll call her later – Ferris races off towards his home. As he leaves, Sloane calls out to Ferris to tell him that she loves him, to which Ferris responds that he reciprocates fully. Smiling, Sloane assures herself aloud that one day the two of them be married.

This scene underscores the depth of affection that exists between Ferris and Sloane, which is hinted at throughout the film. Her consent to the proposal of marriage that he made earlier, though Ferris does not hear it, perhaps undermines his earlier regrets that the two of them are liable to drift apart over the course of the coming year.

Ferris is fighting his way through a patch of greenery

between houses as Jeanie's car heads along a nearby road. In the car, Katie is complaining bitterly about Jeanie's conduct, particularly as she ended up losing a deal at work due to her having to pick Jeanie up from the police station. This is intercut with a shot of Ferris, still racing home on foot, and then quickly returns to Jeanie driving along the road. Unexpectedly, Ferris sprints out of the undergrowth right into the path of Jeanie's car, causing her to make an emergency stop. Ferris is caught right in front of the hood of Jeanie's car, his identity unmistakeable. However, the car's sudden halt has caused Katie's papers to fly up into the air, obscuring her vision. With a tight close-up of Jeanie's eyes, we can see that she is throwing down the gauntlet to Ferris. As he matches her indignant expression and continues his rush towards home, Jeanie hits the accelerator in order to race him to their mutual destination. Katie is totally oblivious to this situation, her papers once again taking to the air (much to her frustration).

As Jeanie continues to pick up speed, Ferris dives through a hedgerow and races through a series of back gardens. The respective householders, some enjoying dinner, watch in surprise as he tears across their property. We cut between Ferris's progress and Jeanie's high-velocity car. Katie is growing more and more agitated at the apparently purposeless acceleration, while Jeanie becomes increasingly hysterical in response. Her progress soon looks to be curtailed by the arrival of a police patrol car. The officer tries to pull her over for speeding. Jeanie, however, appears to be in no mood to slow down.

Still running, Ferris helps himself to a can of cola from an oblivious barbecue enthusiast as he maintains his trajectory towards the Buellers' house. He only stops momentarily to introduce himself to a couple of beautiful sunbathers as he passes through their garden. Tom, meanwhile, is also making his way home from work in his car. He stops momentarily to find a breath mint from his glove compartment. In so doing, he completely misses seeing Jeanie's car speeding past him, followed by an equally swift patrol car.

Further along the road, Jeanie eventually relents and pulls over to be ticketed. Tom, meanwhile, finds his progress impeded by an elderly driver in front of him who is steering slowly and erratically due to the fact that they are too short to see over the dashboard. Ferris is still jogging through the neighbourhood, and is very nearly caught out by Tom – whose car he accidentally ends up running next to – when Tom overtakes the car that has so far been slowing him down. By sheer fluke, Tom looks away at just the right moment and thus does not recognise Ferris as he desperately cuts away behind the car.

Now increasingly frantic, Ferris takes a short-cut straight through someone's house, heads through another garden, climbs over some children's play equipment, and then takes a jump over a high hedge to land in his own backyard. His arrival is simultaneous with the appearance – at the front of the house – of Jeanie, Katie and (seconds later) Tom.

Jeanie tears through the front door while Ferris, at the rear of the house, finds that the back door is locked. Meanwhile, Katie accosts Tom on the house's front entranceway and explains what has happened with Jeanie, describing her trip to the police station. As the discussion of Jeanie's behaviour continues, the deadpan Tom comes to the opinion that a gunshot could improve the situation.

At the back door, Ferris is desperately scrambling about under the doormat in search of a spare house key. A tattered shoe and trouser leg stamp down next to him, and the camera pans up to reveal – much to Ferris's horror – Ed Rooney. (He now appears to have somehow retrieved his missing shoe from the Buellers' guard-dog.) Holding the door key in question, the supremely battered Rooney informs Ferris (with no small amount of jubilation) that he has caught him red-handed at last. This is briefly intercut with Katie and Tom on the front doorstep deciding to go into the house and check on Ferris's wellbeing. Rooney, meanwhile, is absolutely relishing his moment of victory, explaining to Ferris just how long he's waited for this occasion.

There is some interesting symmetry at play in this scene. In an earlier scene, where Ferris telephones Rooney in his office, Rooney is too shocked to speak. Here, as Rooney rants exultantly in the belief that Ferris has finally being called to account for his truancy, the tables are turned and Ferris is the one who finds himself unable to respond. Therefore, although the two engage in direct interaction only rarely throughout the course of the film, in either instance only one speaks while the other listens. (This, of course, is also true of the one-way conversation Rooney has with the recording on the house intercom.) By using this method, Hughes makes the dry observation that the two characters – polar opposites in terms of personality – quite literally have nothing to say to each other.

We then cut to Jeanie, in the kitchen, listening to the exchange between Rooney and Ferris with a look of immense satisfaction on her face. Tom and Katie are moving into the house's main hallway, which is festooned with many different floral bouquets that have obviously been gifted to Ferris throughout the day. Returning to the back door, Jeanie is peering out of the curtains hanging over a small window to witness Rooney, still savouring the moment, telling Ferris to prepare for another full year of high school – this time, under his own direct tutelage. Before the horrified Ferris has a chance to respond, Jeanie abruptly opens the back door and tells him how worried the family have been about him; they expected him back a while ago. Ferris is stunned at this unexpected turnaround in fortune, particularly as it comes from the hand of his oldest adversary (his amazed glance to camera says it all). She also thanks an equally-confused Rooney for driving Ferris home – how, she asks, could such an infirm person expect to get back from hospital on foot? As Ferris heads rapidly into the house before his luck changes, Rooney affects a totally crushed expression as he realises that defeat has been snatched from the jaws of victory. Before he has time to question Jeanie, however, she informs him that she's found his wallet on the kitchen floor, thus proving that he was the intruder from earlier. Rooney's eyes boggle at this revelation as Jeanie tosses the wallet far into the backyard (and, judging from the watery sound that it makes on impact, straight into a garden pond). She then slams the door, which awakens the until-recently unconscious guard-dog. Rooney looks round with disconsolate inevitability as the dog recognises him and begins to snarl. Jeanie stands elatedly, her back to the door, as the deafening sound of Rooney being attacked by the dog once again can be heard from behind her.

Here we witness that Jeanie, like Cameron, has performed a complete one hundred and eighty degree turn as a character. From an initial determination to prove Ferris's dishonesty at any cost, her epiphany at the police station has gifted her enlightenment enough to not only consider her own objectives as the epicentre of her purpose of being, but has actually led her to embrace this philosophy so fully that she can find it in herself to save Ferris from Rooney's clutches – especially significant when she herself seemed ready to inform on Ferris to Rooney earlier in the day.

Safely returning to his bedroom, Ferris rapidly gets undressed and back into his bed. He realises at the last minute that he has left his hi-fi system on, which is still playing a looped sample of his snoring. He has no time to get out of bed before his parents arrive, but suddenly remembers the baseball that he caught at Wrigley Field earlier in the day. Throwing it across the room, he has the good fortune to hit the hi-fi's standby button, silencing the stereo's speakers. He is doubly relieved that the ball miraculously manages to land in a discarded baseball glove lying on the floor (thus making it look totally innocuous), and all literally seconds before his parents arrive.

Katie comes to Ferris's bedside and gently 'wakes' her son. Ferris, who has been feigning sleep with total conviction, assures them when asked that he is feeling much better, but pleads with them not to allow him any further time off school – his studies are important to him, he explains, and he doesn't want to put his future in jeopardy. Tom assures him that the most important thing is his health; he shouldn't rush to get better and inadvertently make himself feel worse. Ferris grudgingly allows that maybe his father knows best. Katie asks him how he ever managed to become so lovable, to which Ferris answers – with more honesty than they realise – that he could only achieve it through years of careful preparation. Still turning on the charm, he invites his mother to pull up his blanket. She assures him that she'll soon return with some hot soup, before leaving with Tom and closing the door quietly behind them.

Ferris, relieved beyond measure that everything has somehow managed to work out, turns directly to camera and reiterates his earlier point that life moves so quickly, it's important to take the time to slow down every so often in order to fully appreciate it. He smiles devilishly as the scene fades out.

It is interesting to note that these closing events mirror the film's opening scenes, with Ferris's dexterous melange of emotional manipulation, precise calculation and blind luck winning the day just as it had back when he was endeavouring to secure the day off in the first place. He also reinforces the film's central theme – the need to enjoy and recognise the value of life rather than simply be swept along by it. It is this realisation that so profoundly transforms the lives of both Cameron and Jeanie, and – to a lesser extent – gives Sloane the determination that she will not willingly let her relationship with Ferris fail. (It is also pleasing to note the Simple Minds poster next to Ferris's bedroom door, which is publicising 'Don't You Forget About Me', the distinctive title song from *The Breakfast Club*.)

As the end credits roll, a bruised and blooded Rooney is gingerly making his way along the street. A reprise of Yello's 'Oh Yeah' begins to play. Rooney is furiously muttering to himself about the injustice of Ferris managing to evade the reach of his authority at the very last minute. As the camera pans up, we realise that Rooney and his suit seem even more dishevelled than they were previously, and his movements are very stiff and painful-looking. Yet just as Rooney must feel that his indignity can increase no further, a school bus packed full of students draws alongside him. The bus driver recognises him, and seems concerned for his wellbeing. Rooney, now humiliated in front of the students (to say nothing of the impotent rage that he is already experiencing), gives no response. However, when the bus driver offers him a lift, he appears so defeated that he silently acquiesces. The bus comes to a halt in order to let him on. Pausing to straighten his tie, Rooney boards the bus only to discover that he is too tall to stand upright in it. He has to stoop in order to avoid hitting his head against the roof. Glowering, he makes his way past rows and rows of students, their expressions bordering on the incredulous. Eventually, he discovers an empty seat near the back of the bus, next to a geeky-looking girl with an unusually conservative taste in fashion. They regard each other in silence. The student tries to engage him in polite conversation, but the shattered Rooney is having none of it. She then offers him a gum sweet, which he takes and then promptly throws further into the bus. The other students don't seem to know where to look, and appear particularly apprehensive when Rooney notices some obscene graffiti about himself scribbled inside the bus. However, the final ignominy comes when he spots one of their folders, which is embellished with a colourful 'Save Ferris' design. Now clearly feeling that his mortification has reached its lowest ebb, Rooney looks straight to camera, a broken man. Seconds later, the bus pulls away from the kerb, heading off into the distance.

If Cameron's story is at the emotional heart of the film's narrative, then Rooney's descent into injury and humiliation forms its counterpoint. Whereas the other main characters discover life-affirming truths about themselves, or – through their self-belief – show appreciation for the importance and worth of life, Rooney's grudge against Ferris instead leads him to spiral into embarrassment and perhaps even a subtle form of borderline psychosis. Growing more and more out of his depth the further he strays from his 'comfort zone' of his high school, Rooney symbolises everything that is hidebound and unimaginative about bureaucratic authoritarianism, and when he makes the decision to turn his suspicions about Ferris into a deeply personal vendetta, he is totally unprepared for the deleterious effect that this will have on him. By the end of the film, his personal and professional reputation are almost as battered as his physical form, and yet from the school bus sequence we are left in no doubt that his ill-fated experiences have done little if anything to actually change his outlook. Thus while Cameron and Jeanie have both been deeply altered, seeking to confront and overcome their personal demons, the most reductive, damaging factor that faces Ed Rooney is in fact revealed to be his own narrow-minded attitude towards life.

After the end credits have rolled, Ferris – back in his bathrobe – heads down the hallway of his home and expresses surprise that anyone is still watching. He assures the audience that the action has now concluded, and urges them to leave and go back to their business – in effect, underscoring one last time the film's central themes of self-determination and making the most of your life for as long as you can.

ILLUSTRATIONS

Illustrations from *Ferris Bueller's Day Off* (1986).

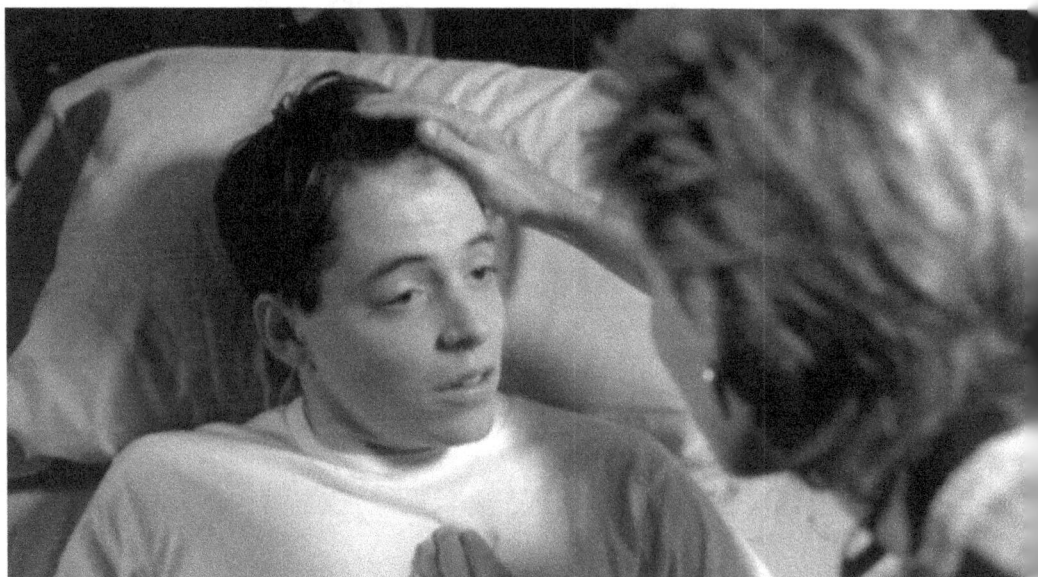

NOTES AND REFERENCES

NATIONAL LAMPOON'S CLASS REUNION (1982)

1. Maura Kelly, 'John Hughes: The films he created in the decade of greed made adolescent angst funny and bearable without romanticising it', in *Salon*, 17 July 2001.
2. For more information about the *National Lampoon* phenomena, one reference resource which is well worth checking out is:
    Josh Karp, *A Futile and Stupid Gesture: How Doug Kenney and National Lampoon Changed Comedy Forever* (Chicago: Chicago Review Press, 2006).
    See also: Matty Simmons, *If You Don't Buy This Book We'll Kill This Dog: Life, Laughs, Love and Death at the National Lampoon* (Fort Lee: Barricade Books, 1995).
3. See, for example: Janet Maslin, 'A *Class Reunion* for *National Lampoon*', in *The New York Times*, 30 October 1982.
4. Norman Short, '*National Lampoon's Class Reunion*', in *DVD Verdict*, 28 March 2000.
    <http://www.dvdverdict.com/reviews/classreunion.php>

MR MOM (1983)

1. Janet Maslin, '*Mr Mom*: Domestic Comedy', in *The New York Times*, 26 August 1983.
2. Roger Ebert, '*Mr Mom*', in *The Chicago Sun-Times*, 22 August 1983.
3. Andrew W.K., '*Mr Mom*', in *Rolling Stone*, 28 August 2003.

NATIONAL LAMPOON'S VACATION (1983)

1. *Variety* Staff, '*National Lampoon's Vacation*', in *Variety*, 3 August 1983.
2. Janet Maslin, '*National Lampoon's Vacation*', in *The New York Times*, 29 July 1983.
3. Patrick Walsh, 'Retro Cinema: *National Lampoon's Vacation*', in *Cinematical*, 21 August 2007.
    <http://www.cinematical.com/2007/08/21/retro-cinema-national-lampoons-vacation/>
4. Patrick Naugle, '*National Lampoon's Vacation: Special Edition*', in *DVD Verdict*, 19 August 2003.
    <http://www.dvdverdict.com/reviews/vacationse.php>

5. Scott Tobias, 'National Lampoon's Vacation' in The Onion A.V. Club, 2 September 2003.
   <http://www.avclub.com/content/node/7354/>

NATE AND HAYES (1983)

1. There is an interesting discussion of Nate and Hayes's place in the wider context of pirate-themed Hollywood films in the following article:
   Bryan Curtis, 'The Celluloid Pirate: Hollywood's strange fascination with buccaneers', in Slate, 11 July 2003.
   <http://www.slate.com/toolbar.aspx?action=print&id=2085480>
2. Vincent Canby, 'Nate and Hayes: Pirates in South Pacific', in The New York Times, 18 November 1983.
3. Roger Ebert, 'Nate and Hayes', in The Chicago Sun-Times, 22 November 1983.
4. A memorably entertaining appraisal of Nate and Hayes in the harsh light of modern action films can be found in Will Helm's excellent article in the 'Misunderstood Masterpieces' section of the 411mania.com website: Will Helm, 'Misunderstood Masterpieces: Nate and Hayes', in 411mania.com, 11 March 2008.
   <http://www.411mania.com/movies/columns/70702>
5. A particularly positive review of the film's DVD release can be found on the DVD Savant website: Glenn Erickson, 'Nate and Hayes', in DVD Savant, 8 July 2006.
   <http://www.dvdtalk.com/dvdsavant/s2055nate.html>

SIXTEEN CANDLES (1984)

1. The significance of Molly Ringwald's performances in three of John Hughes's most prominent teen movies is addressed by Roz Kaveney in her book Teen Dreams: Roz Kaveney, Teen Dreams: Reading Teen Film from Heathers to Veronica Mars (London: I.B. Tauris, 2006), pp.23-30.
2. The lasting significance of Sixteen Candles, and its timeless appeal with audiences, is discussed very effectively by Lisa Borders in the following essay: Lisa Borders, 'Enchanted Night: The Magic of Sixteen Candles', in Don't You Forget About Me: Contemporary Writers on the Films of John Hughes, ed. by Jaime Clarke (New York: Simon

Spotlight, 2007), pp.25-34.

3. Janet Maslin, '*16 Candles*, A Teen-Age Comedy', in *The New York Times*, 4 May 1984.
    For an alternative critical appraisal, see: Scot Haller, '*Sixteen Candles*', in *People*, 14 May 1984.

4. Roger Ebert, '*Sixteen Candles*', in *The Chicago Sun-Times*, 30 April 1984. See also: Pauline Kael, '*Sixteen Candles*', in *The New Yorker*, 28 May 1984.

5. *Variety* Staff, '*Sixteen Candles*', in *Variety*, 2 May 1984.

6. Brad Laidman, '*Sixteen Candles*', in *Film Threat*, 17 October 2000.
    <*http://www.filmthreat.com/index.php?section=reviews&Id=1313*>

7. Marjorie Baumgarten, '*Sixteen Candles*', in *The Austin Chronicle*, 23 April 2002.

8. Anon., '*37 Candles* would make a lot of light', in *The Chicago Sun-Times*, 7 June 2005.

THE BREAKFAST CLUB (1985)

1. Although never confirmed on-screen, the film's title may be a tribute to Don McNeill's affectionately-remembered Illinois radio show *The Breakfast Club*, which ran from June 1933 through to December 1968 on ABC Radio.

2. The term 'Brat Pack', a tongue-in-cheek play on the earlier 'Rat Pack' label ascribed to actors Frank Sinatra, Sammy Davis Jr, Dean Martin, Joey Bishop and Peter Lawford in the 1950s and 60s, is thought to have been originally coined by journalist David Blum:
    David Blum, 'Hollywood's Brat Pack', in *New York Magazine*, 10 June 1985.

3. Mark J. Charney discusses the similarities and variations between *The Breakfast Club* and *St Elmo's Fire*, amongst many other things, in the following chapter: Mark J. Charney, 'It's a Cold World Out There', in *Beyond the Stars: Studies in American Popular Film Volume 5: Themes and Ideologies in American Popular Film*, ed. by Paul Loukides and Linda K. Fuller (Madison: Popular Press, 1996), pp.21-42.

4. Andrew Eaton, 'For a short time they were on fire, then they vanished into obscurity: Whatever happened to the Brat Pack of the 1980s?', in *The Scotsman*, 20 January 2007.

5. The character of Principal Vernon and the strident message of anti-authoritarianism that Hughes injects throughout the course of *The*

Breakfast Club is discussed in specific detail by Mark J. Charney:
Mark J. Charney, in Paul Loukides and Linda K. Fuller, pp.30-31.

6. Roger Ebert, '*The Breakfast Club*', in *The Chicago Sun-Times*, 15
February 1985.
See also: Derek Malcolm, 'Snap, Crackle, Pot', in *The Guardian*, 16
June 1985.

7. Janet Maslin, 'John Hughes's *Breakfast Club*', in *The New York Times*,
15 February 1985.
See also: Ned Corrigan, 'Popular Videos – Counting Down', in *The
Washington Post*, 22 December 1985.

8. Kevin N. Laforest, '*The Breakfast Club*', in *The Montreal Film Journal*,
10 September 2002.
<*http://www.montrealfilmjournal.com/review.asp?R=R0000082*>
See also: Lee Chase IV, '*The Breakfast Club*: It's Hard Out There for a
Teen', in *CultureCartel.com*, 10 July 2006.
<*http://www.culturecartel.com/review.php?rid=10006219*>

9. Anon., 'Enjoy a late *Breakfast*', in *The Topeka Capital-Journal*, 14
March 2008.

10. Michael Booth, '*Breakfast Club* rises, shines' in *The Denver Post*, 24
July 2007.

11. Ethan Aames, 'Estevez on *The Breakfast Club 2*', in *Cinema
Confidential*, 12 July 2005.
<*http://www.cinecon.com/news.php?id=0507126*>

12. The ongoing legacy of *The Breakfast Club* is discussed by Timothy
Shary in his book *Teen Movies: American Youth on Screen*:
Timothy Shary, *Teen Movies: American Youth on Screen* (London:
Wallflower Press, 2005), pp.68-71.
See also: Bob Batchelor, and Scott Stoddart, *The 1980s* (Westport:
Greenwood Publishing Group, 2006), pp.29-30.

13. Philip Martin, 'Flashback 1985: *The Breakfast Club*: Hughes may have
been the first filmmaker to attempt to put plausible teenagers on
screen', in *The Arkansas Democrat-Gazette*, 17 April 2005. See also:
Sarfraz Manzoor, 'More than a quintessential Eighties teen film', in
The Independent, 24 March 2004.

NATIONAL LAMPOON'S EUROPEAN VACATION (1985)

1. Moon Unit Zappa discusses her views on the films of John Hughes,
including *National Lampoon's European Vacation*, in her essay 'How
John Hughes Altered My Life': Moon Unit Zappa, 'How John Hughes

Altered My Life', in *Don't You Forget About Me: Contemporary Writers on the Films of John Hughes*, ed. by Jaime Clarke (New York: Simon Spotlight, 2007), pp.192-204.

2. The variable reception of Heckerling's direction is briefly discussed by Mary G. Hurd in her book *Women Directors and Their Films*: Mary G. Hurd, *Women Directors and Their Films* (Westport: Greenwood Publishing Group, 2006), p.24.

3. *Variety* Staff, '*National Lampoon's European Vacation*', in *Variety*, 9 August 1985.

4. Janet Maslin, '*National Lampoon* in Europe', in *The New York Times*, 27 July 1985.

5. John J. Puccio, '*National Lampoon's European Vacation* (Special Edition)', in *DVD Town*, 23 April 2002.
< *http://www.dvdtown.com/reviews/national-lampoons-european-vacation/1064*>
See also: Patrick Naugle, '*National Lampoon's European Vacation*', in *DVD Verdict*, 20 March 2002.
<*http://www.dvdverdict.com/reviews/europeanvacation.php*>

6. Earl Cressey, '*National Lampoon's European Vacation*', in *DVD Talk*, 22 March 2002.
<*http://www.dvdtalk.com/reviews/3571/national-lampoons-european-vacation/*>

WEIRD SCIENCE (1985)

1. Timothy Shary discusses how *Weird Science* fits into the filmic subgenre of youth science fantasy as part of his chapter 'Simple Science', which appears in: Timothy Shary, *Generation Multiplex: The Image of Youth in Contemporary American Cinema* (Austin: University of Texas Press, 2002), pp.193-94.

2. The central importance of Lisa's character is discussed in Sheila Benson's review of the film in *The Los Angeles Times*:
Sheila Benson, '*Weird Science*', in *The Los Angeles Times*, 2 August 1985.

3. Janet Maslin, '*Weird Science*: Youth Fantasy', in *The New York Times*, 2 August 1985.

4. Roger Ebert, '*Weird Science*' in *The Chicago Sun-Times*, 2 August 1985.

5. Kevin N. Laforest, '*Weird Science*', in *The Montreal Film Journal*, 10 August 2002.

<http://www.montrealfilmjournal.com/review.asp?R=R0000593>

6. Brett Cullum, 'The Brat Pack Movies and Music Collection', in *DVD Verdict*, 14 November 2005.
    <http://www.dvdverdict.com/reviews/bratpack.php>
7. Claudia Springer, 'The Pleasure of the Interface', in *Technology and Culture: The Film Reader*, ed. by Andrew Utterson (London: Routledge, 2005), p.82.

PRETTY IN PINK (1986)

1. Deutch's successful filmic partnerships with Hughes throughout the latter half of the 1980s are briefly discussed by Lesley Speed in 'Pastel Romances: The Teen Films of John Hughes', a valuable journal article centring on Hughes's work in the teen movie genre: Lesley Speed, 'Pastel Romances: The Teen Films of John Hughes', in *Metro Media and Education Magazine*, Issue 113/114, 1998, pp.103-110.
2. Patrick Naugle, '*Pretty in Pink*', in *DVD Verdict*, 5 September 2002.
    <http://www.dvdverdict.com/reviews/prettyinpink.php>
3. Bill Chambers, '*Pretty and Pink* and *Some Kind of Wonderful*', in *Film Freak Central*, 27 August 2000.
    <http://filmfreakcentral.net/dvdreviews/prettywonderful.htm>
4. For an exploration of the importance of music in *Pretty in Pink*, see: Justin Wyatt, *High Concept: Movies and Marketing in Hollywood* (Austin: University of Texas Press, 1994), pp.41-42.
5. Janet Maslin, 'John Hughes's *Pretty in Pink*' in *The New York Times*, 28 February 1986.
6. Roger Ebert, '*Pretty in Pink*', in *The Chicago Sun-Times*, 28 February 1986.
7. *Variety* Staff, '*Pretty in Pink*', in *Variety*, 12 February 1986.
8. Scott Tobias, '*Pretty in Pink*', in *The Onion A.V. Club*, 30 August 2002.
    <http://www.avclub.com/content/node/6367/>
9. Brendan Babish, '*Pretty in Pink*: Everything's Duckie Edition', in *DVD Verdict*, 12 September 2006.
    <http://www.dvdverdict.com/reviews/prettyinpinkse.php>
10. Chris Barsanti, '*Pretty in Pink*', in *CultureCartel.com*, 21 September 2006. <http://www.culturecartel.com/review.php?rid=10006280>
11. Dean Winkelspecht, '*Pretty in Pink*: Everything's Duckie Special Edition', in *DVD Town*, 31 August 2006.
    <http://www.dvdtown.com/reviews/pretty-in-pink/3911>
12. Ringwald discusses her career since the success of her mid-eighties

performances in an interview with Katie Holmes for the September 1999 issue of *Interview* magazine: Katie Holmes, 'Good Golly, Miss Molly! Actress Molly Ringwald', in *Interview*, September 1999.

13. Simon Reynolds, 'Ringwald hopes for *Sixteen Candles* sequel', in *Digital Spy*, 1 July 2008.
<http://www.digitalspy.co.uk/movies/a106300/ringwald-hopes-for-sixteen-candles-sequel>

FERRIS BUELLER'S DAY OFF (1986)

1. The way in which *Ferris Bueller's Day Off* fits into Hughes's wider canon of films is discussed in the following text: Quentin J. Schultze, Roy M. Anker, James D. Bratt, William D. Romanowski, John W. Worst and Lambert Zuidervaart, *Dancing in the Dark: Youth, Popular Culture, and the Electronic Media* (Grand Rapids: William B. Eerdmans Publishing, 1990), pp.230-232.

2. Janet Staiger presents a highly detailed theoretical analysis of Ferris Bueller (both the character and the film) in her valuable book *Perverse Spectators*: Janet Staiger, *Perverse Spectators: The Practices of Film Reception* (New York: New York University Press, 2000), pp.118-123.

3. Roger Ebert, '*Ferris Bueller's Day Off*', in *The Chicago Sun-Times*, 11 June 1986.

4. Rob Salem, 'Adults are the idiots in tale of two kiddies', in *The Toronto Star*, 13 June 1986.

5. Bob Thomas, 'At the Movies: *Ferris Bueller's Day Off*', in *The Associated Press*, 26 June 1986.

6. Nina Darnton, 'Screen: A Youth's *Day Off*', in *The New York Times*, 11 June 1986.

7. Patrick Goldstein, 'Director Has an Off Day in *Day Off*', in *The Los Angeles Times*, 20 June 1986.

8. Noel Megahey, '*Ferris Bueller's Day Off*: Bueller... Bueller... Edition', in *DVD Times*, 29 March 2006.
<http://www.dvdtimes.co.uk/content.php?contentid=60991>

9. Adam Smith, 'Empire Essay: *Ferris Bueller's Day Off*', in *Empire Online*, 5 May 2008.
<http://www.empireonline.com/reviews/reviewcomplete.asp?FID=132851>

10. Gary Panton, '*Ferris Bueller's Day Off*', in *Movie Gazette*, 9 July 2003.
<http://www.movie-gazette.com/cinereviews/313>

SOME KIND OF WONDERFUL (1987)

1. Roz Kaveney draws an interesting thematic comparison between *Pretty in Pink* and *Some Kind of Wonderful* in her thought-provoking text *Teen Dreams*: Roz Kaveney, *Teen Dreams: Reading Teen Film from Heathers to Veronica Mars* (London: I.B. Tauris, 2006), pp.30-40.
2. A discussion of the politics of *Some Kind of Wonderful*, in relation to Hughes's other teen movies, can be found in: Michael Ryan and Douglas Kellner, *Camera Politica: The Politics and Ideology of Contemporary Hollywood* (Indianapolis: Indiana University Press, 1988), p.120.
3. Rita Kempley, '*Some Kind of Wonderful*', in *The Washington Post*, 27 February 1987.
4. Roger Ebert, '*Some Kind of Wonderful*', in *The Chicago Sun-Times*, 27 February 1987.
5. *Variety* Staff, '*Some Kind of Wonderful*', in *Variety*, 25 February 1987.
6. Jamie S. Rich, '*Some Kind of Wonderful*: SE', in *DVD Talk*, 27 August 2006.
   <http://www.dvdtalk.com/reviews/23454/some-kind-of-wonderful-se/>
7. Brett Cullum, '*Some Kind Of Wonderful*: Special Edition', in *DVD Verdict*, 29 August 2006.
   <http://www.dvdverdict.com/reviews/somekindwonderfulse.php>
8. Patrick Naugle, '*Some Kind Of Wonderful*', in *DVD Verdict*, 19 September 2002.
   <http://www.dvdverdict.com/reviews/somekindwonderful.php>

PLANES, TRAINS AND AUTOMOBILES (1987)

1. Roger Ebert, '*Planes, Trains and Automobiles*', in *The Chicago Sun-Times*, 25 November 1987.
2. *Variety* Staff, '*Planes, Trains & Automobiles*', in *Variety*, 25 November 1987.
3. Hal Hinson, '*Planes, Trains and Automobiles*', in *The Washington Post*, 25 November 1987.
4. Janet Maslin, '*Planes, Trains and Automobiles*', in *The New York Times*, 25 November 1987.
5. Norman Short, '*Planes, Trains and Automobiles*', in *DVD Verdict*, 4 December 2000.
   <http://www.dvdverdict.com/reviews/planestrains.php>
6. Gary Panton, '*Planes, Trains and Automobiles*', in *Movie Gazette*, 28

May 2003.
<*http://www.movie-gazette.com/cinereviews/186*>

7.   Jeffrey M. Anderson, '*Planes, Trains & Automobiles*', in *Combustible Celluloid*, 15 November 2006.
     <*http://www.combustiblecelluloid.com/classic/planestrains.shtml*>
8.   Ryan Cracknell, '*Planes, Trains and Automobiles*', in *Movie Views*, 4 December 2003.
<*http://www.movie-
     views.com/films/P/planes_trains_and_automobiles.html*>

SHE'S HAVING A BABY (1988)

1.   The intertextuality of Hughes's films, including *She's Having a Baby*, is discussed in detail by Justin Wyatt in his book *High Concept: Movies and Marketing in Hollywood*: Justin Wyatt, *High Concept: Movies and Marketing in Hollywood* (Austin: University of Texas Press, 1994), pp.58-60.
2.   Hal Hinson, '*She's Having a Baby*', in *The Washington Post*, 6 February 1988.
3.   Roger Ebert, '*She's Having a Baby*', in *The Chicago Sun-Times*, 5 February 1988.
4.   *Variety* Staff, '*She's Having a Baby*', in *Variety*, 3 February 1988.
5.   Norman Short, '*She's Having a Baby*', in *DVD Verdict*, 11 December 2000.
     <*http://www.dvdverdict.com/reviews/sheshavingbaby.php*>
6.   David Nusair, '*She's Having a Baby*', in *Reel Film*, 1 July 2006.
     <*http://www.reelfilm.com/mini58.htm#she*>
7.   Ian Waldron-Mantgani, 'Retrospectives: *She's Having a Baby*', in *The UK Critic*, November 2003.
     <*http://www.ukcritic.com/sheshavingababy_1988.html*>

THE GREAT OUTDOORS (1988)

1.   Janet Maslin, 'Country Life for Aykroyd and Candy', in *The New York Times*, 17 June 1988.
2.   Hal Hinson, '*The Great Outdoors*', in *The Washington Post*, 17 June 1988.
3.   Chris Parry, '*The Great Outdoors*', in *eFilmCritic.com*, 31 July 1999.
     <*http://efilmcritic.com/review.php?movie=1115*>

4.   John Stanley, '*The Great Outdoors*', in *DVD Authority*, July 1999.
    <*http://www.dvdauthority.com/reviews.asp?reviewID=1820*>

UNCLE BUCK (1989)

1.   Vincent Canby, 'An Uncouth Uncle Against the Suburban Grain', in
    The New York Times, 16 August 1989.
2.   Jay Carr, 'Candy's Back with *Buck*', in *The Boston Globe*, 16 August
    1989.
3.   Chris Willman, '*Uncle Buck*: John Hughes' Valentine to Teenhood', in
    The Los Angeles Times, 16 August 1989.
4.   Henry Mietkiewicz, 'Time to cast Candy against type', in *The Toronto
    Star*, 16 August 1989.
5.   Mike Clark, 'Candy's *Buck* is a victim of comedy devaluation', in
    USA Today, 16 August 1989.
6.   Peter Travers, '*Uncle Buck*', in *Rolling Stone*, 7 September 1989.
7.   Gavin Turner, '*Uncle Buck*', in *DVD.net.au*, 2003.
    <*http://www.dvd.net.au/review.cgi?review_id=804*>
8.   Alex F., '*Uncle Buck*', in *DVD Bits*, 18 August 2001.
    <*http://www.dvdbits.com/reviews.asp?id=669*>
9.   Doug Pratt, '*Uncle Buck*', in *DVD Laser*, September 2004.
    <*http://www.dvdlaser.com/search/detail.cfm?id=2192*>

NATIONAL LAMPOON'S CHRISTMAS VACATION (1989)

1.   Roger Ebert, '*National Lampoon's Christmas Vacation*', in *The Chicago
    Sun-Times*, 1 December 1989.
2.   Janet Maslin, 'On *Vacation* Once Again', in *The New York Times*, 1
    December 1989.
3.   Rita Kempley, '*National Lampoon's Christmas Vacation*', in *The
    Washington Post*, 1 December 1989.
4.   *Variety* Staff, '*National Lampoon's Christmas Vacation*', in *Variety*, 1
    December 1989.
5.   Chris Hicks, '*National Lampoon's Christmas Vacation*', in *Deseret
    News*, 16 December 2002.
6.   Patrick Naugle, '*National Lampoon's Christmas Vacation*: Special
    Edition', in *DVD Verdict*, 16 October 2003.
    <*http://www.dvdverdict.com/reviews/christmasvacationse.php*>
7.   Daniel Stephens, '*National Lampoon's Christmas Vacation*', in *DVD*

Times, 17 November 2003.
<*http://www.dvdtimes.co.uk/content.php?contentid=6068*>
8. Ryan Arthur, '*National Lampoon's Christmas Vacation*', in
    eFilmCritic.com, 15 October 1998.
    <*http://efilmcritic.com/review.php?movie=1116*>

CONCLUSION

1. Jaime Clark, 'Introduction', in *Don't You Forget About Me:
    Contemporary Writers on the Films of John Hughes*, ed. by Jaime Clarke
    (New York: Simon Spotlight, 2007), pp.1-3.
2. Michael Ryan and Douglas Kellner, *Camera Politica: The Politics and
    Ideology of Contemporary Hollywood* (Indianapolis: Indiana
    University Press, 1988), p.120.
3. Bob Batchelor and Scott Stoddart, *The 1980s* (Westport: Greenwood
    Publishing Group, 2006), pp.28-30.
4. Stephen Prince, *A New Pot of Gold: Hollywood Under the Electronic
    Rainbow, 1980-1989* (Berkeley: University of California Press, 2002),
    pp.211-13.
5. Leger Grindon, 'Movies and Fissures in Reagan's America', in
    American Cinema of the 1980s: Themes and Variations, ed. by Stephen
    Prince (Chapel Hill: Rutgers University Press, 2007), pp-156-60.
6. Maura Kelly, 'John Hughes: The films he created in the decade of
    greed made adolescent angst funny and bearable without
    romanticising it', in *Salon*, 17 July 2001.
7. Tim Appelo, 'John Huge: John Hughes' view from the top', in
    Entertainment Weekly, 251, 2 December 1994.
8. Mandi Bierly, 'PopWatch Blog: John Hughes Lost, Long Duk Dong
    Found', in *Entertainment Weekly Online*, 25 March 2008.
    <*http://popwatch.ew.com/popwatch/2008/03/john-hughes.html*>

CHRONOLOGICAL FILMOGRAPHY

NATIONAL LAMPOON'S CLASS REUNION (1982)

Production Company: American Broadcasting Company.
Distributor: Twentieth Century Fox.
Director: Michael Miller.
Producer: Matty Simmons.
Screenplay: John Hughes.
Cinematography: Philip H. Lathrop.
Original Score: Peter Bernstein and Mark Goldenberg.
Set Decoration: Mel Cooper.
Running Time: 84 minutes.
Main Cast: Gerrit Graham (Bob Spinnaker), Michael Lerner (Dr Robert Young), Misty Rowe (Cindy Shears), Blackie Dammett (Walter Baylor), Fred McCarren (Gary Nash), Miriam Flynn (Bunny Packard), Stephen Furst (Hubert Downs), Mews Small (Iris Augen), Shelley Smith (Meredith Modess), Zane Buzby (Delores Salk), Jacklyn Zeman (Jane Washburn), Barry Diamond (Chip Hendrix), Art Evans (Carl Clapton), Marla Pennington (Mary Beth), Randy Powell (Jeff Barnes), Anne Ramsey (Mrs Tabazooski), Chuck Berry (Himself), Richard Hawley (Hary Bower), Gary Hibbard (Fritz Shears), Steve Tracy (Milt Friedman), Isabel West (Gloria Barnes).

MR MOM (1983)

Production Company: Sherwood Productions.
Distributor: Twentieth Century Fox.
Director: Stan Dragoti.
Producers: Lynn Loring and Lauren Shuler.
Co-Producer: Harry Colomby.
Associate Producers: Art Levinson and Bill Wilson.
Executive Producer: Aaron Spelling.
Screenplay: John Hughes.
Film Editor: Patrick Kennedy.
Cinematography: Victor J. Kemper.
Unit Production Manager: Art Levinson.
Original Score: Lee Holdridge.
Production Design: Alfred Sweeney.
Casting: Lisa Freiberger.
Set Designer: Sig Tingloff.
Costume Design: Norman A. Burza, Linda Matthews and Nolan

Miller.

Running Time: 91 minutes.

Main Cast: Michael Keaton (Jack), Teri Garr (Caroline), Frederick Koehler (Alex), Taliesin Jaffe (Kenny), Courtney White (Megan), Brittany White (Megan), Martin Mull (Ron), Ann Jillian (Joan), Jeffrey Tambor (Jinx), Christopher Lloyd (Larry), Tom Leopold (Stan), Graham Jarvis (Humphries), Carolyn Seymour (Eve), Michael Alaimo (Bert), Valri Bromfield (Doris), Charles Woolf (Phil), Miriam Flynn (Annette).

NATIONAL LAMPOON'S VACATION (1983)

Production Company: Warner Brothers.
Distributor: Warner Brothers.
Director: Harold Ramis.
Producer: Matty Simmons.
Associate Producer: Robert Grand.
Screenplay: John Hughes, based on his short story 'Vacation '58'.
Film Editor: Pem Herring.
Cinematography: Victor J. Kemper.
Unit Production Manager: Robert Grand.
Original Score: Ralph Burns.
Production Design: Jack Collis.
Casting: Susan Arnold and Phyllis Huffman.
Set Decoration: Joe Mitchell.
Costume Design: Robert Harris Jr and Barbara Siebert.
Running Time: 98 minutes.

Main Cast: Chevy Chase (Clark Griswold), Beverly D'Angelo (Ellen Griswold), Imogene Coca (Aunt Edna), Randy Quaid (Cousin Eddie), Anthony Michael Hall (Russell 'Rusty' Griswold), Dana Barron (Audrey Griswold), Eddie Bracken (Roy Walley), Brian Doyle-Murray (Kamp Komfort Clerk), Miriam Flynn (Cousin Catherine), James Keach (Motorcycle Cop), Eugene Levy (Car Salesman), Frank McRae (Grover), John Candy (Lasky), Christie Brinkley (The Girl in the Ferrari), Jane Krakowski (Cousin Vicki), John Navin (Cousin Dale), Nathan Cook (Man Giving Directions), Christopher Jackson (Pimp), Mickey Jones (Mechanic), John Diehl (Assistant Mechanic), Jeannie Dimter Barton (Dodge City Cashier), Randolph Dreyfuss (Wyatt Earp), Virgil Wyaco II (Indian), Gerry Black (Davenport).

NATE AND HAYES (1983)

Production Company: Paramount Pictures.
Distributor: Paramount Pictures.
Director: Ferdinand Fairfax.
Producers: Lloyd Phillips and Rob Whitehouse.
Screenplay: John Hughes and David Odell; screen story by David
Odell, based on a story by Lloyd Phillips.
Film Editor: John Shirley.
Cinematography: Tony Imi.
Production Manager: Jane Gilbert.
Production Supervisor: Ted Lloyd.
Original Score: Trevor Jones.
Production Design: Maurice Cain.
Casting: Celestia Fox and Penny Perry.
Art Direction: Dan Hennah and Rick Kofoed.
Costume Design: Norma Moriceau.
Running Time: 100 minutes.
Main Cast: Tommy Lee Jones (Captain Bully Hayes), Michael O'Keefe
(Nathaniel Williamson), Max Phipps (Ben Pease), Jenny Seagrove (Sophie),
Grant Tilly (Count Von Rittenberg), Peter Rowley (Louis Beck), Bill
Johnson (Reverend Williamson), Kate Harcourt (Mrs Williamson), Reg
Ruka (Moaka), Roy Billing (Auctioneer), Bruce Allpress (Mr Blake),
David Letch (Ratbag), Prince Tui Teka (King of Ponape), Pudji Waseso
(Fong), Peter Vere-Jones (Gunboat Captain), Tom Vanderlaan (Count's
Lieutenant), Mark Hadlow (Gun Operator), Phillip Gordon (Timmy),
Norman Fairley (Pegleg), Warwick Simmons (Pog).

SIXTEEN CANDLES (1984)

Production Company: Channel Productions/Universal Pictures.
Distributor: Universal Pictures.
Director: John Hughes.
Producer: Hilton A. Green.
Associate Producer: Michelle Manning.
Executive Producer: Ned Tanen.
Screenplay: John Hughes.
Film Editor: Edward Warschilka.
Cinematography: Bobby Byrne.
Unit Production Manager: Daniel Franklin.

Original Score: Ira Newborn.
Production Design: John W. Corso.
Casting: Jackie Burch.
Set Decoration: Jennifer Polito.
Costume Design: Mark Peterson and Marla Denise Schlom.
Running Time: 93 minutes.
Main Cast: Molly Ringwald (Samantha Baker), Justin Henry (Mike Baker), Michael Schoeffling (Jake Ryan), Haviland Morris (Caroline Mulford), Gedde Watanabe (Long Duk Dong), Anthony Michael Hall (Farmer Ted/'The Geek'), Paul Dooley (Jim Baker), Carlin Glynn (Brenda Baker), Blanche Baker (Ginny Baker), Edward Andrews (Howard Baker), Billie Bird (Dorothy Baker), Carole Cook (Grandma Helen), Max Showalter (Grandpa Fred), Liane Curtis (Randy), John Cusack (Bryce), Darren Harris (Cliff), Deborah Pollack (Marlene), Jonathan Chapin (Jimmy Montrose), Jami Gertz (Robin), Cinnamon Idles (Sara Baker), Beth Ringwald (Patty).

THE BREAKFAST CLUB (1985)

Production Company: A&M Films/Universal Pictures.
Distributor: Universal Pictures.
Director: John Hughes.
Producers: John Hughes and Ned Tanen.
Co-Producer: Michelle Manning.
Executive Producer: Gil Friesen and Andrew Meyer.
Screenplay: John Hughes.
Film Editor: Dede Allen.
Director of Photography: Thomas Del Ruth.
Unit Production Managers: John C. Chulay and Richard Hashimoto.
Original Score: Keith Forsey.
Production Design: John W. Corso.
Casting: Jackie Burch.
Set Decoration: Jennifer Polito.
Costume Design: Marilyn Vance.
Running Time: 97 minutes.
Main Cast: Emilio Estevez (Andrew Clark), Anthony Michael Hall (Brian Ralph Johnson), Judd Nelson (John Bender), Molly Ringwald (Claire Standish), Ally Sheedy (Allison Reynolds), Paul Gleason (Principal Richard Vernon), John Kapelos (Carl the Janitor), Ron Dean (Mr Clark), Tim Gamble (Mr Standish), Mercedes Hall (Mrs Johnson), Mary

Christian (Brian's Sister), Perry Crawford (Mr Reynolds), Fran Gargano (Mrs Reynolds).

NATIONAL LAMPOON'S EUROPEAN VACATION (1985)

Production Company: Warner Brothers.
Distributor: Warner Brothers.
Director: Amy Heckerling.
Producer: Matty Simmons.
Co-Producer: Stuart Cornfeld.
Screenplay: John Hughes and Robert Klane, from a story by John Hughes.
Film Editor: Pembroke J. Herring.
Director of Photography: Bob Paynter.
Original Score: Charles Fox.
Production Design: Bob Cartwright.
Casting: Marion Dougherty.
Art Direction: Alan Tomkins and Leslie Tomkins.
Set Decoration: Simon Wakefield.
Costume Design: Graham Williams.
Running Time: 94 minutes.
Main Cast: Chevy Chase (Clark Griswold), Beverly D'Angelo (Ellen Griswold), Dana Hill (Audrey Griswold), Jason Lively (Russell 'Rusty' Griswold), John Astin (Kent Winkdale), William Zabka (Jack), Julie Wooldridge (Princess Diana), Peter Hugo (Prince Charles), Jeannette Charles (Queen Elizabeth), Derek Deadman (Taxi Driver), Mel Smith (Hotel Manager), Robbie Coltrane (Man in the Bathroom), Maureen Lipman (Lady in the Bed), Eric Idle (The Bike Rider), Elizabeth Arlen (Mrs Garland), David Gersh (Mr Garland), Jacques Maury (Hotel's Assistant Manager), Philippe Sturbelle (Café Waiter), Sylvie Badalati (Rusty's French Girl), Didier Pain (Video Camera Thief), William Millowitsch (Fritz Spritz), Erica Wackernagel (Helga Spritz), Claudia Neidig (Claudia), Victor Neidig (The Thief), Massimo Sarchielli (The Other Thief), Jorge Krimer (Unfortunate Express Agent), Moon Zappa (Rusty's California Girl).

WEIRD SCIENCE (1985)

Production Company: Universal Pictures.
Distributor: Universal Pictures.
Director: John Hughes.
Producer: Joel Silver.
Associate Producer: Jane Vickerilla.
Screenplay: John Hughes.
Film Editors: Chris Lebenzon, Scott Wallace and Mark Warner.
Cinematography: Matthew F. Leonetti.
Unit Production Manager: Don Zepfel.
Original Score: Ira Newborn.
Production Design: John W. Corso.
Casting: Jackie Burch.
Art Direction: James Allen.
Set Decoration: Jennifer Polito.
Costume Design: Marilyn Vance.
Running Time: 94 minutes.
Main Cast: Anthony Michael Hall (Gary Wallace), Kelly LeBrock (Lisa), Ilan Mitchell-Smith (Wyatt Donnelly), Bill Paxton (Chet Donnelly), Suzanne Snyder (Deb), Judie Aronson (Hilly), Robert Downey (Ian), Robert Rusler (Max), Vernon Wells (Lord General), Britt Leach (Al Wallace), Barbara Lang (Lucy Wallace), Michael Berryman (Mutant Biker), Ivor Barry (Henry Donnelly), Anne Bernadette Coyle (Carmen Donnelly), Suzy J. Kellems (Gymnast), John Kapelos (Dino), Jill Whitlow (Susan), Wally Ward (Art), D'Mitch Davis (Bartender), Kym Malin (Girl Playing Piano), Jennifer Balgobin (Biker Girl), Jeff Jensen (Metal Face), Doug MacHugh (Wyatt's Father), Pamela Gordon (Wyatt's Mother).

PRETTY IN PINK (1986)

Production Company: Paramount Pictures.
Distributor: Paramount Pictures.
Director: Howard Deutch.
Producer: Lauren Shuler.
Associate Producer: Jane Vickerilla.
Executive Producers: Michael Chinich and John Hughes.
Screenplay: John Hughes.
Film Editor: Richard Marks.
Cinematography: Tak Fujimoto.

Unit Production Manager: Arne Schmidt.
Original Score: Michael Gore.
Production Design: John W. Corso.
Casting: Paula Herold and Marci Liroff.
Set Decoration: Jennifer Polito and Bruce Weintraub.
Costume Design: Marilyn Vance.
Running Time: 96 minutes.
Main Cast: Molly Ringwald (Andie Walsh), Harry Dean Stanton (Jack Walsh), Jon Cryer (Phil 'Duckie' Dale), Annie Potts (Iona), James Spader (Steff), Andrew McCarthy (Blane McDonnagh), Jim Haynie (Donnelly), Alexa Kenin (Jena Hoeman), Kate Vernon (Benny Hanson), Andrew 'Dice' Clay (Bouncer at CATS), Emily Longstreth (Kate), Margaret Colin (English Teacher), Jamie Anders (Terrence), Gina Gershon (Trombley), Audre Johnston (Benny's Mother), Maggie Roswell (Mrs Dietz), Dweezil Zappa (Simon), Kristy Swanson (Duckette), Kevin D. Lindsay (Kevin).

FERRIS BUELLER'S DAY OFF (1986)

Production Company: Paramount Productions.
Distributor: Paramount Productions.
Director: John Hughes.
Producers: John Hughes and Tom Jacobson.
Associate Producer: Jane Vickerilla.
Executive Producer: Michael Cinich.
Screenplay: John Hughes.
Film Editor: Paul Hirsch.
Cinematography: Tak Fujimoto.
Unit Production Manager: Arne Schmidt.
Original Music: Arthur Baker, Ira Newborn and John Robie.
Production Design: John W. Corso.
Casting: Janet Hirshenson and Jane Jenkins.
Set Decoration: Jennifer Polito.
Costume Design: Marilyn Vance.
Running Time: 103 minutes.
Main Cast: Matthew Broderick (Ferris Bueller), Alan Ruck (Cameron Frye), Mia Sara (Sloane Peterson), Jeffrey Jones (Ed Rooney), Jennifer Grey (Jeanie Bueller), Cindy Pickett (Katie Bueller), Lyman Ward (Tom Bueller), Edie McClurg (Grace), Charlie Sheen (Boy in Police Station), Ben Stein (Economics Teacher), Del Close (English Teacher), Virginia Capers (Florence Sparrow), Richard Edson (Garage Attendant), Larry Flash

Jenkins (Attendant's Co-Pilot), Kristy Swanson (Simone Adamley), Lisa Bellard (Economics Student), Max Perlich (Anderson), T. Scott Coffee (Adams), Jonathan Schmock (Chez Quis Maitre D'), Joey Viera (Pizza Man).

SOME KIND OF WONDERFUL (1987)

Production Company: Hughes Entertainment/Paramount Pictures.
Distributor: Paramount Pictures.
Director: Howard Deutch.
Producer: John Hughes.
Executive Producers: Michael Cinich and Ronald Colby.
Screenplay: John Hughes.
Film Editor: Bud Smith and M. Scott Smith.
Cinematography: Jan Kiesser.
Unit Production Managers: Jerry Baerwitz and Ronald Colby.
Original Score: Stephen Hague and John Musser.
Production Design: Josan Russo.
Casting: Judith Wiener.
Art Direction: Gregory Pickrell.
Set Decoration: Linda Spheeris.
Costume Design: Marilyn Vance-Straker.
Running Time: 93 minutes.
Main Cast: Eric Stoltz (Keith Nelson), Mary Stuart Masterson (Watts), Lea Thompson (Amanda Jones), Craig Sheffer (Hardy Jenns), John Ashton (Cliff Nelson), Elias Koteas (Duncan), Molly Hagan (Shayne), Maddie Corman (Laura Nelson), Jane Elliot (Carol Nelson), Candace Cameron (Cindy Nelson), Chynna Phillips (Mia), Scott Coffey (Ray), Carmine Caridi (Museum Guard), Lee Garlington (Gym Instructor), Laura Leigh Hughes (Holly), Peter Elbling (Maitre'D), Patricia Gale (Mrs Gale), Kenneth Kimmins (Detention Teacher).

PLANES, TRAINS AND AUTOMOBILES (1987)

Production Company: Hughes Entertainment/Paramount Pictures.
Distributor: Paramount Pictures.
Director: John Hughes.
Producer: John Hughes.
Associate Producer: Bill Brown.

Executive Producers: Michael Cinich and Neil Machlis.
Screenplay: John Hughes.
Film Editor: Paul Hirsch.
Cinematography: Don Peterman.
Unit Production Manager: Neil A. Machlis.
Original Score: Ira Newborn.
Production Design: John W. Corso.
Casting: Janet Hirshenson and Jane Jenkins.
Art Direction: Harold Michelson.
Set Decoration: Jane Bogart and Linda Spheeris.
Costume Design: April Ferry.
Running Time: 93 minutes.
Main Cast: Steve Martin (Neal Page), John Candy (Del Griffith), Laila Robins (Susan Page), Michael McKean (State Trooper), Kevin Bacon (Taxi Racer), Dylan Baker (Owen), Carol Bruce (Joy Page), Olivia Burnette (Marti Page), Diana Douglas (Peg), Larry Hankin (Doobie), Richard Herd (Walt), Matthew Lawrence (Little Neal Page), Edie McClurg (Car Rental Agent), George O. Petrie (Martin Page), Gary Riley (Motel Thief), Charles Tyner (Gus Mooney), Susan Isaacs (Marie), Lulie Newcomb (Owen's Wife), Bill Erwin (Man on Plane).

SHE'S HAVING A BABY (1988)

Production Company: Hughes Entertainment/Paramount Pictures.
Distributor: Paramount Pictures.
Director: John Hughes.
Producer: John Hughes.
Associate Producer: Bill Brown.
Executive Producer: Ronald Colby.
Screenplay: John Hughes.
Film Editor: Alan Heim.
Cinematography: Don Peterman.
Production Managers: Ronald Colby and James Herbert.
Original Score: Stewart Copeland.
Production Design: John W. Corso.
Casting: Jane Alderman, Janet Hirshenson and Jane Jenkins.
Set Decoration: Jennifer Polito.
Costume Design: April Ferry.
Running Time: 106 minutes.
Main Cast: Kevin Bacon (Jefferson Edward Briggs), Elizabeth

McGovern (Kristen Briggs), Alec Baldwin (Davis McDonald), William
Windom (Russ Bainbridge), Holland Taylor (Sarah Briggs), Cathryn
Damon (Gayle Bainbridge), John Ashton (Ken), James Ray (Jim Briggs),
Dennis Dugan (Bill), Larry Hankin (Hank), Nancy Lenehan (Cynthia),
Isabel Lorca (Fantasy Girl), Reba McKinney (Grandmother), Bill Erwin
(Grandfather), Anthony Mockus Sr (Minister), Steve Tannen (Man with
Bike), Neal Bacon (Young Jake), Laure Aronica (Young Kristy), Valeri
Breiman (Erin), Al Leong (Photographer), Lili Taylor (Girl at Medical
Lab), Sherry Narens (Nurse at Medical Lab), Kellye Nakahara (Nurse at
Hospital), Ellen Dweck (Receptionist).

THE GREAT OUTDOORS (1988)

Production Company: Hughes Entertainment/Universal Pictures.
Distributor: Universal Pictures.
Director: Howard Deutch.
Producer: Arne Schmidt.
Associate Producers: Stephen Lim and Elena Spiotta.
Executive Producers: John Hughes and Tom Jacobson.
Screenplay: John Hughes.
Film Editor: Seth Flaum and Tom Rolf.
Cinematography: Ric Waite.
Unit Production Manager: Charles Newirth.
Original Score: Thomas Newman.
Production Design: John W. Corso.
Set Decoration: John Anderson.
Costume Design: Marilyn Vance.
Running Time: 90 minutes.
Main Cast: Dan Aykroyd (Roman Craig), John Candy (Chet Ripley),
Stephanie Faracy (Connie Ripley), Annette Bening (Kate Craig), Chris
Young (Buck Ripley), Ian Giatti (Ben Ripley), Hilary Gordon (Cara Craig),
Rebecca Gordon (Mara Craig), Robert Prosky (Wally), Zoaunne LeRoy
(Juanita), Lucy Deakins (Cammie), Nancy Lenehan (Waitress), John Bloom
(Jimbo), Lewis Arquette (Herm), Britt Leach (Reg), Cliff Bemis (Boat Yard
Owner), Paul Hansen (Hot Dog Vendor).

UNCLE BUCK (1989)

Production Company: Hughes Entertainment/Universal Pictures.
Distributor: Universal Pictures.
Director: John Hughes.
Producers: John Hughes and Tom Jacobson.
Associate Producers: Bill Brown and Ramey E. Ward.
Screenplay: John Hughes.
Film Editors: Lou Lombardo, Tony Lombardo and Peck Prior.
Cinematography: Ralf Bode.
Unit Production Managers: Alan C. Blomquist, Ray Hartwick and Tom Udell.
Original Score: Ira Newborn.
Production Design: John W. Corso and Doug Kraner.
Casting: Risa Bramon and Billy Hopkins.
Set Decoration: Dan May.
Costume Design: Marilyn Vance-Straker.
Running Time: 100 minutes.
Main Cast: John Candy (Buck Russell), Jean Louisa Kelly (Tia Russell), Gaby Hoffman (Maizy Russell), Macaulay Culkin (Miles Russell), Amy Madigan (Chanice Kobolowski), Elaine Bromka (Cindy Russell), Garrett M. Brown (Bob Russell), Laurie Metcalf (Marcie Dahlgren-Frost), Jay Underwood (Bug), Brian Tarantina (E. Roger Coswell), Mike Starr (Pooter the Clown), Suzanne Shepherd (Mrs Anita Hoargarth), William Windom (Mr Hatfield), Dennis Cockrum (Pal).

NATIONAL LAMPOON'S CHRISTMAS VACATION (1989)

Production Company: Hughes Entertainment/Warner Brothers.
Distributor: Warner Brothers.
Director: Jeremiah Chechik.
Producers: John Hughes and Tom Jacobson.
Associate Producers: William S. Beasley, Mauri Syd Gayton and Ramey E. Ward.
Executive Producer: Matty Simmons.
Screenplay: John Hughes.
Film Editor: Jerry Greenberg and Michael Stevenson.
Director of Photography: Thomas Ackerman.
Unit Production Manager: William S. Beasley.
Original Score: Angelo Badalamenti.

Production Design: Stephen Marsh.

Casting: Risa Bramon, Billy Hopkins and Heidi Levitt.

Art Direction: Beala B. Neel.

Set Decoration: Lisa Fischer.

Costume Design: Michael Kaplan.

Running Time: 97 minutes.

Main Cast: Chevy Chase (Clark Griswold), Beverly D'Angelo (Ellen Griswold), Juliette Lewis (Audrey Griswold), Johnny Galecki (Russell 'Rusty' Griswold), John Randolph (Clark Wilhelm Griswold Sr), Diane Ladd (Nora Griswold), E.G. Marshall (Art Smith), Doris Roberts (Frances Smith), Randy Quaid (Cousin Eddie Johnson), Miriam Flynn (Cousin Catherine Johnson), Cody Burger (Cousin Rocky Johnson), Ellen Hamilton Latzen (Cousin Ruby Sue Johnson), William Hickey (Uncle Lewis), Mae Questel (Aunt Bethany), Sam McMurray (Bill), Nicholas Guest (Todd Chester), Julia Louis-Dreyfus (Margo Chester), Nicolette Scorsese (Mary), Keith MacKechnie (Delivery Boy), Brian Doyle-Murray (Frank Shirley), Natalia Nogulich (Helen Shirley), Michael Kaufman (Young Executive).

THE FILMS OF JOHN HUGHES: A TIMELINE

1. *National Lampoon's Class Reunion* (1982)
   Dir. Michael Miller
   (as screenwriter)

2. *Mr Mom* (1982)
   Dir. Stan Dragoti
   (as screenwriter)

3. *National Lampoon's Vacation* (1983)
   Dir. Harold Ramis
   (as screenwriter)

4. *Nate and Hayes* (1983)
   Dir. Ferdinand Fairfax
   (as screenwriter)

5. *Sixteen Candles* (1984)
   Dir. John Hughes
   (as director and screenwriter)

6. *The Breakfast Club* (1985)
   Dir. John Hughes
   (as producer, director and screenwriter)

7. *National Lampoon's European Vacation* (1985)
   Dir. Amy Heckerling
   (as screenwriter)

8. *Weird Science* (1985)
   Dir. John Hughes
   (as director and screenwriter)

9. *Pretty in Pink* (1986)
   Dir. Howard Deutch
   (as executive producer and screenwriter)

10. *Ferris Bueller's Day Off* (1986)
    Dir. John Hughes
    (as producer, director and screenwriter)

11. *Some Kind of Wonderful* (1987)

Dir. Howard Deutch
(as producer and screenwriter)

12. *Planes, Trains and Automobiles* (1987)
Dir. John Hughes
(as producer, director and screenwriter)

13. *She's Having a Baby* (1988)
Dir. John Hughes
(as producer, director and screenwriter)

14. *The Great Outdoors* (1988)
Dir. Howard Deutch
(as executive producer and screenwriter)

15. *Uncle Buck* (1989)
Dir. John Hughes
(as producer, director and screenwriter)

16. *National Lampoon's Christmas Vacation* (1989)
Dir. Jeremiah S. Chechik
(as producer and screenwriter)

17. *Home Alone* (1990)
Dir. Chris Columbus
(as producer and screenwriter)

18. *Career Opportunities* (1991)
Dir. Bryan Gordon
(as producer and screenwriter)

19. *Only the Lonely* (1991)
Dir. Chris Columbus
(as producer)

20. *Dutch* (1991)
Dir. Peter Faiman
(as producer and screenwriter)

21. *Curly Sue* (1991)
Dir. John Hughes

(as producer, director and screenwriter)

22. *Beethoven* (1992)
    Dir. Brian Levant
    (as screenwriter, writing as Edmond Dantès)

23. *Home Alone 2: Lost in New York* (1992)
    Dir. Chris Columbus
    (as producer and screenwriter)

24. *Dennis the Menace* (1993)
    Dir. Nick Castle
    (as producer and screenwriter)

25. *Baby's Day Out* (1994)
    Dir. Patrick Read Johnson
    (as producer and screenwriter)

26. *Miracle on 34th Street* (1994)
    Dir. Les Mayfield
    (as producer and screenwriter)

27. *101 Dalmatians* (1996)
    Dir. Stephen Herek
    (as producer and screenwriter)

28. *Flubber* (1997)
    Dir. Les Mayfield
    (as producer and screenwriter)

29. *Home Alone 3* (1997)
    Dir. Raja Gosnell
    (as producer and screenwriter)

30. *Reach the Rock* (1998)
    Dir. William Ryan
    (as producer and screenwriter)

31. *Les Visiteurs en Amérique/Just Visiting* (2001)
    Dir. Jean-Marie Poiré
    (as screenwriter)

32. *New Port South* (2001)
    Dir. Kyle Cooper
    (as executive producer)

33. *Maid in Manhattan* (2002)
    Dir. Wayne Wang
    (story, writing as Edmond Dantès)

34. *Drillbit Taylor* (2008)
    Dir. Steven Brill
    (story, writing as Edmond Dantès)

SELECT BIBLIOGRAPHY

BOOKS AND REFERENCE GUIDES

Annesley, James, *Blank Fictions: Consumerism, Culture and the Contemporary American Novel* (London: Pluto Press, 1998).

Austin, Joe, and Michael Nevin Willard, eds, *Generations of Youth: Youth Cultures and History in Twentieth-Century America* (New York: NYU Press, 1998).

Batchelor, Bob, and Scott Stoddart, *The 1980s* (Westport: Greenwood Publishing Group, 2006).

Base, Ron, and David Haslam, *The Movies of the Eighties* (London: Portland, 1990).

Benshoff, Harry M., and Sean Griffin, *America on Film: Representing Race, Class, Gender and Sexuality at the Movies* (Oxford: Blackwell Publishing, 2004).

Bernstein, Jonathan, *Pretty in Pink: The Golden Age of Teenage Movies* (New York: St. Martin's Griffin, 1997).

Browne, Ray Broadus, and Pat Browne, *The Guide to United States Popular Culture* (Madison: Popular Press, 2001).

Clarke, Jaime, ed., *Don't You Forget About Me: Contemporary Writers on the Films of John Hughes* (New York: Simon Spotlight, 2007).

Docker, John, *Postmodernism and Popular Culture: A Cultural History* (Cambridge: Cambridge University Press, 1994).

Ellis, John, *Visible Fictions: Cinema, Television, Video* (London: Routledge, 1989) [1982].

Falk, Gerhard, and Ursula A. Falk, *Youth Culture and the Generation Gap* (New York: Algora Publishing, 2005).

Frow, John, *Genre* (London: Routledge, 2006).

Hardy, Phil, ed., *The Aurum Film Encyclopedia: Science Fiction* (London: Aurum Press, 1995).

Hollows, Joanne, and Mark Jancovich, eds, *Approaches to Popular Film* (Manchester: Manchester University Press, 1995).

Hurd, Mary G., *Women Directors and Their Films* (Westport: Greenwood Publishing Group, 2006).

Jordan, Chris, *Movies and the Reagan Presidency: Success and Ethics* (Westport: Greenwood Publishing Group, 2003).

Kael, Pauline, *Hooked: Film Writings, 1985-88* (London: Marion Boyars Publishers, 1990).

Kael, Pauline, *State of the Art* (London: Marion Boyars Publishers, 1987).

Karp, Josh, *A Futile and Stupid Gesture: How Doug Kenney and National Lampoon Changed Comedy Forever* (Chicago: Chicago Review Press, 2006).

Kaveney, Roz, *Teen Dreams: Reading Teen Film from Heathers to Veronica Mars* (London: I.B. Tauris, 2006).

Lewis, Jon, *The Road to Romance & Ruin: Teen Films and Youth Culture* (London: Routledge, 1992).

Loukides, Paul, and Linda K. Fuller, eds, *Beyond the Stars: Studies in American Popular Film Volume 5: Themes and Ideologies in American Popular Film* (Madison: Popular Press, 1996).

Mallan, Kerry, and Sharyn Pearce, *Youth Cultures: Texts, Images, and Identities* (Westport: Greenwood Publishing Group, 2003).

Mansour, David, *From Abba to Zoom: A Pop Culture Encyclopedia of the Late 20th Century* (Riverside: Andrews McMeel Publishing, 2005).

McMahon, Robert, *The Cold War: A Very Short Introduction* (Oxford: Oxford University Press, 2003).

Miller, Toby, and Robert Stam, eds., *A Companion to Film Theory* (Oxford: Blackwell, 2004) [1999].

Mitchell, Jeremy, and Richard Maidment, eds., *The United States in the Twentieth Century: Culture* (London: Hodder and Stoughton, 1994).

Müller, Jürgen, *Movies of the 80s* (Köln: Taschen Books, 2002).

Neale, Steve, *Genre and Hollywood* (London: Routledge, 2000).

Palmer, William J., *The Films of the Eighties: A Social History* (Carbondale: Southern Illinois University Press, 1993).

Prince, Stephen, *A New Pot of Gold: Hollywood Under the Electronic Rainbow, 1980-1989* (Berkeley: University of California Press, 2002).

Prince, Stephen, ed., *American Cinema of the 1980s: Themes and Variations* (Chapel Hill: Rutgers University Press, 2007).

Quart, Alissa, *Branded: The Buying and Selling of Teenagers* (Jackson: Basic Books, 2004).

Rettenmund, Matthew, *Totally Awesome 80s* (New York: Saint Martin's Press, 1996).

Ryan, Michael, and Douglas Kellner, *Camera Politica: The Politics and Ideology of Contemporary Hollywood* (Indianapolis: Indiana University Press, 1988).

Schultze, Quentin J., Roy M. Anker, James D. Bratt, William D. Romanowski, John W. Worst and Lambert Zuidervaart, *Dancing in the Dark: Youth, Popular Culture, and the Electronic Media* (Grand Rapids: William B. Eerdmans Publishing, 1990).

Shary, Timothy, *Generation Multiplex: The Image of Youth in Contemporary American Cinema* (Austin: University of Texas Press, 2002).

Shary, Timothy, *Teen Movies: American Youth on Screen* (London: Wallflower Press, 2005).

Simmons, Matty, *If You Don't Buy This Book We'll Kill This Dog: Life,*

Laughs, Love and Death at the National Lampoon (Fort Lee: Barricade Books, 1995).

Simpson, Paul, ed., The Rough Guide to Cult Movies (London: Haymarket Customer Publishing, 2001).

Staiger, Janet, Perverse Spectators: The Practices of Film Reception (New York: New York University Press, 2000).

Tropiano, Stephen, Rebels and Chicks: A History of the Hollywood Teen Movie (New York: Back Stage Books, 2006).

Turner, Graeme, Film as Social Practice (London: Routledge, 1999).

Utterson, Andrew, ed., Technology and Culture: The Film Reader (London: Routledge, 2005).

Wyatt, Justin, High Concept: Movies and Marketing in Hollywood (Austin: University of Texas Press, 1994).

ARTICLES, INTERVIEWS AND REVIEWS

Aames, Ethan, 'Estevez on The Breakfast Club 2', in Cinema Confidential, 12 July 2005. <http://www.cinecon.com/news.php?id=0507126>

Anderson, Jeffrey M., 'National Lampoon's Vacation', in Combustible Celluloid, 16 November 2003.
<http://www.combustiblecelluloid.com/classic/nlvacation.shtml>

—, 'Planes, Trains & Automobiles', in Combustible Celluloid, 15 November 2006.
<http://www.combustiblecelluloid.com/classic/planestrains.shtml>

Anon., '37 Candles would make a lot of light', in The Chicago Sun-Times, 7 June 2005.

Anon., 'Enjoy a late Breakfast', in The Topeka Capital-Journal, 14 March 2008.

Ansen, David, 'A Mixed Bag for Labor Day', in Newsweek, 4 September 1989.

Appelo, Tim, 'John Huge: John Hughes' view from the top', in Entertainment Weekly, 251, 2 December 1994.

Arthur, Ryan, 'National Lampoon's Christmas Vacation', in eFilmCritic.com, 15 October 1998. <http://efilmcritic.com/review.php?movie=1116>

Asperschlager, Erich, 'Uncle Buck', in DVD Verdict, 20 August 2011.
<http://www.dvdverdict.com/reviews/unclebuckbluray.php>

Attanasio, Paul, 'Ferris: More Teen Tedium', in The Washington Post, 12 June 1986.

Babish, Brendan, 'Pretty in Pink: Everything's Duckie Edition', in DVD Verdict, 12 September 2006.
<http://www.dvdverdict/reviews/prettyinpinkse.php>

Barsanti, Chris, 'Pretty in Pink', in CultureCartel.com, 21 September 2006.
<http://www.culturecartel.com/review.php?rid=10006280>

Barsanti, Chris, 'Weird Science', in FilmCritic.com, 31 October 2004.
<http://www.filmcritic.com/misc/emporium.nsf/ddb5490109a79f598625623
d0015f1e4/c6afd7555e1baa8688256d9600654fc4?OpenDocument>

Baumgarten, Marjorie, 'Ferris Bueller's Day Off', in The Austin Chronicle, 15 August 2001.

—, 'Sixteen Candles', in The Austin Chronicle, 23 April 2002.

—, 'Some Kind of Wonderful', in The Austin Chronicle, 6 June 2001.

—, 'The Breakfast Club', in The Austin Chronicle, 5 July 2000.

Benson, Sheila, 'Weird Science', in The Los Angeles Times, 2 August 1985.

Bierly, Mandi, 'PopWatch Blog: John Hughes Lost, Long Duk Dong Found', in Entertainment Weekly Online, 25 March 2008.
<http://popwatch.ew.com/popwatch/2008/03/john-hughes.html>

Blum, David, 'Hollywood's Brat Pack', in New York Magazine, 10 June 1985.

Booth, Michael, 'Breakfast Club rises, shines' in The Denver Post, 24 July 2007.

Brussat, Frederic, and Mary Ann Brussat, 'Weird Science', in Spirituality and Practice, 22 August 2004.
<http://www.spiritualityandpractice.com/films/films.php?id=8927>

Canby, Vincent, 'An Uncouth Uncle Against the Suburban Grain', in The New York Times, 16 August 1989.

—, 'Nate and Hayes: Pirates in South Pacific', in The New York Times, 18 November 1983.

Carr, Jay, 'Candy's Back with Buck', in The Boston Globe, 16 August 1989.

Chambers, Bill, 'Pretty and Pink and Some Kind of Wonderful', in Film Freak Central, 27 August 2000.
<http://filmfreakcentral.net/dvdreviews/prettywonderful.htm>

Chase IV, Lee, 'The Breakfast Club: It's Hard Out There for a Teen', in CultureCartel.com, 10 July 2006.
<http://www.culturecartel.com/review.php?rid=10006219>

Clark, Mike, 'Candy's Buck is a victim of comedy devaluation', in USA Today, 16 August 1989.

Collins, Leah, and Miranda Furtado, 'Who doesn't love high school reunions?: Not everybody can relive the past as a hit man, porn star, Lothario – or psycho killer', in The Montreal Gazette, 7 April 2012.

Corrigan, Ned, 'Popular Videos – Counting Down', in The Washington

Post, 22 December 1985.

Cracknell, Ryan, '*Planes, Trains and Automobiles*', in *Movie Views*, 4 December 2003. <*http://www.movie-views.com/films/P/planes_trains_and_automobiles.html*>

Cressey, Earl, '*National Lampoon's European Vacation*', in *DVD Talk*, 22 March 2002.

<*http://www.dvdtalk.com/reviews/3571/national-lampoons-european-vacation/*>

Crook, Simon, '*The Breakfast Club*', in *Empire Online*, 4 February 2006.

<*http://www.empireonline.com/reviews/reviewcomplete.asp?FID=14432*>

Cullum, Brett, '*Some Kind of Wonderful*: Special Edition', in *DVD Verdict*, 29 August 2006.

<*http://www.dvdverdict.com/reviews/somekindwonderfulse.php*>

—, 'The Brat Pack Movies and Music Collection', in *DVD Verdict*, 14 November 2005. <*http://www.dvdverdict.com/reviews/bratpack.php*>

Curtis, Bryan, 'The Celluloid Pirate: Hollywood's strange fascination with buccaneers', in *Slate*, 11 July 2003.

<*http://www.slate.com/toolbar.aspx?action=print&id=2085480*>

Darnton, Nina, 'Screen: A Youth's *Day Off*', in *The New York Times*, 11 June 1986.

Denby, David, 'Happy Birthday, Sweet Sixteen', in *New York*, 28 May 1984.

Eaton, Andrew, 'For a short time they were on fire, then they vanished into obscurity: Whatever happened to the Brat Pack of the 1980s?', in *The Scotsman*, 20 January 2007.

Ebert, Roger, '*Ferris Bueller's Day Off*', in *The Chicago Sun-Times*, 11 June 1986.

—, '*Mr Mom*', in *The Chicago Sun-Times*, 22 August 1983.

—, '*Nate and Hayes*', in *The Chicago Sun-Times*, 22 November 1983.

—, '*National Lampoon's Christmas Vacation*', in *The Chicago Sun-Times*, 1 December 1989.

—, '*Planes, Trains and Automobiles*', in *The Chicago Sun-Times*, 25 November 1987.

—, '*Pretty in Pink*', in *The Chicago Sun-Times*, 28 February 1986.

—, '*She's Having a Baby*', in *The Chicago Sun-Times*, 5 February 1988.

—, '*Sixteen Candles*', in *The Chicago Sun-Times*, 30 April 1984.

—, '*Some Kind of Wonderful*', in *The Chicago Sun-Times*, 27 February 1987.

—, '*The Breakfast Club*', in *The Chicago Sun-Times*, 15 February 1985.

—, '*Uncle Buck*', in *The Chicago Sun-Times*, 16 August 1989.

—, '*Weird Science*' in *The Chicago Sun-Times*, 2 August 1985.

Erickson, Glenn, '*Nate and Hayes*', in *DVD Savant*, 8 July 2006.

<http://www.dvdtalk.com/dvdsavant/s2055nate.html>

Evenson, Bill, 'Ferris Bueller's Day Off', in DVD Review, 25 October 1999.

<http://www.dvdreview.com/html/ferris_bueller_s_day_off.shtml>

F., Alex, 'Uncle Buck', in DVD Bits, 18 August 2001.

<http://www.dvdbits.com/reviews.asp?id=669>

Gillette, Britt, 'National Lampoon's Christmas Vacation', in The DVD
  Report, 17 February 2006.

<http://thedvdreport.blogspot.com/2006/02/national-lampoons-christmas-
  vacation.html>

Goldstein, Patrick, 'Director Has an Off Day in Day Off', in The Los
  Angeles Times, 20 June 1986.

Haller, Scot, ' Sixteen Candles', in People, 14 May 1984.

Harrington, Richard, 'Some Kind of Wonderful', in The Washington Post, 28
  February 1987.

Helm, Will, 'Misunderstood Masterpieces: Nate and Hayes', in
  411mania.com, 11 March 2008.

<http://www.411mania.com/movies/columns/70702>

Hicks, Chris, 'National Lampoon's Christmas Vacation', in Deseret News, 16
  December 2002.

Hicks, Chris, 'Uncle Buck', in the Deseret News, 16 August 1989.

Hinson, Hal, 'Planes, Trains and Automobiles', in The Washington Post, 25
  November 1987.

— , 'She's Having a Baby', in The Washington Post, 6 February 1988.

Hinson, Hal, 'The Great Outdoors', in The Washington Post, 17 June 1988.

Holmes, Katie, 'Good Golly, Miss Molly! Actress Molly Ringwald', in
  Interview, September 1999.

Howe, Desson, 'Planes, Trains and Automobiles', in The Washington Post,
  27 November 1987.

Kael, Pauline, ' Sixteen Candles', in The New Yorker, 28 May 1984.

Kehr, Dave, 'National Lampoon's Vacation', in The Chicago Reader Film
  Search, 18 May 2010.

<http://www.chicagoreader.com/chicago/national-lampoons-
  vacation/Film?oid=1843274>

Kelly, Maura, 'John Hughes: The films he created in the decade of greed
  made adolescent angst funny and bearable without romanticising it',
  in Salon, 17 July 2001.

Kempley, Rita, 'John Candy's Sugar Pop', in The Washington Post, 16
  August 1989.

— , 'National Lampoon's Christmas Vacation', in The Washington Post, 1
  December 1989.

— , 'Some Kind of Wonderful', in The Washington Post, 27 February 1987.

Klady, Leonard, 'Cinefile: Uncle Buck', in *The Los Angeles Times*, 30 October 1988.

Laforest, Kevin N., '*Ferris Bueller's Day Off*', in *The Montreal Film Journal*, 10 September 2002.

<http://www.montrealfilmjournal.com/review.asp?R=R0000205>

— , '*The Breakfast Club*', in *The Montreal Film Journal*, 10 September 2002.

<http://www.montrealfilmjournal.com/review.asp?R=R0000082>

— , '*Weird Science*', in *The Montreal Film Journal*, 10 August 2002.

<http://www.montrealfilmjournal.com/review.asp?R=R0000593>

Laidman, Brad, '*Ferris Bueller's Day Off*', in *Film Threat*, 17 October 2000.

<http://www.filmthreat.com/index.php?section=reviews&Id=1316>

— , '*Pretty in Pink*', in *Film Threat*, 17 October 2000.

<http://www.filmthreat.com/index.php?section=reviews&Id=1315>

— , '*Sixteen Candles*', in *Film Threat*, 17 October 2000.

<http://www.filmthreat.com/index.php?section=reviews&Id=1313>

— , '*The Breakfast Club*', in *Film Threat*, 17 October 2000.

<http://www.filmthreat.com/index.php?section=reviews&Id=1314>

Malcolm, Derek, 'Snap, Crackle, Pot', in *The Guardian*, 16 June 1985.

Manzoor, Sarfraz, 'More than a quintessential Eighties teen film', in *The Independent*, 24 March 2004.

Martin, Philip, 'Flashback 1985: *The Breakfast Club*: Hughes may have been the first filmmaker to attempt to put plausible teenagers on screen', in *The Arkansas Democrat-Gazette*, 17 April 2005.

— , 'Flashback 1986: *Ferris Bueller's Day Off*: Removed from the moment, the high capitalism of the 1980s, the movie seems mild and pleasantly whimsical', in *The Arkansas Democrat-Gazette*, 24 January 2006.

Maslin, Janet, '*16 Candles*, A Teen-Age Comedy', in *The New York Times*, 4 May 1984.

— , 'A *Class Reunion* for *National Lampoon*', in *The New York Times*, 30 October 1982.

— , 'Country Life for Aykroyd and Candy', in *The New York Times*, 17 June 1988.

— , 'John Hughes's *Breakfast Club*', in *The New York Times*, 15 February 1985.

— , 'John Hughes's *Pretty in Pink*' in *The New York Times*, 28 February 1986.

— , '*Mr Mom*: Domestic Comedy', in *The New York Times*, 26 August 1983.

— , '*National Lampoon's Vacation*', in *The New York Times*, 29 July 1983.

— , '*National Lampoon* in Europe', in *The New York Times*, 27 July 1985.

— , 'On *Vacation* Once Again', in *The New York Times*, 1 December 1989.

—, 'Planes, Trains and Automobiles', in *The New York Times*, 25 November 1987.

—, '*She's Having a Baby*, From John Hughes', in *The New York Times*, 5 February 1988.

—, '*Some Kind of Wonderful*', in *The New York Times*, 27 February 1987.

—, '*Weird Science*: Youth Fantasy', in *The New York Times*, 2 August 1985.

Megahey, Noel, '*Ferris Bueller's Day Off*: Bueller... Bueller... Edition', in *DVD Times*, 29 March 2006.

<*http://www.dvdtimes.co.uk/content.php?contentid=60991*>

Mietkiewicz, Henry, 'Time to cast Candy against type', in *The Toronto Star*, 16 August 1989.

Naugle, Patrick, '*National Lampoon's Christmas Vacation*', in *DVD Verdict*, 19 December 2000.

<*http://www.dvdverdict.com/reviews/christmasvacation.php*>

—, '*National Lampoon's Christmas Vacation*: Special Edition', in *DVD Verdict*, 16 October 2003.

<*http://www.dvdverdict.com/reviews/christmasvacationse.php*>

—, '*National Lampoon's European Vacation*', in *DVD Verdict*, 20 March 2002.

<*http://www.dvdverdict.com/reviews/europeanvacation.php*>

—, '*National Lampoon's European Vacation*', in *DVD Verdict*, 10 August 2010.

<*http://www.dvdverdict.com/reviews/europeanvacationbluray.php*>

—, '*National Lampoon's Vacation: Special Edition*', in *DVD Verdict*, 19 August 2003.

<*http://www.dvdverdict.com/reviews/vacationse.php*>

—, '*Pretty in Pink*', in *DVD Verdict*, 5 September 2002.

<*http://www.dvdverdict.com/reviews/prettyinpink.php*>

—, '*Some Kind Of Wonderful*', in *DVD Verdict*, 19 September 2002.

<*http://www.dvdverdict.com/reviews/somekindwonderful.php*>

Null, Christopher, '*National Lampoon's Vacation*', in *FilmCritic.com*, 19 August 2003.

<*http://www.filmcritic.com/misc/emporium.nsf/reviews/National-Lampoons-Vacation*>

Nusair, David, '*She's Having a Baby*', in *Reel Film*, 1 July 2006.

<*http://www.reelfilm.com/mini58.htm#she*>

—, 'The Films of John Hughes: *Sixteen Candles*', in *Reel Film Reviews*, 13 February 2012. <*http://reelfilm.com/johnhugh.htm#six*>

Orndorf, Brian, 'John Hughes: The High School Flashback Collection (*Sixteen Candles, The Breakfast Club* and *Weird Science*)', in *DVD Talk*, 16 September 2008.

<http://www.dvdtalk.com/reviews/34539/john-hughes-the-high-school-flashback-collection-sixteen-candles-the-breakfast-club-and-weird-science/?___rd=1>

Panton, Gary, 'Ferris Bueller's Day Off', in Movie Gazette, 9 July 2003.
<http://www.movie-gazette.com/cinereviews/313>

—, 'Planes, Trains and Automobiles', in Movie Gazette, 28 May 2003.
<http://www.movie-gazette.com/cinereviews/186>

Parry, Chris, 'The Great Outdoors', in eFilmCritic.com, 31 July 1999.
<http://efilmcritic.com/review.php?movie=1115>

Pratt, Doug, 'Uncle Buck', in DVD Laser, September 2004.
<http://www.dvdlaser.com/search/detail.cfm?id=2192>

Puccio, John J., 'National Lampoon's European Vacation (Special Edition)', in DVD Town, 23 April 2002.
< http://www.dvdtown.com/reviews/national-lampoons-european-vacation/1064>

—, 'National Lampoon's Vacation: DVD Review', in DVD Town, 17 August 2003.
<http://moviemet.com/review/national-lampoons-vacation-dvd-review>

—, 'Pretty in Pink', in DVD Town, 12 August 2008.
<http://moviemet.com/review/pretty-pink-dvd-review-0>

—, and Justin Cleveland, 'Ferris Bueller's Day Off: I Love the 80s Edition', in DVD Town, 24 July 2008.
<http://www.dvdtown.com/reviews/ferris-buellers-day-off/6129>

Reynolds, Simon, 'Ringwald hopes for Sixteen Candles sequel', in Digital Spy, 1 July 2008.
<http://www.digitalspy.co.uk/movies/a106300/ringwald-hopes-for-sixteen-candles-sequel>

Rich, Jamie S., 'Some Kind of Wonderful: SE', in DVD Talk, 27 August 2006.
<http://www.dvdtalk.com/reviews/23454/some-kind-of-wonderful-se/>

Rogers, David, 'The Breakfast Club', in DVD Verdict, 24 May 2000.
<http://www.dvdverdict.com/reviews/breakfastclub.php>

Rubinow, Alexander, 'American Teen Maestro', in The John Hughes Retrospective, 10 May 2000.
<http://www.geocities.com/xanderubi/html/body_teen_maestro.html>

Rubinow, Alexander, 'Hughes the Ad', in The John Hughes Retrospective, 26 March 1998.
<http://www.geocities.com/xanderubi/html/body_hughes_the_ad.html>

—, 'Hughesdom', in The John Hughes Retrospective, 7 December 1998.
<http://www.geocities.com/xanderubi/html/body_hughesdom.html>

Salem, Rob, 'Adults are the idiots in tale of two kiddies', in The Toronto Star, 13 June 1986.

Short, Norman, 'National Lampoon's Class Reunion', in DVD Verdict, 28
    March 2000.
<http://www.dvdverdict.com/reviews/classreunion.php>
—, 'Planes, Trains and Automobiles', in DVD Verdict, 4 December 2000.
<http://www.dvdverdict.com/reviews/planestrains.php>
—, 'She's Having a Baby', in DVD Verdict, 11 December 2000.
<http://www.dvdverdict.com/reviews/sheshavingbaby.php>
Siegel, Lee, 'At the Movies: Real Genius, My Science Project, Weird
    Science', in The Associated Press, 26 August 1985.
Smith, Adam, 'Empire Essay: Ferris Bueller's Day Off', in Empire Online,
    5 May 2008.
<http://www.empireonline.com/reviews/reviewcomplete.asp?FID=132851>
Speed, Lesley, 'Pastel Romances: The Teen Films of John Hughes', in Metro
    Media and Education Magazine, Issue 113/114, 1998.
Stanley, John, 'The Great Outdoors', in DVD Authority, July 1999.
<http://www.dvdauthority.com/reviews.asp?reviewID=1820>
Stephens, Daniel, 'National Lampoon's Christmas Vacation', in DVD Times,
    17 November 2003.
<http://www.dvdtimes.co.uk/content.php?contentid=6068>
Sterritt, David, 'A film going along for the ride, tracking teens playing
    hooky', in The Christian Science Monitor, 18 June 1986.
Thomas, Bob, 'At the Movies: Ferris Bueller's Day Off', in The Associated
    Press, 26 June 1986.
Tobias, Scott, 'National Lampoon's Vacation' in The Onion A.V. Club, 2
    September 2003. <http://www.avclub.com/content/node//354/>
Tobias, Scott, 'Old School: Ferris Bueller's Day Off', in The Onion A.V.
    Club, 25 January 2006. <http://www.avclub.com/content/node/44746/>
Tobias, Scott, 'Pretty in Pink', in The Onion A.V. Club, 30 August 2002.
<http://www.avclub.com/content/node/6367/>
Travers, Peter, 'Uncle Buck', in Rolling Stone, 7 September 1989.
Turner, Gavin, 'Uncle Buck', in DVD.net.au, 2003.
<http://www.dvd.net.au/review.cgi?review_id=804>
Variety Staff, 'Ferris Bueller's Day Off', in Variety, 4 June 1986.
—, 'National Lampoon's Christmas Vacation', in Variety, 1 December 1989.
—, 'National Lampoon's European Vacation', in Variety, 9 August 1985.
—, 'National Lampoon's Vacation', in Variety, 3 August 1983.
—, 'Planes, Trains & Automobiles', in Variety, 25 November 1987.
—, 'Pretty in Pink', in Variety, 12 February 1986.
—, 'She's Having a Baby', in Variety, 3 February 1988.
—, 'Sixteen Candles', in Variety, 2 May 1984.
—, 'Some Kind of Wonderful', in Variety, 25 February 1987.

–, 'Weird Science', in *Variety*, 7 August 1985.

W.K., Andrew, '*Mr Mom*', in *Rolling Stone*, 28 August 2003.

Waldron-Mantgani, Ian, 'Retrospectives: *She's Having a Baby*', in *The UK Critic*, November 2003.

<*http://www.ukcritic.com/sheshavingababy_1988.html*>

Walsh, Maeve, 'It was 15 years ago today: The Bratpack meets at *The Breakfast Club*', in *The Independent*, 13 February 2000.

Walsh, Patrick, 'Retro Cinema: *National Lampoon's Vacation*', in *Cinematical*, 21 August 2007.

<*http://www.cinematical.com/2007/08/21/retro-cinema-national-lampoons-vacation/*>

Weinberg, Scott, '*Nate and Hayes*', in *DVD Talk*, 2 June 2006.

<*http://www.dvdtalk.com/reviews/21999/nate-and-hayes/*>

Willman, Chris, '*Uncle Buck*: John Hughes' Valentine to Teenhood', in *The Los Angeles Times*, 16 August 1989.

Wilson, Linda J., 'Movies Were Popular Pastime in 1982', in *The Queens Gazette*, 27 June 2007.

Winkelspecht, Dean, '*Pretty in Pink*: Everything's Duckie Special Edition', in *DVD Town*, 31 August 2006.

<*http://www.dvdtown.com/reviews/pretty-in-pink/3911*>

Wrightson, Berni, and Michele Wrightson, 'A Peek At *National Lampoon's Class Reunion*', in *Heavy Metal*, Vol.6, No.8, November 1982.

About the Author

Thomas Christie has a life-long fascination with films and the people who make them. Currently reading for a PhD in Scottish literature, he lives in Scotland with his family.

He holds a first-class Honours degree in Literature and a Masters degree in Humanities, specialising with distinction in British Cinema History, from the Open University in Milton Keynes.

Books by Thomas Christie include *Liv Tyler, Star in Ascendance: Her First Decade in Film* (2007), *John Hughes and Eighties Cinema* (2009), *Ferris Bueller's Day Off: Pocket Movie Guide* (2010) and *The Cinema of Richard Linklater* (2011). Available from Crescent Moon Publishing. For more information about Tom and his books, visit his website at: http://www.tomchristiebooks.co.uk

CRESCENT MOON PUBLISHING

ARTS, PAINTING, SCULPTURE

The Art of Andy Goldsworthy
Andy Goldsworthy: Touching Nature
Andy Goldsworthy in Close-Up
Andy Goldsworthy: Pocket Guide
Andy Goldsworthy In America
Land Art: A Complete Guide
The Art of Richard Long
Richard Long: Pocket Guide
Land Art In the UK
Land Art in Close-Up
Land Art In the U.S.A.
Land Art: Pocket Guide
Installation Art in Close-Up
Minimal Art and Artists In the 1960s and After
Colourfield Painting
Land Art DVD, TV documentary
Andy Goldsworthy DVD, TV documentary
The Erotic Object: Sexuality in Sculpture From Prehistory to the Present Day
Sex in Art: Pornography and Pleasure in Painting and Sculpture
Postwar Art
Sacred Gardens: The Garden in Myth, Religion and Art
Glorification: Religious Abstraction in Renaissance and 20th Century Art
Early Netherlandish Painting
Leonardo da Vinci
Piero della Francesca
Giovanni Bellini
Fra Angelico: Art and Religion in the Renaissance
Mark Rothko: The Art of Transcendence
Frank Stella: American Abstract Artist
Jasper Johns
Brice Marden
Alison Wilding: The Embrace of Sculpture
Vincent van Gogh: Visionary Landscapes
Eric Gill: Nuptials of God
Constantin Brancusi: Sculpting the Essence of Things
Max Beckmann
Caravaggio
Gustave Moreau
Egon Schiele: Sex and Death In Purple Stockings
Delizioso Fotografico Fervore: Works In Process I
Sacro Cuore: Works In Process 2
The Light Eternal: J.M.W. Turner
The Madonna Glorified: Karen Arthurs

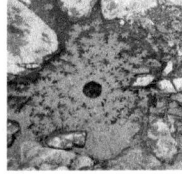

LITERATURE

J.R.R. Tolkien: The Books, The Films, The Whole Cultural Phenomenon
J.R.R. Tolkien: Pocket Guide
Tolkien's Heroic Quest
The *Earthsea* Books of Ursula Le Guin
Beauties, Beasts and Enchantment: Classic French Fairy Tales
German Popular Stories by the Brothers Grimm
Philip Pullman and *His Dark Materials*
Sexing Hardy: Thomas Hardy and Feminism
Thomas Hardy's *Tess of the d'Urbervilles*
Thomas Hardy's *Jude the Obscure*
Thomas Hardy: The Tragic Novels

Love and Tragedy: Thomas Hardy
The Poetry of Landscape in Hardy
Wessex Revisited: Thomas Hardy and John Cowper Powys
Wolfgang Iser: Essays and Interviews
Petrarch, Dante and the Troubadours

Maurice Sendak and the Art of Children's Book Illustration
Andrea Dworkin
Cixous, Irigaray, Kristeva: The *Jouissance* of French Feminism
Julia Kristeva: Art, Love, Melancholy, Philosophy, Semiotics and Psychoanalysis
Hélène Cixous I Love You: The *Jouissance* of Writing
Luce Irigaray: Lips, Kissing, and the Politics of Sexual Difference

Peter Redgrove: Here Comes the Flood
Peter Redgrove: Sex-Magic-Poetry-Cornwall
Lawrence Durrell: Between Love and Death, East and West
Love, Culture & Poetry: Lawrence Durrell

Cavafy: Anatomy of a Soul
German Romantic Poetry: Goethe, Novalis, Heine, Hölderlin
Feminism and Shakespeare
Shakespeare: Love, Poetry & Magic
The Passion of D.H. Lawrence
D.H. Lawrence: Symbolic Landscapes
D.H. Lawrence: Infinite Sensual Violence

Rimbaud: Arthur Rimbaud and the Magic of Poetry
The Ecstasies of John Cowper Powys
Sensualism and Mythology: The Wessex Novels of John Cowper Powys
Amorous Life: John Cowper Powys and the Manifestation of Affectivity (H.W. Fawkner)
Postmodern Powys: New Essays on John Cowper Powys (Joe Boulter)
Rethinking Powys: Critical Essays on John Cowper Powys
Paul Bowles & Bernardo Bertolucci
Rainer Maria Rilke
Joseph Conrad: *Heart of Darkness*

In the Dim Void: Samuel Beckett
Samuel Beckett Goes into the Silence
André Gide: Fiction and Fervour
Jackie Collins and the Blockbuster Novel
Blinded By Her Light: The Love-Poetry of Robert Graves
The Passion of Colours: Travels In Mediterranean Lands
Poetic Forms

POETRY

Ursula Le Guin: Walking In Cornwall
Peter Redgrove: Here Comes The Flood
Peter Redgrove: Sex-Magic-Poetry-Cornwall
Dante: Selections From the Vita Nuova
Petrarch, Dante and the Troubadours
William Shakespeare: Sonnets
William Shakespeare: Complete Poems
Blinded By Her Light: The Love-Poetry of Robert Graves
Emily Dickinson: Selected Poems
Emily Brontë: Poems
Thomas Hardy: Selected Poems
Percy Bysshe Shelley: Poems
John Keats: Selected Poems
Joh n Keats: Poems of 1820
D.H. Lawrence: Selected Poems
Edmund Spenser: Poems
Edmund Spenser: Amoretti
John Donne: Poems
Henry Vaughan: Poems
Sir Thomas Wyatt: Poems
Robert Herrick: Selected Poems
Rilke: Space, Essence and Angels in the Poetry of Rainer Maria Rilke
Rainer Maria Rilke: Selected Poems
Friedrich Hölderlin: Selected Poems
Arseny Tarkovsky: Selected Poems
Arthur Rimbaud: Selected Poems
Arthur Rimbaud: A Season in Hell
Arthur Rimbaud and the Magic of Poetry
Novalis: Hymns To the Night
German Romantic Poetry
Paul Verlaine: Selected Poems
Elizaethan Sonnet Cycles
D.J. Enright: By-Blows
Jeremy Reed: Brigitte's Blue Heart
Jeremy Reed: Claudia Schiffer's Red Shoes
Gorgeous Little Orpheus
Radiance: New Poems
Crescent Moon Book of Nature Poetry
Crescent Moon Book of Love Poetry
Crescent Moon Book of Mystical Poetry
Crescent Moon Book of Elizabethan Love Poetry
Crescent Moon Book of Metaphysical Poetry
Crescent Moon Book of Romantic Poetry
Pagan America: New American Poetry

MEDIA, CINEMA, FEMINISM and CULTURAL STUDIES

J.R.R. Tolkien: The Books, The Films, The Whole Cultural Phenomenon
J.R.R. Tolkien: Pocket Guide
The *Lord of the Rings* Movies: Pocket Guide
The Cinema of Hayao Miyazaki
Hayao Miyazaki: *Princess Mononoke*: Pocket Movie Guide
Hayao Miyazaki: *Spirited Away*: Pocket Movie Guide
Tim Burton
Ken Russell
Ken Russell: *Tommy*: Pocket Movie Guide
The Ghost Dance: The Origins of Religion
The Peyote Cult
Cixous, Irigaray, Kristeva: The *Jouissance* of French Feminism
Julia Kristeva: Art, Love, Melancholy, Philosophy, Semiotics and Psychoanalysis
Luce Irigaray: Lips, Kissing, and the Politics of Sexual Difference
Hélene Cixous I Love You: The *Jouissance* of Writing
Andrea Dworkin
'Cosmo Woman': The World of Women's Magazines
Women in Pop Music
Discovering the Goddess (Geoffrey Ashe)
The Poetry of Cinema
The Sacred Cinema of Andrei Tarkovsky
Andrei Tarkovsky: Pocket Guide
Andrei Tarkovsky: *Mirror*: Pocket Movie Guide
Andrei Tarkovsky: *The Sacrifice*: Pocket Movie Guide
Walerian Borowczyk: Cinema of Erotic Dreams
Jean-Luc Godard: The Passion of Cinema
Jean-Luc Godard: *Hail Mary*: Pocket Movie Guide
Jean-Luc Godard: *Contempt*: Pocket Movie Guide
Jean-Luc Godard: *Pierrot le Fou*: Pocket Movie Guide
John Hughes and Eighties Cinema
Ferris Bueller's Day Off: Pocket Movie Guide
Jean-Luc Godard: Pocket Guide
The Cinema of Richard Linklater
Liv Tyler: Star In Ascendance
Blade Runner and the Films of Philip K. Dick
Paul Bowles and Bernardo Bertolucci
Media Hell: Radio, TV and the Press
An Open Letter to the BBC
Detonation Britain: Nuclear War in the UK
Feminism and Shakespeare
Wild Zones: Pornography, Art and Feminism
Sex in Art: Pornography and Pleasure in Painting and Sculpture
Sexing Hardy: Thomas Hardy and Feminism

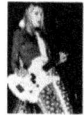

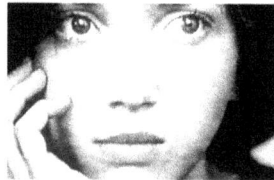

CRESCENT MOON PUBLISHING
P.O. Box 1312, Maidstone, Kent, ME14 5XU, Great Britain. www.crmoon.com

www.ingramcontent.com/pod-product-compliance
Lightning Source LLC
Chambersburg PA
CBHW070410100426
42812CB00005B/1688